Advanced Research on Asian Economy and Economies of Other Continents – Vol. 8

Resilient States from a Comparative Regional Perspective

Central and Eastern Europe and Southeast Asia

Advanced Research on Asian Economy and Economies of Other Continents

(ISSN: 1793-0944)

Series Editor: Manoranjan DUTTA
(Rutgers, The State University of New Jersey, USA)

Published

Vol. 1   Asian Economic Cooperation in the New Millennium:
China's Economic Presence
Edited by Calla Wiemer (East Asian Institute, National
University of Singapore) & Heping Cao (Peking University, China)

Vol. 2   China's Industrial Revolution and Economic Presence
by Manoranjan Dutta (Rutgers, The State University of New Jersey, USA)

Vol. 3   International Economic Integration and Asia
Edited by Michael G Plummer & Erik Jones
(Johns Hopkins University SAIS-Bologna, Italy)

Vol. 4   Economic Dynamism of Asia in the New Millenium:
From the Asian Crisis to a New Stage of Growth
Edited by Yoshinori Shimizu (Hitotsubashi University, Japan)

Vol. 5   Future Perspectives on the Economic Development of Asia
by John Malcolm Dowling (Singapore Management University, Singapore)

Vol. 6   Asean Economic Integration: Trade, Foreign Direct Investment, and Finance
by Michael G Plummer (Johns Hopkins University, SAIS-Bologna, and
East-West Center, Italy)

Vol. 7   EU-Asia and the Re-Polarization of the Global Economic Arena
Edited by Lars Oxelheim (Lund University, Sweden & Research Institute of
Industrial Economics, Sweden)

Vol. 8   Resilient States from a Comparative Regional Perspective:
Central and Eastern Europe and Southeast Asia
by Bafoil François (Sciences Po Paris, France)

Advanced Research on Asian Economy and Economies of Other Continents – Vol. 8

Resilient States from a Comparative Regional Perspective

Central and Eastern Europe and Southeast Asia

François BAFOIL

Sciences Po Paris, France

World Scientific

NEW JERSEY · LONDON · SINGAPORE · BEIJING · SHANGHAI · HONG KONG · TAIPEI · CHENNAI

Published by

World Scientific Publishing Co. Pte. Ltd.

5 Toh Tuck Link, Singapore 596224

USA office: 27 Warren Street, Suite 401-402, Hackensack, NJ 07601

UK office: 57 Shelton Street, Covent Garden, London WC2H 9HE

Library of Congress Cataloging-in-Publication Data
Bafoil, François.
   Resilient states from a comparative regional perspective : Central and Eastern Europe and Southeast Asia / by François Bafoil.
      p. cm. -- (Advanced research on Asian economy and economics of other continent ISSN 1793-0944 ; vol. 8)
   Includes bibliographical references and index.
   ISBN 978-9814417464
   1. Europe, Central--Economic policy--1989– 2. Europe, Eastern--Economic policy--198
3. Southeast Asia--Economic policy. 4. Europe, Eastern--Politics and government--198
5. Europe, Central--Politics and government--1989– 6. Southeast Asia--Politics and governmen
I. Title.
   HC244.B323 2013
   330.9--dc23
                                                          2012032308

British Library Cataloguing-in-Publication Data
A catalogue record for this book is available from the British Library.

In-house Editors: Sandhya Venkatesh/Dipasri Sardar

Typeset by Stallion Press
Email: enquiries@stallionpress.com

Printed in Singapore.

CONTENTS

ABOUT THE AUTHOR

 **François Bafoil** is a sociologist and Senior Research Fellow at the French National Center of Research (CNRS), and at Sciences Po Paris. He holds degrees in Philosophy, Polish and Sociology. In 1986, he obtained his PhD from the Institut d'Etudes Politiques de Paris (IEP), and in 1994 he obtained a Habilitation from University of Grenoble II in Sociology. He has undertaken extended research fellowships at the Lodz University, Poland (1984). He is a Humboldt Foundation Fellow at the die Freie Universität and WZB in Berlin. He lived in Berlin for eight years, 1988–1994, during which the Berlin Wall fell. Then he returned to France in 1994 (Grenoble), and came to Paris in 2003. Before joining CERI, François Bafoil served as the EU expert in charge of *ex-ante* assessment in Poland and advisor at the Ministry of Economy in Warsaw (2002–2003). After that he became a special advisor to the OECD for the Territorial Review of Poland in 2008/2009. He was an invited professor at the University of Köln and Frankfurt an der Oder (Germany), Fudan (Shangai), and Bilgi (Turkey). For 4 years from 2006 to 2009, he organized training sessions for the ADB and worked therefore in the Great Mekong Subregion. Since 2010, he has been leading a research group on the Cohesion Policy and regional development in a comparative perspective. François Bafoil is a member of the scientific boards of the Institut für Europäische Politik in Berlin, the Centre for Social Studies (PAN)

in Warsaw, the Institut des Hautes Etudes Internationales (CIFE) in Berlin and Nice. At Sciences Po, he teaches at the Master of Public Affairs at Sciences Po, "Regional development Policies in a Comparative Perspective — Eastern Europe/South East Asia". He teaches in Berlin, Istanbul. He is also a member of the European Online Academy: "Theoretical, political and economic aspects of transition in Eastern Europe". He wrote 10 books and co-edited 8, edited 12 reviews, wrote more than 47 chapters in books, and 55 articles in per review journals.

His research interests include "Central and Eastern Europe: economic and social transformations since 1990" and "Central and Eastern Europe/Mekong region: regional integration and cross-border cooperation".

INTRODUCTION

This book offers a comparison of Central and East European (CEE) and Southeast Asian states using one empirical observation as a point of departure: All these states — with the single exception of Thailand — have been destroyed several times throughout history as a result of occupation by colonial or imperialist powers. Observation of this single fact leads to a four-fold approach to any study of these two regions: the state, regional integration, political economy, and capitalism. These four approaches form the basis of this book, which aims to offer a better understanding of these states' resilience from a comparative perspective. It also focuses on providing a clearer explanation of the type of political economies and the brand of capitalism emerging in each of the regions considered.

One dimension of this approach is that it calls for the application of a particular theoretical framework: The so-called "Bringing the State Back In" approach, in reference to a well-known work, which analyses "reorganizational episodes" during which state structures are transformed taking market factors and political constituencies into account. This is analyzed in Chapter 2. Transformation policies for property rights and regionalization provide an illustration of this. They are analyzed in Chapters 3 and 4.

A second dimension should be added to this initial framework: the processes of integration used by the different states for entry into supranational ensembles and in this case the EU and ASEAN. These first two dimensions, which can be described as internal and external, show the resilience of these states as they respond to a two-fold challenge. On the one hand, they have to deal with the pressure to

globalize trade using privatization, regionalization policies and industrial relations to do so. On the other hand, they must negotiate their
membership within these supranational ensembles that guarantee
both their external security and, for most of them, their internal
development.

Third, political economies within these states were rebuilt as part
of their internal and external (dialectical) processes of adaptation to
market constraints and economic globalization. This sometimes happened in continuity with previous trajectories and sometimes by
breaking with these trajectories but always in keeping with national
legacies. The institutions that were created when these different
"reorganizational episodes" took place bear witness to this. The range
of these institutions and the different ways in which they are managed
are indicative of the varying degrees to which the states are "open" or
"closed". They provide a clearer understanding of what is usually seen
as their "strengths" or "weaknesses".

Finally, given the fact that these states have fallen behind economically, politically and socially, their strategies for catching up have
been dominated by the concern to attract the greatest possible number of foreign direct investments by putting attractive and largely
deregulated fiscal and social policies in place. For this reason, these
states can be seen as fertile grounds for extending the globalization of
capitalist trade. Chapters 5 and 8 explore this idea focusing on industrial relations and enlargement policies.

The present work is structured by four theses. The first of these
underlines the primacy of national sovereignty in the processes of the
internal and external rebuilding of new EU and ASEAN member
states. This is reflected in the notion of 'state resilience'. The second
thesis postulates that the rebuilding of national political economies
enables the process of regional integration to be understood. The
third thesis explores the relative nature of the notions of 'weakness'
and 'strength' drawing on internal (public policy) and external
(regional belonging) aspects to do so. The fourth thesis stresses that
the new members of each regional ensemble (the EU and ASEAN)
have become vectors of globalized capitalism. This has resulted in
deregulation in all cases.

A number of fallacious arguments against comparison of these regions exist, all of which are based on a culturalist vision of modernization. Their only effect is to discredit valid comparisons whose justification cannot be denied as described below.

1. Fallacious Arguments Against Comparison

History is often said to radically differentiate both regions from the perspective of "modernization": The western world has been a place of economic and political modernization since the Enlightenment in the 18th century. Subsequent to that period, it exported capitalist methods, technical advances and systems for the organization of work practices around the world. Ultimately, the general view is that of a supposedly recognized opposition between a "dynamic" modern Europe on the one hand and a passive Southeast Asia, anchored in ancient tradition on the other. Throughout history, various authors influenced by Montesquieu and Hegel have written about a series of deficits in Southeast Asia such as the rule of law, civil society and legal and monetary systems. All these features characterizing the transformation of Western Europe are seen to be absent from Southeast Asia. Marx spoke of an "Asian mode of production" meaning a lack of clear rules and a society deeply embedded in paternalist authority. In Weberian terms, the technical rationality underpinning legal rational rule is opposed to the traditional values underpinning patrimonial authority, of which Asia is seen to be a major example. Clear Anglo-Saxon rules of governance are deemed to be the opposite of "crony capitalism" and "nomenklatura" types of capitalism.[1] Within such a mindset, pre-colonial Southeast Asia is seen as having no experience of the manor economy. Lastly, state jobs are not awarded on the basis of inherited titles or property but rather through pre-bends.[2] On the other hand, in Europe, long-term transformations are described as

---

[1] "The term 'Nomenklatura capitalism' is used to highlight the close connection between political elites and insulated domestic cartels" (Jayasurija, 2003).

[2] For a re-examination of pre-colonial histories, which can in no way be described as "blank pages" (Murray and Rees, 2010).

the result of increasing endogenous merchant and working classes, urban networks, and an ever developing dynamic of technological innovation (Lieberman, 1993). As Richard Higgott argues, the comparison very often discriminates against ASEAN, which is less rule-oriented (Higgott, 1998). From this remark, it may be derived causally that ASEAN is less economically developed, less consensual, less politically developed and consequently less moral. The EU is always seen as exemplary and defined as a model with Asia lagging far behind because of its so-called deficiencies.

This cleaved vision of development in each region is widely supported by an erroneous culturalist approach defining a scale of progress that always places Europe at the top and Southeast Asia at the bottom. The approach exemplifies a progressive EU versus a "backward" Southeast Asian region. This scale of values depicts maturity and self-awareness as characteristic of the western world. It assigns the core concept of patrimonialism to Southeast Asia, which is seen as regulating relationships between people, from childhood at home right up to the workplace.[3] The core idea of equality between citizens within western societies is seen to be deeply challenged in Asia by the supremacy of the father figure or the boss.[4] In contrast to western values where individualism and self-interest are promoted, Asian values are seen to highlight community and filial piety, dependence and submission to authority. Indeed, in radical opposition to western values,[5] Asian values structure the discourses of most colonialists and many leaders in Southeast Asia struggling to guarantee national sovereignty.

---

[3] Lucien Pye (1985), writes in his major book: "The model of all relationships is the family and therefore the sentiments at the heart of power in the various Asian countries reflect the family values of the individual cultures.

[4] "One element of continuity in their lives was kinship.... In business, family loyalties accounted for much of what unsympathetic Westerners saw as 'corruption', but locals regarded as simple fulfillment of familial obligations" (Tarling, 2000).

[5] "To some extent, this expression of an 'Asian' identity is viewed as a reaction to the way in which the US treats the region. The notion of an Asian identity is an exercise in invention, seen by leaders who advance such notions as a way of stemming the intrusion of western cultural and moral value systems without rejecting the dynamics aspects of western economic and technological modernization" (Higgott, 1997).

From these two major constraints — history and values — there results a vision of institutions based on formal, written, and predictable rules on the one hand and informal practices on the other. This vision identifies two different types of bureaucracy and political economy.

The first type of bureaucracy is proper to the western trajectory, based on rational bureaucracies served by impartial civil servants, as opposed to more patrimonial bureaucracies, which blend formal and informal rules backed by strong interpersonal links. In the first type, political economy is (formally) based on a strict distinction between politics and economics, while the second type is characterized by a strong interconnection between business and political interests where kinship plays a major role. Consequently, the EU framework, strongly institutionalized by means of rules, objectives and agencies differs from the rather weak, informal cooperation found between actors at different levels in ASEAN countries. The vision of a market, which is more or less constrained by common rules, can easily be contrasted to the vision of another more loosely coordinated market. Institutional matter and the fundamental difference between both regions lies in the distinction between the rule of law and the rule by law.[6] This approach is of course limited by the fact that the "ideal type" and "concrete reality" have been largely mixed together to the advantage of the former, reproducing an ideal and perfect table of the empirical and historical data (Jayasurija, 1999).

Finally, within each supranational ensemble a radically different feeling of belonging may be inferred from the previous discussion. In Europe, the so-called European identity built over several centuries is seen to be more likely to give birth to a supranational entity. Such "pooled sovereignty" is conceivable because belonging is based on the principle of equality among all members and because the general

---

[6] Rule by law has "represented the attempt to codify Vietnamese laws and regulation into a coherent and internally consistent system to increase the transparency of bureaucratic process and to eliminate opportunities for corruption, nepotism, favoritism and arbitrariness from their implementation. As such it implied reforms of the bureaucracy as well as the rewriting of many laws to make them applicable to a market economy" (Beresford, 2001) (see Chapter 7).

interest is considered to guarantee the security of individual interests. The shared principle of common law secures private interests; the more collective norms and rules there are, the greater is the feeling of security. Mutual agreements are based on formal rules. On the other hand, in Southeast Asia, which was so often broken up under the domination of numerous foreign interests, "pooled sovereignty" can be seen as an additional constraint. ASEAN is fundamentally based on principles of "sovereignty", "non-interference", and "mutual accommodation", in order to better reject any submission to foreign rule.[7] This is seen as a necessary condition for the securing of private interests. It would be a mistake to conclude that there is no shared identity among Southeast Asian countries. As Acharya writes, this identity which did not exist prior to the birth of ASEAN — as it did in the EU — is gradually being built as continuous negotiations take place.[8]

1.1. *Better arguments in favor of comparing*

Approaches comparing Europe with Southeast Asia — for the main data see Table 1 — are empirically valid for two main reasons: Because of long-term history together with concerns about national sovereignty and the negotiations of shared rules; and because both regions are facing the challenge of combining efficiency and the reduction of social, economic and territorial inequality, thanks to efficient institutions. These reasons ground the theoretical framework using the "strong and weak States" and the "patrimonial bureaucracy" approaches. Four arguments support the legitimacy of the comparison.

The first argument is based on fact that the ASEAN has existed for more than 40 years, and the EU for more than 50 years. History matters. Moreover, in the past few decades, both ensembles have

---

[7]The principles of ASEAN are the following: "mutual respect of the independence, sovereignty, equality, territorial integrity and national identity of all nations; the right of every state to lead its national existence free from external interference, subversion or coercion; non-interference in the internal affairs of one another; settlement of differences or disputes by peaceful manner; renunciation of the threat or use of force; effective cooperation among themselves" (Beeson, 2009).
[8]See Chapter 7.

Table 1.   Population and GDP in the EU and in ASEAN.

In CEE	Population in millions 2008	GDP/ Hab SPA (% UE27)	In Southeast Asia/ASEAN and the three ASEAN +3 countries 2010	GDP $ billion	GNP per capita ($)	Populations in millions
Bulgaria	7,6	41 (2008)	Brunei	12	26,930	0.4
Estonia	1,3	62	Cambodia	9	540	14
Hungary	10	63	Indonesia	433	1,650	226
Latvia	2,3	49	Laos PDR	4	580	6
Lithuania	3,4	53	Malaysia	181	6,540	27
Poland	38,1	56 (2008)	Myanmar	—	—	49
Czech Republic	10,5	80	The Philippines	144	1,620	88
Romania	21,5	42 (2008)	Singapore	161	32,470	5
Slovakia	5,4	72	Thailand	246	3,400	64
Slovenia	2,0	86	Vietnam	71	790	85
EU 27	499,7	100	ASEAN	1.261	8,280	544
CEE 10	104		Japan	4.377	37,670	128
EU 15		111	South Korea	970	19,690	49
			China	3.280	2,360	1,320

Source: http://web.worldbank.org.

enlarged and have also expanded their initial common design by adding on new tasks (Yeo, 2009). Both CEE and Southeast Asian states have achieved remarkable economic development, placing them at the top of the list of emerging countries (see Tables 2 and 3), even if they differ in timing and speed, mirroring important differences from an institutional perspective.[9]

---

[9] "Both the Southeast Asian countries and the new Member States have grown more rapidly and more steadily than any other regions in the world over the last decade. Due to the ever closer trade and financial linkages with the old Member States in the

Second, the counter argument that weakens the notion of a supposedly "backward" SEA cites the remarkable way in which Asian economies have "caught up" during the last 20 years.[10] Moreover, the huge negative effects of the worldwide economic crisis that started in 2008 have cast doubts on this notion given that the more open economies have suffered less from the crisis than more protected economies. Overall, ASEAN members appear to have responded better to current economic challenges than EU member states have. Several studies now converge in their assessment of the way in which

Table 2.   ASEAN GDP Growth 2006–2010.

	2006	2007	2008	2009	2010
Brunei	4.4	0.2	−1.9	−1.8	2
Cambodia	10.8	10.2	6.7	0.1	6.3
Indonesia	5.5	6.3	6	4.6	6.1
Laos PDR	8.1	7.9	7.2	7.3	7.5
Malaysia	5.6	6.5	4.7	−1.7	7.2
Myanmar[11]	7	5.5	3.6	5.1	5.3
Philippines	5.3	7.1	3.7	1.1	7.3
Singapore	8.6	8.8	1.5	−0.8	14.5
Thailand	5.1	5	2.5	−2.3	7.8
Vietnam	8.2	8.5	6.3	5.3	6.8
ASEAN	6.1	6.7	4.2	1.2	7.8
China	12.7	14.2	9.6	9.2	10.3

Source: Asian Development Outlook 2011 cited in Verbiest (p. 8).

run-up to accession, the new Member States have been able to achieve better economic performances than other emerging economies with similar income levels" (EU Report, 2009b).

[10] "Economic integration has taken place mainly via the rapid expansion of intra-regional trade and the remarkable growth of supply-chain networks. However, from an institutional point of view, integration has been largely uncoordinated, focusing mainly on trade agreements, currency swap arrangements among central banks, or initiatives to create regional bond markets, with often overlapping memberships and ultimately limited commitment". See the EU Report, Five Years After Enlargement, "Does the EU Make a Difference", Chapters 2 and 3, p. 44.

[11] Adjusted based on weighted exchange rate, IMF.

Table 3. Eastern, Central and Western European Countries: GDP Growth (real) 2007–2001.

	GDP Growth				
	2007	2008	2009	2010	2011 Forecasts
Europe	4.0	1.4	−4.6	2.3	2.2
Advanced European countries	3.0	0.5	−4.0	1.7	1.6
Emerging European countries	7.0	4.1	−6.0	3.9	3.8
European Union	3.2	0.8	−4.1	1.7	1.7
Emerging EU countries	6.0	4.4	−3.0	1.6	2.9
Bulgaria	6.2	6.0	−5.0	0.0	2.0
Estonia	6.9	−5.1	−13.9	1.8	3.5
Hungary	1.0	0.6	−6.3	0.6	2.0
Latvia	10.0	−4.2	−18.0	−1.0	3.3
Lithuania	9.8	2.8	−14.8	1.3	3.1
Poland	6.8	5.0	1.7	3.4	3.7
Roumania	6.3	7.3	−7.1	−1.9	1.5

Source: http://www.imf.org/external/french/np/sec/pr/2010/pr10391f.htm.

Table 4. Population and World Income in 1820, 1951, 2000 and 2025.

	Population			World income GDP			
	1820	1951	2000	1820	1950	2000	2025
Western world	14%	17%	13%	25%	56%	45%	30%
Asian world	66%	66%	70%	58%	19%	33%	55–60%

Source: Radelet and Sachs (1997).

Asia as a whole has caught up this century. They also point out the important balance of world wealth obtained in the region in just a few short decades, to the detriment of the current western position, built up over the last two centuries. As Radelet and Sachs write, "in the next two decades China/India/Indonesia could reach 58% of world-wide income (GDP=) and in this way regain the level they obtained in 1820" (see Table 4).

Third, both sub-regions — Eastern Europe and the Mekong region (with the exception of Thailand[12]) — have faced major historical challenges in the area of national sovereignty during the past few decades. At precisely the same time that they became independent and sovereign, they were forced to take on globalization and all its implications. In other words, at the very moment they had to ensure internal security, they also had to find adequate channels to cope with external pressures. Belonging to a supranational ensemble was the only guaranteed way to increase economic wealth and stabilize political regimes. For CEE, there was no alternative to EU integration in 1990. For Southeast Asian states — or at the very least the newest ASEAN members — belonging to ASEAN was the only way to reach worldwide markets and to pave the way for the adoption of WTO rules. However, becoming a member simultaneously required negotiating the loss of a certain degree of sovereignty. The resulting tension between membership and loss of power explains why some new members of each regional ensemble have tried to limit further "pooling of sovereignty".

Lastly concerning formal rules, considered in the EU to refer to a legal rational system, and in ASEAN to a more patrimonial order, legal bureaucracy might be considered to be an ideal type and as such, rarely (and perhaps never) appropriate to a given concrete historical situation. Singapore could be described as a state based on a type of rational patrimonial legality, and on the other hand, the Greek crisis has shown the presence of patrimonial behavior within EU states. In the same way, the category of Sultanism directly used by Weber might have been applied to the Balkan States before 1989 and even afterwards (Linz and Stepan, 1996; Kitschelt *et al.*, 1999). In both regions — CEE and Southeast Asia — the weight of historical legacies accompanying the transitory periods of systemic change have contributed to the setting up of insecure and rather obscure rules. For this

---

[12] Although Thailand, or more precisely Siam, never disappeared under colonial rule, several authors have underlined the intense "westernization" of its elites notably under pressure from the British and French empires. Some have gone as far as to call it a "semi-colonial" state. See Harrison and Jackson (2010).

reason, a much more appropriate form of bureaucracy has emerged: "patrimonial bureaucracy" to use Weberian terms (Weber, 1958).[13] "Patrimonial bureaucracy" is a complex mix of rational rules and personal connections, proper to transitory periods shifting from traditional orders dominated by the father figure, to more legal rational ones placed under the responsibility of civil servants capturing the dynamics of State — society, Evan uses the term "embedded autonomy" to indicate the same features of bureaucracy made of neutral rules and communities ties, which allow the states to be anchored in society.[14] To this extent, there is no difference between states emerging from a Soviet type system or from Communist rule, whether they are in Europe or Asia. Patrimonial bureaucracy plays the same role in the administrative order as political capitalism does in the realm of economic: A mix of legal rules requiring discipline and appropriate behavior from neutral civil servants. Relationships between people are regulated much more by personal links, loyalty and trust than by a respect for rules. This provides an important reason to compare both areas, not only because they share comparable bureaucracies, but also because these bureaucracies support different types of political economies. The term "political economy" as used here is understood to mean the theory targeting blended political and economic influences within closed or open systems, from a disciplinary perspective.[15] From an empirical perspective it includes the notion of the intertwined relationship of political elites and business backed by military powers

---

[13] Concerning the use of the term "patrimonial bureaucracy" in Asia see (Evans and Rausch, 1999; Rudolf and Rudolf, 1979). Concerning CEE (Bafoil, 2010a).

[14] Informal networks give the bureaucracy an internal coherence and corporate identity that meritocracy alone could not provide, but the character and consequences of these networks depend fundamentally on the strict selection process through which civil servants are chosen"... later, he adds "This 'embedded autonomy', which is precisely the mirror image of the incoherent despotism of the predatory state, is the key to the developmental state's effectiveness" (Evans, 1995, pp. 49–50).

[15] " . . . political economy, an emerging subfield within political science whose broad focus is the ways in which politics influences aspects of economic policymaking and economic interests and outcomes influence political processes and outcomes" (Doner, 1991).

embedded in authoritarian regimes and even dictatorship.[16] From a comprehensive perspective, Ravi Harvind Palat has defined the term in this field as referring to relationships between political and business elites in each location (as) conditioned by the nature and structure of state power and the organizational strength and technological maturity of the bourgeoisie, by the size of their domestic markets and their varied endowments of natural resources, by the extent of the dislocation of the pre-war production and sales networks, and by the pattern of political and economic linkages in which they were enmeshed. In spite of institutional differences, the varying historical trajectories and differentiated political economies that characterize Europe and Asia, the conclusion must be drawn that a dynamic of convergence exists between them. This convergence can be seen in responses to pressure exerted by the markets on privatization (Chapter 3) and regionalization policies (Chapter 4). Policy in both these domains has given rise to considerable deregulation within industrial organizations (Chapter 5) aimed in both cases at encouraging FDI. One of the main theses in this book postulates that, for these states, membership of the EU or ASEAN has accentuated globalization by turning them into privileged vectors for the extension of largely unregulated capitalism (Chapters 6, 7, and 8).

2. Book Outline

What these two regions have in common is the fact that almost every country belonging to them lost its national sovereignty to a foreign empire at one point or another. This single fact provides the fundamental starting point of this study. The rediscovery of national independence became the highest collective value in each of these countries: The national state was re-embedded in national history and

---

[16] What Haggard defines as following: "First, the coherence of government policy does depend on the nature of the political institutions structuring business — government relations.…these institutional arrangements themselves are partly explained by the broader political relationship between the government and the private sector at critical historical junctures" (Haggard, 1994).

secured within internationally recognized borders. The state became the central actor once it had become legitimized in its fundamental monopoly of legal violence exercised within limited territories and secured by international organizations. This intentional reference to a Weberian definition of the state embraces two dimensions analyzed in the two parts below.

The first dimension concerns the process of consolidation within the state, which is shaped by changing policies such as privatization, regionalization and industrial relations. The first step is to analyze the political economy in each area. Far from emerging from nothing or resulting from the transitory period alone, political economies in these two regions are made up of long-term periods of colonialism and Soviet-type imperialism, combined with new rules. Rules imported from abroad cannot succeed unless they are adapted by domestic actors to fit in with national contexts.[17] Interests and ideas are recombined within the new architecture of rules according to the domestic level firstly, then to the global and lastly to the regional level.

The second dimension concerns intergovernmental relationships, resulting from the setting up of regional areas created in order to secure borders and guarantee internal development. This has been of utmost importance as the re-emergence of independent states very often occurred within unsecured environments marked by external insecurities caused by the surrounding "great powers" that had previously shaped the destiny of each region. The first objective of both the European Community and ASEAN as regional bodies was to ensure security based on a strong political determination to achieve it, even if both subsequently followed a more economic path. The EU founders wanted to eliminate any possibility of war in Europe by pooling economic resources (mainly coal and steel) and in this way they hoped to reduce German power. The ASEAN founders wanted to breathe life into a region which had been broken by the conflicts

---

[17] For Central and Eastern Europe, see Stark and Bruszt (1998). For Southeast Asia, see Acharya (1997).

between the Great Powers, US–USSR–China. Both were created in reaction to the threat of Communism.[18]

The book is divided into three parts. The first part covers the empirical and theoretical background of the content. The second part focuses on three public policies implemented by the CEE and Southeast Asian states: Privatization, regionalization, and industrial relations policies. The third part deals with integration into both regional ensembles (the EU and ASEAN) and enlargement policies.

2.1. *Part I*

The first chapter explains the empirical background of the book, focusing on how history matters by highlighting the similarities between shared features relative to the gradual disappearance of the state over a long period of time. Indeed, in both regions, the national states disappeared either under colonial or imperial rule, or indeed capitalist or Communist rule. However particular the cultural, political, economic and social experiences of each of them were, the fact is that after colonial or imperial occupation, national sovereignty became the highest value underpinning public policies.

Chapter 2 presents the theoretical framework of the book based on the "Bringing the State Báck in" approach which fuels the concepts of "strong" and "weak" states by discussing how they relate to concepts of "patrimonial bureaucracy", and to different kinds of political economies in both regions and at different periods of time.

The first part concludes with a presentation of the different states belonging to the CEE region and to Southeast Asia.

2.2. *Part II*

Part II addresses issues surrounding privatization, regionalization and social policies by focusing on the institutions, which support them.

---

[18] Anti communism provided a sense of identity to states that were otherwise so diverse that they were referred to collectively as the 'Balkan' of Asia. They joined forces primarily for "political objectives, stability and security", Lee Kuan Yew quoted in Webber (2001). See also Tarling (2006).

The third chapter analyzes the economic dynamics of transformation during the last 40 years by stressing the shift from very protective policies (*Import Substitution Industrialization* or "Big Push" policies) to more export-oriented economies and indeed very liberalized ones. By focusing on the economic process, it analyzes how national states have set up economic priorities that can be briefly summarized as "liberal" in order to adequately address issues arising from globalization. All of them are very distinct from each other depending on the historical path and the different ways of combining protective measures and export-oriented vision. During these economic transformations later called "privatizations", states never abandoned their sovereignty. Relationships between ruling authorities did not change very much, at least for a certain period. This lack of change, or in other words, the continuity of ruling economic and political elites and their intertwined activity reflects not only the extent of corruption present, but also the capacity of ruling groups to exercise strict control over economic and social changes.

Chapter 4 analyzes the type of transformation states have undergone during globalization. Such transformation essentially results from the regionalization process that has impacted all states. The process is characterized by economic pressures, linked to territorial embeddedness and political pressures linked to the challenges of democracy. But although the pressures have been the same everywhere, regionalization as such has been implemented very differently by individual states, in accordance with their own historical, social, and ethnic composition. The whole process has given rise to numerous conflicts and, to a large extent, regionalization is still very much a work in progress.

Chapter 5 analyzes the accompanying dynamic of the liberalization process from the industrial relations perspective. In both cases, trade unions are more or less absent and collective bargaining and collective rules remain the exception. The liberalization process has been accompanied by what is known as "management by flexibility". In all cases, the state remains an important actor, either by being a member of tripartite forums, or by breaking any alternative and emerging trade union.

Part II concludes by strengthening the comparison between policies aimed at transformation in both regions.

2.3. Part III

The last part of the book addresses issues surrounding regional development by examining different links between strong and weak states, and strong and weak regional ensembles in order to understand how the development of capitalism is organized within each region. Enlargement policies are dealt with in the final chapter.

Whatever the forms adopted by each type of regional development, both regions set up their own strategy by mapping certain territories and by distinguishing between micro-, meso-, and macro-regions. Chapter 6 compares the EU "grand theory" of cohesion policy: Its strategies, tools and objectives with the equivalent ASEAN policy, which receives greater support from regional business networks than its European counterpart.

Turning the analysis to local development, Chapter 7 focuses on different and particular economic zones on the one hand, and on various examples of cross-border cooperation on the other. In both cases, difficulties in lifting historical barriers continue to exist. Collective memory has a huge impact in these border areas. Riparian populations have always been divided by war. In both areas, micro-cooperation largely depends on well-functioning governance between central and local political, administrative and economic actors.

The last chapter deals with the consequences of the most recent periods of enlargement: The 1990s for Southeast Asia and the 2000s for CEE. In both regions, enlargement has highlighted the success of small nationalist sovereign states rather than entailing more "sovereignty pooling" as in former times when sovereignty pooling was the only option for new member states. By joining regional entities, new member states in each regional ensemble in Europe and in Southeast Asia have contributed to diversity in and have halted the global dynamics of political widening apparent during previous decades in both regions.

The third part concludes that the categories of "strong" and "weak" states are only partially relevant.

The general conclusion is that capitalism has taken different forms in each region and that the systems are hybrids.

PART I
INTRODUCTION — THE DESTRUCTION
OF HISTORICAL STATES

One of the central theses of this book postulates that the fate shared by almost all the states considered in the CEE region and in Southeast Asia is that they were all destroyed several times in the course of their history. As a result of this, they have fallen behind in political, economic and social terms. They fell behind politically because of the failure of national elites to emerge and because power was concentrated in the hands of the occupying powers. They fell behind economically because of their dependence on a foreign metropolis. Finally, they fell behind in social terms as a result of very harsh conditions within labor organizations. Once national independence had been recovered, three decisive phenomena became apparent, all of which were the direct result of their falling behind. These were: The absence of national institutions — whose creation took some time to accomplish; the close relations between political, economic and at times military elites which were often made up of individuals who had accumulated resources during the former regime; the strong promotion of the principle of sovereignty. Any attempt to negotiate even the slightest element of this sovereignty has encountered huge resistance from the new elites. This is what happened with internal negotiations aiming to decentralise public policy — through privatization and regionalization policies — and external negotiations with respectively, the EU or ASEAN. The concept of the resilient state stems from these phenomena. It can be grasped internally by examining public policy and externally by examining negotiations with the EU and ASEAN.

The first chapter deals with the legacies proper to each country in terms of the spatial distribution of resources, territorial inequalities and poverty, and finally minorities.

The second chapter provides a theoretical framework for this category of resilient state which allows an understanding of the notions of "strength" and "weakness" to emerge.

HISTORY AND GEOGRAPHY MATTER — BUT FOR WHAT KIND OF LEGACIES?

The first point to be made here is that most of the countries under consideration, belonging to the current European Union (EU) and Association of Southeast Asian Nations (ASEAN), have been in existence for a relatively short time. Central and Eastern Europe (CEE) countries were broken up by the four empires that had dominated Central Europe since the end of the 18th century: Russia, Prussia (becoming the German Empire after the defeat of France in 1870), the Austro-Hungarian Empire and lastly, the Ottoman Empire (Berendt and Ranki, 1974). Liberated from these empires at the end of WW1, they were sovereign states from 1919 to 1939.[1] Most of them then disappeared under Nazi rule, followed by more than four decades under Soviet occupation. By the end of the 19th century, most Southeast Asian countries had disappeared under the foreign rule of Britain, France, the Netherlands, Spain, or, later, the United States and to a very minor extent, Germany. In the second half of the 20th century, the Mekong region played host to a struggle between the great powers, the USSR, the US and China (Tarling, 1999; Osborne, 2005; Owen, 2006; Tarling, 2001).

In her masterpiece, *The Origins of Totalitarianism*, the German philosopher Hannah Arendt argues that what best defines Western Europe historically is the union between historical borders, unity of nations and the continuity of the State. She speaks therefore of the "holy trinity", which gave continuity to Western Europe and allowed identities to be forged, in contrast to Eastern Europe, which was

---

[1] Cekoslovakia disappeared under the Nazi rule in 1938.

constantly destroyed, and whose populations were blended together without sovereign states being created. The lack of continuity in borders in this part of Central Europe resulted in a scattering of ethnic groups, differing minorities and majorities, a great sense of community derived from local embeddedness, and a conspicuous lack of nation states caused by the domination of foreign empires. Despite this situation, there was a tremendous nationalistic feeling within some groups, which was overvalued by intellectuals wanting to hypostasize traditional values and myths of origin. This causal link between a lack of continuity in historical borders and an absence of nation states seems equally true for the Mekong region, where the features of blending populations, an absence of national unity and a disappearance of national states can also be observed. Benedict Anderson has highlighted the role of communities of young scholars and students, educated in different universities within Southeast Asia and less commonly in foreign metropolises, to explain the emergence of the sense of shared identity throughout the whole region (Anderson, 1983; Owen, 2005). Milton Osborne has underscored the difference between the Indonesian and Vietnamese nationalism that was strongly opposed to the foreign Dutch or French occupation, and the cooperative attitudes adopted by Cambodian, Laotian (and to a lesser extent Thai) elites, who sought not to be subjected to either Dutch or French rule over the Islands and the Mekong region (Osborne, 2005). Such a comparison allows us to understand that national sovereignty became the core value for new states *vis-à-vis* both domestic and foreign actors in the form of states or supranational regions. We will further analyze this phenomenon in the next chapters by considering, privatization, regionalization, industrial relations and regional development. But first, we should consider the important impact of historical and geographic legacies, by adopting two perspectives — territorial and social — in order to understand the legacies that produced the state in both regions. From this perspective, and for purposes of demonstration, we will isolate only a few useful variables, leaving aside many others that deal with education, nationalism and the political landscape.

The first part of this chapter defines the historical importance of the gradual disappearance over time of most countries' national sovereignty in both regions, whether because of imperialism in Europe or colonialism in Southeast Asia. Three types of legacies are highlighted: First, the lack of territorial continuity, followed by territorial inequalities, and finally poverty. Taken as a whole, these phenomena have marked social structures and notably the status of minorities in a lasting manner.

1.1. Lack of Territorial Continuity and Borders: Lack of Sovereign States

Historically, in both Europe and Southeast Asia, disputed borders have been a source of conflict. In both regions, borders have been frequently moved, checkpoints destroyed, and populations separated from each other. Rather than connecting territories and populations, borders have generated hatred and wars.

For centuries there were no clear borders in the Mekong regions.[2] States did not exist as such.[3] Kingdoms were constituted by the territory over which various subjugated groups paid tribute to the landlord, or to the dominant kingdom. Because borders were mostly mapped in the 19th century by colonial occupiers who "racialized" populations (Anderson, 1983; Winichakul, 1997), borders were experienced by local people as being highly arbitrary and were subjects of dispute between central and regional authorities. They are, therefore, a relatively recent innovation, but one that has not succeeded in creating the conditions for peaceful exchange. No supranational attempt to create a regional identity — whether colonial or communist — has succeeded in the long term. All foreign attempts to create something akin to an Asian identity failed. The Japanese project failed because their "grand" strategy of creating an "East Asian Co-Prosperity Area"

---

[2] "The concept of a frontier was uncommon if not unknown in SEA. The idea that the ambit of a state was geographically fixed was rarely accepted. What counted in SAE sparse in population was allegiance" (Tarling, 1998, p. 47).

[3] "Prior to European colonization the demarcation of political space, which we take to be such a familiar part of national and international life, was unknown in SEA" (Beeson, 2007, p. 47).

consisted of merely subjugating Southeast Asia, as Japan had previously done with Korea from 1910 onwards (Cumings, 2005). Despite its success at ousting former Western occupants, Japan very quickly alienated its Southeast Asian allies.[4] Britain failed as well because they focused almost exclusively on India and, to a certain extent, Malaysia, because of Singapore. Their main objective was to carry the "white's man burden", whereas Dutch authorities were intent on imposing upon Indonesia the "ethical mission" and its inhumane system of work, called the "culture system" (SarDesai, 1994). French occupiers also failed in their goal of imposing their *mission civilisatrice* on an ill-defined historical region called Indochina. But by favoring the Vietnamese, they disregarded tensions resulting from the constant role of "boss" played by Vietnam *vis-à-vis* Cambodia and Laos (Pholsena, 2006b; Pholsena and Banomyong, 2004). Finally, during the second half of the 20th century, the United States also failed in its attempt to create a Southeast Asian identity, largely because they resorted to extensive bombing to do so. Unsurprisingly, this action was unlikely to spread anticommunist sentiments among a civil population who suffered a great deal.

In the end, no imperial project managed to create a sense of common Southeast Asian spirit, or a shared identity. There was no language likely to become a lingua franca, neither was there a common religion. Buddhism, Confucianism, Islam, and Christianity tended to split countries rather to unite them. Identity was nurtured on a national level during clashes and fighting with immediate neighbors. All of the Mekong countries have always had conflictual relations with their neighbors. Burma and Thailand, for example, have been enemies for centuries, Burma having completely destroyed the Siamese capital in 1772. Similarly Cambodia and Thailand, and Thailand and Laos, have all been involved in protracted territorial disputes. Finally, Vietnam attracted hostility from all quarters due to its imperialistic designs on the entire Mekong basin, elaborated first by its emperors and subsequently by French occupiers. Everywhere there were disputes about land ownership,

---

[4] As Beeson (2007, p. 47) says "Strategically and economically the Great East Asian Co-Prosperity sphere was ill-conceived and unsuccessful" (see also Osborne, 2005).

razzia, and local wars to extract tribute from reluctant vassals. Meanwhile, local populations migrated across borders, ignoring the warlord they were subject to, having no geographical identity other than a very local one, which changed with the shifting of village boundaries.

CEE and Southeastern Asia have in common the fact that over the centuries most of their constituent countries disappeared gradually, both before and during the rule of the main European empires. If we consider CEE, the first occupier to be mentioned is Prussia, which became the German empire in 1871. For 123 years, from 1795 up to 1918, the Western part of Poland, which was the most developed part of the country, was occupied by its Western neighbor and the inhabitants were forced to be "German". What this meant in practice was that Polish citizens were compelled to become second-class German citizens.[5] In the Central part of the European continent, from the 16th century onwards, the Habsburg Empire dominated the Hungarian kingdom, including Slovak territories on its Northern outskirts. In the 1620s, it annexed Bohemia and Moravia, including the highly developed region of Prague. Most of CEE became part of the Russian empire, which advanced victoriously Westwards, capturing the Eastern part of Poland along with Warsaw at the end of the 18th Century, and Southwards, annexing Central Asia and taking over the territory between the Mediterranean Sea and the Black Sea by expelling the Ottoman Empire from Europe. The Ottoman Empire at its height, between the 16th and 18th centuries, spanned what is now Bosnia, Herzegovina, Macedonia, Bulgaria, Walachia and Moldavia (parts of the present-day Romania) in Europe, and extended up to Central Asia, and South into Syria, Iran, Iraq, and Egypt.

Finally, although the communist and postcolonial periods contributed to stabilizing borders, they did not create better communication among people. The strong assertion of national sovereignty by the new elites was mainly seen as a historic victory over the class or racial conflicts that had resulted from capitalism's destruction of traditional values and communities. These conflicts resulted in protectionist

---

[5] In the part dedicated to the nation, Weber speaks of Silesian people as "passive but docile German citizens" (*Wirtschaft und Gesellschaft*, 5te Auflage, p. 527).

policies, which encompassed not only economic but political life. Modernization, as we will show in the fifth chapter, was considered an inclusive and even closed vision of development thanks to protectionist economic policies which supported "big push" policies. They were based on the development of heavy industry, just like "import substitute industrialization", which had the same goal, though it was based on more tariff barriers. All of them were backed by authoritarian regimes or dictatorships which imposed highly centralized decision-making and concentration of industrial relations within a unified labor confederation with strong links to the political elites.[6]

From the political perspective, protectionism adopted defensive measures aimed at completely closing off territories, even from bordering neighbors considered to be "brothers". In the Mekong region, all the borders were heavily militarized, leading to considerable environmental and human destruction. The Cold War brought barbed wires to the borders of CEE, and despite the fact that borders between "brother countries" were known as "borders of friendship", citizens living in the East were not allowed cross-border visits, even to see their own families. These rules were only relaxed during the 1970s, and then just for a few citizens of Poland. In the same period, retired people won the right to visit family on the Western side, and in the 1970s students were permitted to work in Northern and Western Europe during their summer holidays. After the Solidarity period ended in December 1981, it was forbidden for East German citizens to cross the Eastern border to visit Poland.[7] Communist bosses were afraid that the Solidarity revolutionary spirit would spread.

Two major legacies stem from these very rapidly squeezed historical and geographical features. The first regards territorial distribution,

---

[6] For Asia, see Deyo (1989). For Eastern Europe, see Kaeser and Radice (1977).

[7] Solidarity started at the end of August 1980 and soon had some 10 million members. It was the first free trade union in the Soviet bloc (apart from some short-lived experiments in the USSR in the 70s). Its creation can be considered as marking the beginning of the end of Communism in Europe. It lost its legal status on December 13, 1981, before being banned.

the second social structures. These different legacies allow us to construct our comparison by emphasizing the importance of the state, bureaucracy, and civil societies.

1.2. Territorial Imbalances: Inter- and Intra-Regional Disparities

In both regional areas, the territorial differentiations anchored in different historical experiences have reinforced the major cleavage between urban and rural areas, a cleavage, which could more accurately be described as a break between the capital and the rest of the country. Huge territorial inequality — much bigger in Southeast Asia than in Eastern Europe — is coupled with a geographical cleavage. In Southeast Asia, this divide has set apart the coastal and riverside cities of Bangkok, Saigon, and to a lesser extent Phnom Penh and Hanoi, from the small cities of the interior. In CEE, the Soviet type political development has created a very deep divide between the previously developed Western regions, which were later undermined by the new Communist authorities, and the previously economically underdeveloped Eastern regions, which under the new Soviet regime became targeted for economic development. The Eastern territories bordering the Soviet Union were thus deliberately and rapidly developed with industrial plants and collective farms, while the Western borders were equipped with military barracks, miradors and checkpoints.

Huge territorial inequalities in both regions result in large disparities of income and, therefore, different levels of wealth and poverty.[8]

---

[8] How to define poverty? As Rigg (2003) says, it is difficult to have one definition for everyone. It depends on different variables such as per capita income, per capita consumption, educational level of adult household members, per capita agricultural land. The problem is that different definitions target different populations. Moreover in SEA a lot of experts criticized the fact that many categories of people are not considered poor because they are not "targeted" by the public policies. Furthermore, a lot of public policies fail to succeed because they do not target the "right" poor. The same observation is made by experts who analyze poverty in the "backward" EU regions, see Barca (2009, Chapter 7). For the definition of "backward" region, see Chapter 7.

1.2.1. *Disparities between member states and within both regions*

Huge differences can be observed between countries in Southeast Asia (see Table 1.1). First of all, if we look at the ASEAN 6, namely the founders of ASEAN (Indonesia, Malaysia, the Philippines, Singapore, Thailand, and later Brunei), in 2000 the average per capita GDP was over USD 13,000. This represents more than 13 times the equivalent figure for ASEAN's new members, the so-called CLMV (Cambodia, Laos, Myanmar, Vietnam), whose per capita GDP averaged less than USD 1,000. Even this gap is dwarfed by the ratio (40:1) between the GDP per capita of the most highly–developed country, Singapore (USD 25,000), and that of the least developed country, Laos (USD 600).

Although these disparities are huge, it should be noted that equivalent differences in Europe are also large (see Table 1.2). Indeed, before 2004, the ratio of differences between the populations living in the top 10% of the 15 richest EU regions and the bottom 10% living in the 15 poorest EU regions was less than one to three, or 61% and 161% of the European average. After enlargement, the gap has more than doubled to one to seven, or between 31% and 177%. From a regional perspective, the most highly developed region — Inner London — has a GDP per capita of 334% of the European average, while the least developed region has a GDP of 26% of the EU average.

Table 1.1. Differential between most and least developed Southeast Asian countries (Purchasing power annual rate and population) 2010.

	Highest	Lowest	Ratio (*x* times)
GDP/PPP	Singapore USD 25,000	Laos USD 600	40
Population	Indonesia 220 million	Brunei 404,000	500
		Laos 5 million	40

Table 1.2. Differential between the most and least developed European countries (Purchasing power annual rate and population).

	Highest	Lowest	Ratio
GDP PPP	Luxembourg 32,000 euros	Bulgaria 2,500 euros	15
Population	Germany 82.5 millions	Malta 404,000	204

Nevertheless, the differences within the ASEAN states are much more complex: Even within the ASEAN 6, Singapore's per capita GDP is seven times higher than that of Indonesia. Pre-2004 in Europe, the difference between Luxembourg, the richest country, and Portugal, the poorest, was not comparable to this. Moreover, there are also significant differences between Vietnam and the other three newer members (Cambodia, Laos, and Myanmar).

1.2.2. *Capital cities versus surrounding regions*

Concentration of wealth and capacities in urban centers results in huge territorial imbalances. At this stage, Southeast Asia is experiencing a degree of concentration in capital cities that is generally much higher than that seen in CEE. If we compare the number of inhabitants in the capital and the second biggest city, the Thai capital, Bangkok, is 10 times bigger than the second Thai city, Chiang Mai, and Phnom Penh is ten times bigger than Cambodia's next biggest city, Battambang. Moreover, the average income is three times higher in the most highly developed part of Bangkok than in Chang Mai, and is 10 times higher than in the poorest region, Isan, in North East Thailand. But the differences lay not so much between city populations within a particular country than between income levels.

In the more developed European countries, differences between metropolises and the rest of the country are smaller than in the less developed areas, located in Europe's Southern or Eastern peripheries. According to a report from the DG Regio,[9] growth in the most highly developed countries is far less concentrated, as opposed to less developed regions where metropolitan economies are relatively more important. CEE has three characteristics which distinguish it from Western Europe. The first factor is the huge gap between capital cities and other metropolises. For instance, Bratislava's GDP per head is three times higher than that of Slovakia's second city, Kosice. These countries are therefore considered monocentric. The second factor is the high concentration of assets that induce a strong divide between the core city

---

[9] See EU Report (2009a).

and surrounding regions. Finally, the third factor is the huge risk associated with this concentration. These different data indicate that the "catching up" that characterizes less developed countries leads to high levels of concentration. The capital cities often tend to suck resources in from the periphery and to attract most of the FDI at the expense of other regions. In this regard, Poland presents something of an exception, with eight major cities spread out across its territory.[10] Regional capitals have a much greater importance than they have in neighboring countries. While Warsaw has the highest GDP per capita at almost 150% of the national average, figures for Katowice, Poland's second city, correspond to about 110% of the national average, and GDP per capita in Wroclaw and Gdansk are also both higher than the national average.[11] This greater regional and metropolitan distribution may partially explain Polish resilience to the current crisis.

However, while the interregional disparities are larger in Southeast Asia, the intraregional ones are bigger in both CEE and Southeast Asia. High levels of disparities have been detected in both EU members who joined in 2004 and in East Asian states (Balisican *et al.*, 2006). Growth does not necessarily spill over into regions, which have been lagging behind. In fact, on the contrary, it seems to deepen initial territorial inequalities. If territorial balance is an important challenge for the public authorities at the national level, it is equally important at the local level, namely within each region (NUTS3). It raises issues concerning what kind of policies can be delegated from the regional urban centers to their peripheries. In Europe the "place-based approach" seeks to foster local strategies that are theoretically much better placed to achieve their objectives than central strategies, because local actors have a much better knowledge of their own needs and environment than their central partners do (Barca, 2009). Only

---

[10] These cities are Warsaw, Lodz, Cracow, Katowice, Wroclaw, Poznan, Szczecin, and Gdansk. Some analysts and regional authorities consider that there are not eight but 11, if regional cities from the Eastern side are taken into consideration (Balystok, Lublin, and Rzeszow).

[11] "Countries with several metropolises with a high quality business environment offer a large range of locations to entrepreneurs and investors, instead of just one high quality location and the others lagging behind" (EU Report, 2009a).

local actors can tackle and exploit the "hidden resources" that are the key to development (as we will see in Chapter 7).

1.2.3. *Poverty*

However, poverty is defined and calculated, it is inevitably more widespread in certain territories and among certain populations — particularly those located close to borders (see Fig. 1.1).

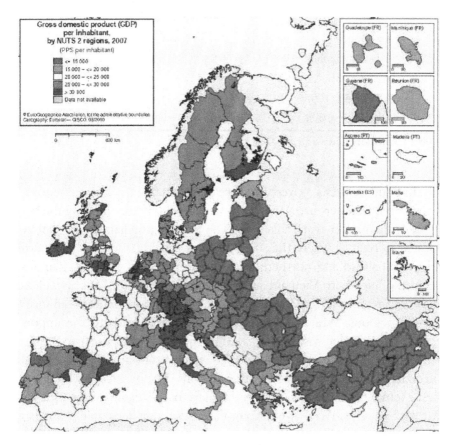

Fig. 1.1.   GDP per inhabitant, by NUTS 2 regions in PPS.[12]

Source: Eurostat (2007).

---

[12] "A so-called 'backward' region is a region having a GDP/per capita less than 75% of the EU average", see Chapter 7.

Table 1.3. The geographical distribution of the poor in Southeast Asia: Rural and urban levels of poverty.

	Incidence of poverty		
	Rural	Urban	Total
Brunei	—	—	—
Cambodia (1999)	40.0	25.5	35.9
Indonesia (1999)	26.1	19.5	23.4
Laos (1997/1998)	40.0	17.5	36.3
Malaysia (1999)	13.2	3.8	8.1
Myanmar	—	—	—
The Philippines (2000)	54.4	25.0	40.0
Singapore	—	—	—
Thailand (1998)	17.2	1.5	12.9
Vietnam (1998)	45.0	9.0	37.

Source: www.adb.org/2001, p. 93.

In Southeast Asia, poverty is more of a rural than an urban phenomenon, although there are also zones of great poverty surrounding the big cities of the region (see Table 1.3). The poorest populations are mainly located in regions where the soil is of poor quality, in the northeastern part of Thailand and northern part of Cambodia, in the mountainous regions of Northern Vietnam and between Vietnam and Laos, as well as in border regions affected by long conflicts, and more generally in inaccessible regions. While the development dynamic leads to the importance of capitals increasing compared to the other cities or surrounding rural areas, the poverty dynamic is made more pronounced by territorial inequality between capitals and other regions. The megacity of Bangkok best exemplifies the two cleavages that have been steadily widening over the past 40 years. Why? Even though all regions are developing, the gap between the capital and the rest of the country will continue to widen, because Bangkok is growing faster than other regions are. More generally, although lagging regions are growing and becoming less backward, the most highly developed regions are growing even faster. Thus, the backwardness of the less developed regions will continue to grow.

Table 1.4. Regional and rural–urban incidences of poverty in Thailand 1975–1994 (%).

	1975/76	1988	1992	1994	1996	1998
Entire country	30	22.2	13.1	14.3	11.4	13.0
Villages	36	25.5	15.5	18.7	15	22
Municipal areas	13	6.4	2.4	1.8	2	1

Source: Rigg (2003, p. 115).

There are three populations which are most affected by poverty. The first is the immigrant population. In 2004, Thailand hosted 1.5 million illegal immigrants, mainly from Myanmar and from Laos, 70,000 of whom would end up working in Cambodia. These workers have very poor working conditions. The second is the HIV Aids and drug-addicted population. HIV-positive individuals number 750,000 in Thailand, 530,000 in Myanmar, 220,000 in Cambodia, and 100,000 in Vietnam, and 1,400 in Laos (Data from 2000; Rigg, 2003). Members of the third and last group are victims of people trafficking — the women and young girls, who are generally children, who are forced into employment as sex workers. Finally, in Southeast Asia overall poverty is declining rapidly while the relative backwardness of certain areas is becoming more pronounced. This means that even if lagging regions can combat and reduce poverty, if poverty declines even more quickly and more substantially in other regions, the gap is widening. Poverty is a multifaceted problem that requires multiple interventions in the areas of family, education, health, employment and income distribution.

Poverty in CEE presents particular features linked to the restructuring process which occurred after 1990, and which has strongly impacted particular territories over the last two decades. We shall start with some general observations about the European dimension of poverty. Poverty in Europe is particularly associated with certain types of territory, such as sparsely populated regions (SPRs), which are affected by a lack of accessibility to public goods; islands, mainly those far from their metropolis; and the outermost regions, which are impacted by their distance from the capital,[13] and which are among the very poorest regions (for example, Kardzhali in Bulgaria with a GDP per head of 27% of the EU average) (Monfort, 2009). What is much more relevant for our purposes, however, is the significance of borders. In the 27 country EU, more than 195 million people live in regional border areas which amounts to 39.5% of the EU population, including the 35% of the EU population who live mainly in Central–Eastern external border areas.[14] The level of development of EU inhabitants living near borders is lower than the EU average (GDP per head in 2006: 88.3%). Several differences distinguish highly developed internal border regions from the less developed external ones. Within this last group, maritime borders are much more developed (92% of the EU average) than some external borders areas which are mainly located in Eastern Europe (GDP less than 64% of the EU average) (see Table 1.5). In these external borders, unemployment is generally higher and accessibility to public services is more problematic than in

Table 1.5. Categories of regions, number of regions, share of EU population, population, GDP.

Regions	Number of regions	Share of EU pop %	Population 1000 hab	GDP : Head PPS Index EU 27 = 100
Borders	547	39.5%	195,184	88,3
internal	488	35.3%	174,297	91.5
external	124	9.1%	45,060	64
terrestrial	389	27%	133,435	83.2
maritime	194	16%	79,017	99.2
Mountainous	168	8%	39,514	77.0
Islands	56	3%	14,870	79.2
SPRs	18	0.6%	3,023	96
Outermost	13	0.9%	4,267	79.5
Total	642	44.3%		100

Source: Monfort (2009).

[13] Like La Réunion, 9,400 kms away from Paris.
[14] With 27% of EU population in terrestrial border.

other regions. Finally, these Eastern borders are disadvantaged because they border even poorer states and regions, like Belarus and Ukraine. On the other hand, the Western borders of Polish, Czech or Hungarian regions are more developed than their Eastern borders because they are next to highly developed countries like Germany and Austria.

Eastern regions of the Eastern states have suffered greatly from the major restructuring process of both industrial plants and state-owned farms. Poverty has rapidly increased in these territories which were already quite poor before 1939, before being artificially strengthened during the Communist period by industrial investments, then largely abandoned in the aftermath of 1989. These territories have, moreover, been almost completely ignored by Foreign Direct Investments, which principally targeted developed cities equipped with amenities that small and medium-sized cities lacked. These small and medium-sized cities suffered doubly in the first post-communist decade. This was, first, because they were suppliers of big firms who, during restructuring, had cut off their provincial partners. Having mainly worked as mono-industrial structures creation of new jobs was particularly difficult. Second, the administrative restructuring process at the end of the 1990s took administrative functions away from the majority of small and medium cities, with the result that many people were forced to either leave the labor market or emigrate. Lastly, poverty is particularly acute in rural areas for a number of other reasons, ranging from the inadequate size of new farms, lack of equipment, the inability of new farmers to adapt to new market rules, and the post-1989 liquidation of state-owned enterprises, whose unskilled employees were unable to find alternative employment. Some Polish studies estimate that in the 1990s there were around 400,000 people heavily dependent on public assistance and afflicted with various social ills (alcoholism, prostitution, etc.) (Bafoil, 2007).

1.3. Social Structures: Intermediaries and Minorities

The third set of legacies concern populations, and more precisely, the relationships between majorities and minorities, insiders and outsiders, and native people and foreigners, which, as we saw above, were of primary importance because of the lack of a constituent state. Hannah Arendt defined Eastern European populations as a "belt of mixed populations". Her definition can also be usefully applied to Southeast Asian populations. Indeed in both regions, because of the long-term disappearance of borders due to foreign occupation, one can observe shared characteristics in political and social structures. All of these structures include two main features.

The first feature, referred to earlier, is the blending of populations which results from the very frequent shifting of borders, and the inability of a stable and sovereign state to organize collective rights and duties. As mentioned above, what Arendt identified as the "holy trinity" — characteristic of the Western European countries of Great Britain, France and Spain — namely, the unique concordance of historical borders, embedded in long-term history with unified peoples recognizing themselves as national unities, is not present in CEE. There, constant border violations, huge population migrations and the inclusion of regions within larger empires are associated with both a lack of unity at the national level and a deep localism stressing the importance of language, religious rituals, and closed communities (Bibo, 1984). Before World War I, the Austro-Hungarian empire was divided into three parts. The Western part contained 10 million German-Austrians, 6.5 m Czechs, 1.3 m Slovenians and a million each of Croatians, Serbians, and Italians. Ethnic Germans made up 25% of the population in the Czech regions. Lastly, the Hungarian Empire numbered 10 million Hungarians, three million Romanians, two million Germans, two million Slovakians, and 1.3 million Romanians. During the interwar period, Poland included 68% Poles, 10% Germans and 7% Jews. Although the Balkan States were more homogenous, Bulgaria was still 30% Turkish, and the Serbian population included 20% non-ethnic Serbs (Janos, 2000). Geographical and historical turmoil led to strong tensions between social groups. Certain individuals were discriminated against because of their social origins and/or professions. The top positions were mostly occupied by foreigners who had removed indigenous former occupants from these posts, usually by force. In CEE, under Soviet rule, most former ruling families were deposed and often murdered.

A similar picture emerged in Southeastern Asian under colonial rule, even though different strategies were applied by the occupiers. Regardless of whether they imposed "direct" or "indirect" rule, according to Furnivall's (1948) categories, the result was the same: The violent liquidation of the former authorities or their relegation to very minor positions, and their replacement by the new occupiers. Even Siam, which was the only kingdom not to be occupied, had to submit to British and French territorial claims and to relinquish ownership of some territory (Wyatt, 2002; Baker and Phongpaichit, 2006). In the cases of Burma and Cochinchina, ruling authorities were removed from office and assassinated. In Malaysia and the Philippines, ruling monarchies remained in office but had no power, and intermediary levels of government were placed under strict control.[15] A particular form of domination was represented by the occupation of Cambodia, Northern and Southern Vietnam, and in Java where the central authorities remained in place and the indigenous population supported the burden of occupation.[16] In all cases, these strategies resulted in a situation where, far from taking on entire responsibility for public affairs, the foreign occupier would manipulate intermediaries who were often chosen from the former upper classes. The governor came from the imperial or foreign court, assisted by the representatives of the local aristocracy. In central bureaucracies, factories, and plantations, a thin stratum of indigenous families filled the role of intermediaries, gaining prestige and

---

[15] As Beeson (2007) writes: "the main impact of American colonialism was to consolidate the position of an indigenous oligarchy which was able to opportunistically enrich itself and use the State as a vehicle to maintain its own position, rather than a vehicle for nationally based economic development".

[16] "The consolidation of Dutch rule tended still further to the weakening of native society. Under native rule authority was an expression of will or not of law, but at the same time, it rested also on custom and consent; the strong man governed but he governed by consent, even if consent was rooted in fear...the native prince or regent with Dutch power behind him was much stronger than he had ever been, much less dependent on consent and far better able to act arbitrarily than former rulers who had depended solely on their force or will..." (Furnivall, 1944; quoted in SarDesai, 1994, p. 89).

wealth by keeping tight control on a large serf population, which was reduced to poverty and misery. Those people, such as translators or fiscal managers, who worked as "intermediaries" between the native people and foreigners ignorant of local customs and languages, were able to amass considerable savings which they could build upon once independence was won. Moreover, there was an emergence of a new elite who tended to go to the same universities, most of which were mostly located in Southeast Asia, though a few were educated in the metropolitan cities (Owen, 2005). Independence, far from bringing a halt to the cultural and education models inherited from colonialism, allowed these new elites to upgrade their positions and to occupy leading posts.[17] Very often related by marriage, these leading families have occupied a central role throughout the bureaucracy, business affairs, and military services ever since (Tipton, 2009).

1.3.1. *Active minorities*

A particular attention has to be paid here to several minorities that have played a definite role in supporting foreigners, and who, as a result, were segregated by the other indigenous elites and sometimes even deeply hated, namely German and Jewish minorities in CEE and Chinese minorities in Southeast Asia. Notwithstanding the similarities, a very important difference between these two minority groups needs to be pointed out. While the German and Jews disappeared en masse after World War II, leaving room for a much more "endogenous" middle class, the Chinese stayed and remained powerful, mainly through deep assimilation dynamics.

In CEE, two minorities enjoyed a special status: First, there were the Germans, who were disseminated in Eastern and far Eastern Europe from the 13th century onwards, and who were merchants,

---

[17] "On occasion independence meant transferring power from foreigners into the hands of a traditional elite or Westernized privileged class, which tried, at least in the early years, to maintain the economic and social status quo with a minimum of disruption, as in the Philippines and Malaysia" (Turnbull, 1992).

landowners, officers, bureaucrats, and, in general, well-integrated into local communities. In this respect they were very different from the second "active" minority, the Jews, who were generally much less integrated and very often discriminated against. Denied the right to serve in the army and bureaucracy and considered incapable of managing a farm because forbidden to buy soil, they were for the most part restricted to certain service activities like medicine, handicrafts, and money-lending. According to Janos, during the interwar period there were around five million Jews in CEE, including 3.5 million in Poland. About 100,000 of these Jews belonged to the upper middle class, two million to the middle and lower class, and 700,000 to the proletarian class.[18] Although part of this minority was fully integrated, all members experienced waves of hate and bloody pogroms. During the industrialization dynamic, some Jews coming from Western Europe occupied managerial positions, even owning big factories. In Romania, three quarters of bank managers and a quarter of doctors were Jewish. In Hungary, a third of doctors were Jews. They were targeted by German citizens because of their financial resources, and hated by the indigenous workers, who had been reduced to being the Polish, Czech or Hungarian proletariat under "foreign" rule. During the 19th century, anti-Semitism flourished as defense of the nation became a rallying call for native elites. In this part of Europe, an uncertain assimilation emerged that was a mix of the foreign occupiers, cooperative minorities and all of the beneficiaries of capitalism, which was now in the rise. The people belonging to this group were considered to be the "non-national" or "non-natural" people, as opposed to the true defenders of tradition and "natural" virtues, namely rural people, peasants, native elites, poor intellectuals and nobles who had lost their leadership positions, but who "rightly" argued for morality, a sense of history and defense of the national soil (Bauvois *et al.*, 2004).

---

[18] Other data indicate different quantities: 9.9% of the Jewish population would belong to the upper class, 28.3% to the middle class, 37.6% to the lower one and 24.2% in the lowest class (see Janos, 2000).

In Southeast Asia, these "active minorities" were Chinese, Arabs and Indian people.[19] Alongside a huge Chinese proletariat, there were many educated Chinese engaged in handicrafts, the export of spices and food products, management of businesses, mines and manufacturing plants, as well as the organization of trade, harbors and supply chains. Like the Jews in the Middle Ages, the Chinese were forbidden to exercise certain activities,[20] and were put in charge of collecting taxes for landlords. Both minorities were able, therefore, to accumulate considerable financial reserves which they could use to help finance the aristocracy's expenditures for their private courts and military conquests. Discriminated against in both regions, these minorities therefore developed strong community links and rituals, protecting themselves by strengthening family ties and by exerting strict control over their own members.[21] Consequently the Chinese, like the Jewish minorities, have reinforced the strong divisions between "them" and "us", which thus created an opposition between "the society", referring to the lords and their servants, and the "community", backed by moral non-material virtues (see Table 1.6).

Once indigenous and native people had the opportunity to envisage the possibility of changing the national rules through upheaval, revolution or other forms of violence, these minorities became the targets of hysterical hatred and a desire for revenge among the rest of

---

[19] ... "In Southeast Asia this role was filled by the ethnic Chinese, including most of the prominent domestic capitalists who emerged in the postcolonial period (Forbes magazine calculated in 1994 that people with some degree of Chinese ethnicity accounted for 86% of Southeast Asia's billionaires" (Owen, 2005).

[20] "The history of economic growth shows over and over again the importance of creative minorities who deviate from, or are marginalized by, the dominant practices of their societies" (Owen, 2005, p. 389).

[21] As Owen (2005) writes, it is nevertheless neither Confucianism nor the ethnic Chinese that have produced capitalism in Southeast Asia. "Both factors had existed in China itself for centuries but China had never produced capitalists as formidable as those in postcolonial Southeast Asia. A unique historical environment in Southeast Asia — which both by discrimination against the Chinese and patronage of them deflected their energies almost entirely into commerce — accounts for their particular inspiration" (p. 390).

Table 1.6. Amount and percentage of Chinese among the workforce and their role in the different economies.

Pays	Number of Chinese	% of total	Role in economy
Brunei	42,800	15% (25% in Rigg)	Dominant in commerce
Cambodia	200,000 to 300,000 (500,000 before 1975)	1.9 to 2.8 (4.0 in Rigg)	Dominant in commerce, 70% of industry before 1975
Indonesia	3,250,000	3.5	73% of listed share capital, 68% of top 300 conglomerate groups
Laos	50,000	1.3 (0.2% Rigg)	Dominant in commerce and service industries
Malaysia	5,400,000	29%	61% of listed share capital, 60% of private sector managers, overrepresented in all professions
Myanmar	—	15 to 7% (3.4% Rigg)	Dominant in commerce and industry before 1962 majority of business created under "new" opening policy
The Philippines	1,200,000?	2%? (1.3% Rigg)	50% to 60% of listed share capital; 35% of sales
Singapore	2,079,000	77% (70% Rigg)	81% of listed share capital
Thailand	5,800,000?	10%?	81% of listed share capital; 100% of wholesale and foreign trade; 50% of retail trade
Vietnam	1,000,000	1.5%	Before 1975, 80% of industry, 100% of wholesale and foreign trade; 50% of retail trade. Since 1986, dominant in private sector, 45% of registered private firms in 1992
Total	23,9 (Rigg, p. 158)		

Source: Australia, 1995, quoted in Tipton (2009).

the populace. Central authorities allowed these desires to be satisfied, and let these minorities become scapegoats, despite the fact that they had been financially supported by them during more peaceful periods. In both Europe and Asia, public authorities skillfully incited calls for "ethnic cleansing", in order to regain legitimacy by taking the side of native people against "the rich", and the side of the exploited against "profiteers" and "exploiters". Nevertheless, these same authorities continued to use Chinese services, but often through hidden channels like Malaysia and Indonesia.

For these reasons, national policies launched against Chinese minorities reflect the increasing influence of nationalism in business, leading first to the construction of domestic conglomerates con-nected to foreign investors and finally to parallel economies. Chinese are scattered across the whole of Southeast Asia and are important economic players. As far as the treatment of Chinese is concerned, Southeastern Asian states can be divided in three groups. The first group includes states which actually expelled ethnic Chinese: Burma, during the 1950s and 1960s, and Vietnam, who did the same thing in the 1970s and 1980s. The consequences of these expulsions were very negative and, for some scholars, the Doi Moi reform launched in 1986 was a way of attempting to win back Chinese business. The second group refers to those states that, while using very nationalist rhetoric and being "inward oriented", as well as officially criticizing the Chinese for exploiting people, nevertheless allowed Chinese to continue to occupy key positions in the trade and finance sectors. In return, they financially support Malays and the Philippines occupying official jobs — the so-called "Ali Baba" agreement.[22] Indonesia,

---

[22] The Malay state developed hostile policies against the Chinese minority by support-ing a discriminatory policy in favor of the native Malays called *Bumiputras*. The state project was to create state-owned enterprises dedicated to Malay employment and to develop a middle class connected to business affairs strongly supporting the ruling party, the United Malays National Organization (UMNO). The privatization policy of the 1980s has therefore fostered Malaysian interests by creating only a few con-glomerates connected to FDI. But if some foreign firms became more competitive, Malay firms were becoming more rent seeking in some non-manufacturing sectors, with the same result experienced everywhere: A dual economy with a very few high

Thailand and Singapore, on the other hand, offered the Chinese a particular form of integration by "nationalizing" them. Once the period of strong nationalism was over in Indonesia, under Sukarno's "guided democracy" (MacIntyre, 1995) political authorities looked for capital and joined forces with them. But because they monopolized trade, despite representing only 5% of the population, they provoked huge resentment from the Indonesia's Muslim population. In Thailand, where as an assimilated group they have dominated small and large business activity since the mid 19th century, they were first persecuted under Phibun and Sarit (Wyatt, 2002), then invited to "Thaicize" their names and participate in economic growth as Thai people, while continuing to be harassed by political elites (Laothamatas, 1995).

1.3.2. *Roms: The combination of territorialization, poverty and political extremism*

Lastly, a particular population has to be mentioned in connection with poverty: The minority that has been the most discriminated against by both societies and states: The Roms (or gypsies). Before 1989, male Roms, who were predominantly unskilled, tended to be employed in unsafe, low-paid jobs, mainly in heavy industry. Women received some social benefits and generally had large families. Although they suffered discrimination under Communist regimes, who in Romania in particular manipulated ethnic hostility in order to strengthen their own political legitimacy, Rom populations still received much better treatment during the Communist era. Even though in the 1950s and 1960s they had been forced to settle in designated parts of the territory, they were still able to benefit from the welfare system. In Hungary as of 1985, 85.2% of the Rom population

---

performing foreign firms in the manufacturing sector, and a domestic sector made up of a ruling bureaucratic elite and domestic niches, leading to more and more lack of efficiency, corruption, and increasing poverty among the people "This politically influential domestic business community had become part of the governing elite" Nesadurai (2003).

was employed (compared to 65% in 1958), and 77.5% of Rom children had completed primary school (for children up to eight years old), compared to just 2.5% in 1961.

The large-scale industrial unemployment and cutting off former social subsidies, which occurred during the 1990s, not only reduced the standard of living of family members, but also increased the dynamics of social intolerance and racism. There were countless violent acts against these populations already reduced to deep poverty and deprived of any public support. Many Bulgarian and Romanian studies have highlighted the fact that in this deprivation process, women suffer more (Bafoil and Beichelt, 2008). Many extremist parties in CEE are openly racist, circulating anti-Rom and anti-Semitic propaganda. Some politicians, and not only those belonging to these extremist parties, have even openly advocated ethnic cleansing. A strong correlation exists between the territorial concentration of these minorities and poverty and political extremism. Bulgaria, Romania, Macedonia, Serbia, Bosnia and Herzegovina, Hungary and Slovakia are a group of countries where between 7% and 10% of the population are Roms. Roms tend to be located either in former industrial regions, such as the Northern part of Moravia in the Czech Republic and Eastern parts of Bulgaria, Slovakia and Hungary, or concentrated on the outskirts of main cities, or even within capital cities such as Fakulteta in Sofia.

1.4. Conclusion

Three major conclusions can be drawn from this brief presentation of the historical backgrounds and legacies of both regions. The first concerns minorities and civil societies, the second addresses "big families" and the last concerns territorial discrepancies. Both structural features help us to understand the issues that new states have faced in the last decades.

As mentioned earlier, minorities are numerically significant in both regions. Classification systems to identify minorities and their respective economic power differ from one region to the other. In CEE, there are three main categories of minorities. The first comprises the former foreign occupiers, namely Turks in Bulgaria or Russians in the Baltic states. Both minorities are also deeply rooted, either in capitals, in the case of the Russian natives, or at the periphery, in the case of the Turks. The second type of minority came about as a result of historical territorial divisions which had scattered populations and separated families from their homelands. This is mainly the case for the five million Hungarians who, since 1920, have been living in territories surrounding present day Hungary, in Voivodine (Serbia), Transylvania (Romania), and in the Southeastern Slovak region. The ethnic Hungarians living in Southeastern Slovakia are in a completely different situation from the former two minorities because their economic power is much higher than the domestic average (at least for some groups within these minorities), leading to tension with the central majority authorities. The last minority group to be accounted for is the Roms, who are scattered throughout CEE, but mainly in Romania and Bulgaria, Slovakia and the Czech Republic. Roms have experienced the worst of all worlds: They are the most excluded population, they live in the worst conditions and earn the lowest wages. Minorities in Southeast Asia are also excluded in a similar way, because most migrant immigrants are also members of minorities. Human Rights Watch in 2003 counted two million Burmese living in Thailand, with approximately 125,000 living in camps close to the border and 500,000 to 1 million working in textile mills and on construction jobs (Jönsson, 2010). Moreover, they are severely discriminated against by the majority populations. For example, in Laos it is said that people from the Hmong minority are maltreated by Laotian Communists because the Hmongs had previously supported the royal regime.[23] Therefore, some observers speak of ethno-nationalism based on the division between the ruling majority and persecuted minorities.

Considering these different minority issues makes us aware of the huge challenges that a new sovereign state faces, in dealing with the privatization dynamic, because of the economic strength of some

---

[23] French racialisation with Laos (Evans, 2002; Ivarson, 2008; Jönsson, 2010; Pholsena, 2002).

minorities and secondly with its internal administrative and regional restructuring process, because of the huge territorial density of minorities. Chapters 2 and 3 will address these challenges.

On the other hand, in focusing on the importance of some powerful minorities we intend to show how different forms of political economy are connected with a complex mix of bureaucratic, military and ruling elites who have ties with "big families". But who are the "big families"? In 1997, Suehiro analyzed the 100 most important families, whose combined revenues were equal to at least half of Thai GDP. The 30 largest own three quarters of total national capital, including 11 banking groups and four agro-businesses. Growth has dramatically increased since 1999 and the 49 biggest families were already ranked in the top 100, 20 years before. The main growth sectors are telecoms, energy, retailing and the alcoholic beverages industry. This concentration led to the creation of big holding companies. In 2004, in order to assess the impact of the Thai crisis of 1997, the same author analyzed data for the 220 groups who had 62% of GDP at their disposal. A total of 212 were originally Chinese and 87 were concentrated in one single activity. Around 106 were semi-conglomerates (having a core business and one or two non-core businesses), and 24 were conglomerates involved in more than four activities. Although most of them were listed on the stock exchange they retained the "Chinese" management model, the so-called "Kongsi", based on kinship and the central figure of the patriarch, who controlled the conglomerate and kept the internal organization secret. "*This was done by forming one or more investment firms that were not listed on the exchange and that were wholly owned by the members of the kongsi*".[24] Chapters 2, 4 and 5 will address the following

---

[24] "Kongsi" means partnership. It refers to the central authority of the patriarch over his whole property, led by members of his own family. He allocates the management of the main parts of his holding to his sons but maintains his final control. It is said that most of these patriarchs practice polygamy in order to diversify strategically their alliances, thanks to the wedding of their daughters. In this sense, the crisis can be analyzed as the result of an unsuccessful type of governance based on too strong intertwining of private interests, backed by deep concentration in the hands of the patriarch or of his sons; resulting in the too deep diversification of their holdings.

four topics: The importance of the crisis for understanding the dynamics of historical and economic change; the ability of certain elites to reshape their alliances in order to retain political and economic control; the importance of corruption resulting from such mixed alliances; and the very particular style of industrial relations resulting from such a crisis and economic liberalization, often referred to as "management by flexibility".

Lastly, from examining territorial dynamics, we have come to realize the importance in both regions of two major divides. The first divide is that between the capital city and the surrounding environment. A strong dynamic may be observed: That of highly developed urban centers attracting, even "sucking in" most technical and human resources at the expense of other areas. Such a dichotomy highlights the necessity for the ruling authorities to reduce such imbalances, by improving efficiency and paying more attention to equity. The second divide refers to the urban–rural one that is particularly apparent when we consider certain types of territory such as the mountain and border regions of Southeast Asia, and the Eastern borders of CEE. Both regions' borders are of utmost importance not only from a historical perspective, since borders were regularly displaced and abolished, but also because the poorest groups live near borders. To this extent, developing border areas was a major challenge, not only to secure peace and security but also to reduce the gap between them and more developed areas. The third part looks at the shared vision of member states within each region, and the regional strategy that is put in place to reduce territorial disparities. In the case of the EU, the regional development strategy is backed by a "grand" vision of economic, social and territorial cohesion — "The Cohesion Policy" — that favors support of national and regional (sub-state) development projects. In the case of Southeast Asia, regional strategy is based more on export-oriented projects likely to anchor regional development to

---

"The disadvantage was that the capacity to achieve this vision (of Thai 'khongsi' capitalism, FB) was wholly dependent on the management resources within the family. Such firms were reluctant to hire outside professionals who would be difficult to integrate with the family structure" (Phongpaichit and Baker, 2008, p. 45).

worldwide development. As Chapter 6 will show, a highly protected and internally oriented market is thus juxtaposed with a very open and worldwide-oriented market. Chapter 7 will analyze the impact of territorial divides in both regions in order to understand why special economic zones are located close to borders and capital cities. Finally Chapter 8 looks at the latest series of enlargements in each area to revisit preceding problematical areas. On the one hand, it focuses on the importance of politics in the decision to proceed to these enlargements and on the other hand, the capacity of new member states to use their national sovereignty as a means to display their strength. This poses the question of the "return of the state", which is the focus of the following chapter.

2 DEFINING A STATE IN TRANSITION

"Bringing the State Back in", to borrow a recently much used term from a well-known book title *Bringing The State Back In* (Evans *et al.*, 1985) is of primary importance to this analysis (Beeson, 2007). In his book, Evans argues that the loss of "the historical liquidation of the national sovereignties in order to understand the recombination of internal organization of states and their integration into the international order", must be taken seriously. Recombining domestic organizations and institutions is a way of recognizing historical dynamics, and more precisely, "the inherent historicity of sociopolitical structures" (Evans *et al.*, 1985, p. 28) that interact within the state. These structures which are historically embedded, combine different historical trajectories as highlighted by Migal's theory of the "state in society" (Migdal, 2001). According to Migdal, the main question concerns the state's ability to remain cohesive by reducing any centrifugal dynamics represented by ethnic minorities, regional peripheries, clans or whatever interest groups. The second question refers to the interactions between the state and its global environment.[1] Here, the main issue concerns the state's ability to draw benefit from belonging to a supranational ensemble. Taken together, these dimensions allow a better understanding of what exactly is meant by these categories of "strong" and "weak" states.

The coupled concepts of "strong" versus "weak" states refer to the huge tensions that characterize modern states forced to

---

[1] "The state necessarily stands at the intersection between domestic sociopolitical orders and the transnational relations within which they must maneuver for survival in relation to other states" (Evans *et al.*, 1985, p. 8).

maintain territorial unity by controlling their internal political and social components. Before defining these dimensions more precisely, it must first be acknowledged that these characterizations are rather ambiguous given that strong states can nurture weaknesses and weak states can be "remarkably resilient" (Dauvergne, 1998; Migdal, 2001). Moreover, it would be a mistake to associate strong states with Central and Eastern Europe (CEE) and weak states with Southeastern Asia. Policies such as regionalization or privatization reveal profound weaknesses in CEE as shall be seen below. Social policies should also be mentioned. The European Union (EU) commission was blamed for having exclusively fostered growth at the expense of social dynamics during the transition process, neglecting large numbers of people who lost their jobs as a result of the transition and who expected financial support from the EU (Landvai, 2004). Although the newly independent Eastern states were strong enough to rapidly implement market and democracy rules just after 1990, their institutions were very weak when it came to the management of EU rules. The process of adjustment to EU integration has aggravated these difficulties (Sissenich, 2010). In Southeast Asia, the ability to shift from a closed protective economic policy (such as "import substitution industrialization") to a much more open one, as characterized by export-oriented economies and "developmental states", would suggest rather that these are strong states. However, states may be defined where corruption is a plain matter of fact in both regions; for this reason alone, both regions could be considered to be rather weak. Lastly, when comparing the ability of different states to prevent attempts to deepen the process of "pooling sovereignty" once they have become members of supranational organizations (the EU and Association of Southeast Asian Nations (ASEAN)), caution should be exercised when using the terms strength and weakness. While they are sometimes described as weak, it might be more apt to describe them as strong in that they restrict other hegemonic powers. These different European and Asian states show their strength by transforming their initial weaknesses into strengths, by blocking certain dynamics and by preventing partners from becoming leaders.

Three dimensions help us to understand "weak" and "strong" states approaches: the polity and coherence of policies, the economic and technological independence, the link with the supranational region. The first part of this chapter examines the states from the perspective of their ability to design and implement public policies coherently. The second part draws up an inventory of the different types of economic and technological dependence that might justify the use of the term "weak" state. The third part links these categories to supranational dimensions.

2.1. Bureaucracies and Political Economies

In terms of the state, "strength" means its ability to make public policies coherent from government level at the top all the way down to local units.[2] To this extent, a strong state can be defined as a state, which is capable of controlling its periphery by mastering its various centrifugal forces, and by privileging particular social groups.[3] Acharya defines a "weak state structure" as a "e.g., lack of a close congruence between ethnic groups and territorial boundaries" (Acharya, 2009, p. 71). These different positions owe something to the thinking of Max Weber for whom the state is defined by its ability to exercise a monopoly over legitimate violence in a given territory (Weber, 1991). The question of legitimacy is decisive for the two aspects he describes: On the one hand, formal order that implies a respect for hierarchy, and on the other hand, the order accepted by citizens who are subject to it. In order to be considered legitimate, public institutions must be seen to be efficient and fair.

---

[2] Peter Dauvergne defines state strength in his introduction as "the willingness and the ability of a state to maintain social control, ensure societal compliance with official laws, act decisively, make effective policies, preserve stability and cohesion, encourage societal participation in state institutions, provide basic services, manage and control the national economy, and retain legitimacy" (Dauvergne, 1998, p. 2).

[3] "In the Mekong regions, the internal territories were for a long period of time abandoned to punishing activities and other razzia military raids. The main durable activities were concentrated close to the sea, in the delta, and far from the main basin of the Mekong. This particular territorial development that distinguished the border peripheries indicated their marginalization *vis-à-vis* the center. It reflected the structure of domination existing in Southeast Asia, which following the 'Mandala' system, allocated the source of power to the central king, and in decreasing degrees to its periphery. In this so-called 'Mandala system', the decentralization of power was perceived to be the major risk of the dilution of power and therefore decentralized levels were the least powerful of all levels" (Rigg, 2003, p. 125).

For Haggard, a strong state unifies the polity and is organized enough internally to launch unified policies (Haggard, 1994). Similarly for Doner, strong states remain independent of various forces, launch public policies independently from interest groups, and are well-organized (Doner, 1992). Here, the nature of the regime — whether democratic or despotic — plays no role at all. When European states are encouraged to combine efficient and equitable rules to support regional development policies under the pressure of the Lisbon Strategy, they may also be defined as strong states. However, this objective is much more an ideal than a reality. In the end, European targets have not been reached and the new programming period (2014–2020) has been placed under the umbrella of more demanding regulation.[4]

Apart from police and army services, bureaucracy is a critical tool that guarantees order and unity thanks to regulated control. Dispensing privileges and distinctions is another one. But as Weber clearly demonstrates, although bureaucracy may be the agent of freedom from the King by delivering fairer rules, it may also be the agent of inequality as nobody can control it and the state can develop rules confined only to a small group of leaders strongly backed up by military force. As long as the state can use force to impose the option of privatizing public rule it remains a strong state. However, simultaneously centrifugal forces can appear within such an organization. Interest groups develop particular preferences. As many American and French sociologists have shown using Weberian analysis, civil servants can sometimes develop their own system of rules — even of values — in order to protect themselves against overly burdensome bureaucratic rules that may threaten the organization.[5] However, when "sub-systems" of

---

[4] None of the targets set up in 2000 for the decade have been reached; neither has the level of employment (70%), nor the level of R&D (3% of expenditure).

[5] As Dauvergne explains, patronage reinforces state strength as long as state authorities are in step with the business milieu. If top officials feel they are not being sufficiently rewarded for their efforts, they will become involved with business people who break state rules. Mid-level officers can support the activities of business patrons to the detriment of state authorities.

rules are increased there is a risk that organizational disorder will be aggravated. In this case, a weak state can be defined as a state where civil servants develop their own rules. This type of behavior results in individual opportunism, disorganization, and conflict. Observers of Soviet bureaucracy have highlighted the dimension of "protective" behaviors developed by civil servants in order to cope with unpredictable central rules (Wnuk-Linpinski, 1982).

On the other hand, as Migdal rightly highlights, delivering privileges to only certain groups runs the risk of raising the dissatisfaction levels of non-elected groups which might subsequently be tempted to find another protector (Migdal, 1994). Moreover, because resources are limited, the strong state is constantly forced to fuel its allies in order to preclude any secessionist dynamic. However, the more supportive groups are empowered, the more they are in a position to secede. Indeed, decentralization creates a risk of rent capture by interest groups who are capable of contesting central power. When this happens, the state is likely to find allies among groups that have been discriminated against by offering them new incentives. In both cases, modernization promoted by the centralized states faces huge opposition from the surrounding periphery, and the decentralized units endanger the collective unity. The real issue for principal and agent is the balance between incentives and rewards.[6]

Finally, a strong state can limit the opportunism of different actors and for this reason, is able to draw upon the relevant resources (raw materials and fiscal revenues) to better master the unavoidable risks of decentralization. However, there is a risk here of creating a type of authoritarianism that relies heavily on the trust of only the closest allies and mistrusts all others, who are naturally suspected of plotting against the leader. Such a choice obviously tends towards dictatorship where

---

[6] "(...) state leaders need a set of strong state agencies to be able to make their own strategy of survival acceptable to the peasants and laborers of the third world" (Migdal, *op. cit.*, p. 402). He adds further, "The potentially damaging groups for the implementer are the regional officials from other state agencies or the government-sponsored party and the local strongmen themselves, whose rules are threatened by the new policy" (*ibid.*, p. 402).

legitimacy is strictly limited to kinship, clan and/or ethnicity, all of whom are rewarded with pre-bends while the majority of people remain deprived in all respects. However, a system of pre-bends can only work if resources are not limited which is never the case.[7] Such a regime faces three major risks: Vassals who can offer better incentives; Bureaucrats who can invent other goals; and, Peripheral players who can outweigh central support. Finally, a strong state is one that can force respect for the boss through regulated rules and relevant incentives. In contrast, a weak state is one that is bound to private interests, is in the hands of new powers, and is unable to impose the general interest as a common goal. For both regions under study here, legitimacy is the major issue.

This "strong states/weak states" approach is relevant to both regions for several reasons. First, Southeast Asian states could be defined as "strong states" because of the kind of political economy they articulate, strongly characterized by the intertwining of business and politics and very often, backed up by military groups. Moreover, this form of bureaucracy can be defined as patrimonial because of the strong patron–client relationship that dominates different forms of exchanges within a highly systemic cohesive unit. Backed by the widespread dissemination of collective values that enhance the role of authority and father figures, these relationships allow states to capture natural and industrial resources. As Dauvergne (1998, p. 142) says "Patron–clients are a key avenue by which non-state organizations, and especially executives, interact and influence the state". The term "rent capture" is being used here to refer to strong states with highly centralized political resources and the capacity to make the redistribution of goods possible.[8] This is the

---

[7] "The problem is that as long as strongmen continue to offer viable strategies of survival to those of their villages, ethnic groups, etc., there are no channels for state leaders to marshal public support and there is little motivation for the populations to lend such support. In other words, state leaders need a set of strong state agencies to be able to make their own strategy of survival acceptable to the peasants and laborers of the third world" (*ibid.*, p. 402).

[8] This definition can be countered by the significant amount of literature, which deals with the "resource curse", stressing the strong correlation between resource endowment and growth decay in the long term (Karl, 1997).

basis of the other fundamental definition of those states perceived as "developmental".[9] While the central state can manipulate prices, most public incentives and rewards are geared towards entrepreneurs who respect central directives.[10] In contrast, firms that do not respect central directives find themselves severely punished and excluded from public calls to tender. Industrial policies target the so-called "export-oriented" economy and huge public funds support the emergence of big-firm entrepreneurs that blend private interests and public elites (Beeson, 2007, p. 160). The Korean *Chaebols* can be considered the ultimate model of this kind of "developmental state" political economy.[11]After the Northeastern Asian states partially based on the Japanese model, Singapore is closest to exemplifying this kind of development. The island city looks like an "Asian miracle" because of its low level of bureaucratic corruption and strong business efficiency (Turner, 2002).[12] Finally, this type of patrimonial bureaucracy is based on informal and personal relations, which lead to the loosest of connections. Such features are fully compatible with the informal networks and loose connections between partners that characterize both regionalization, backed by

---

[9] See Chapter 4.

[10] This model can be found in Korean politics where "the main goal of Korea's finance was to hemorrhage as much capital as possible into the heavy industrialization program...the financial policy of Yushin was this: The government set financial prices at an artificial low to subsidize import-substituting, heavy chemical and export industries...The political economy of this bifurcated financial system was illiberal, undemocratic and statist...Every bank in the nation was owned and controlled by the State; bankers were bureaucrats and not entrepreneurs, they thought in terms of GNP and not profit and they loaned to those favored by the State" (Cumings, 2005, p. 352).

[11] Woo defined a *Chaebol* as "a family-owned and managed group of companies that exercises monopolistic or oligopolistic control in product lines and industries" (Woo, 1991, quoted in Cumings, 2005, p. 149).

[12] However, measures of corruption only cover criteria established by business. They do not refer to the political control exercised over bureaucracy. King clearly shows how much Singaporean bureaucracy is dominated by a culture of secrecy which is imposed by the monopoly party the PAP and which allows a high level of corruption among the ruling elites to exist (King, 2008).

business networks and the ASEAN-backed lack of "pooled sovereignty".[13]

However, states where rent seeking prevails, (in other words where the mix of private and public interests dominate to the exclusive benefit of a small elite), are unlikely to undergo reform and find it very difficult to legitimize their authority. They tend to be characterized by protected "niches" where corruption flourishes and huge inequalities are reflected. These become apparent when external threats occur. Because of this, a crisis (be it financial or political) always provides an ultimate and inescapable reason to change. The weakest states are those who are unable to secure the transition process and who are vulnerable to social unrest and the emergence of new regimes. The strongest ones are those who can face political and economic transition by securing the assets owned by elites or by opening up to completely different regimes. In both cases, external support is of absolute importance.

Finally, looking at the past few decades of development, a comparison of both these regions shows that a state can be characterized by a strong intertwining of political interests and business backed by a type of centralization which is reluctant to share its power with any decentralized or alternative type of power. Such a state can be qualified as strong as long as it can contain centrifugal forces. On the other hand, a strong state can also be characterized by the rule of law, meaning a clear and strong division of powers between public institutions — central or regional — and a legal rational bureaucracy backed by the criteria used to define a meritocracy. The process of transformation in CEE since 1990 has revealed the importance of the rule of law. This is understood to mean the clear demarcation between public and private interests, the need to impose rules of control on bureaucratic activities and the division of power between the center and the periphery. During this process, the states involved were able to assert their sovereignty

---

[13] As Lay Hwee Yeo points out "...networked regionalism is a formula that may suit weak states...ASEAN, an organization of relatively weak, developing states, is in fact a pioneer of networked regionalism" (see Yeo, 2010).

thanks to guarantees put in place by external organizations, such as NATO and by recombining historical legacies. However, even if the EU was massively present in the process of adjustment to EU rules by the candidates, some of them were beset by huge corruption. The Balkan states provide a major example of this although, generally speaking, all the candidate countries experienced some such failure.[14] Despite the adoption of democracy and the market economy, they did not fully comply with a rule of law system. Decentralization and regionalization policies were the theater of huge corruption.

One of the most important questions is to explain why and how corrupt organizations become more legal and better regulated by adopting more predictable rules. This involves identifying the necessary endogenous prerequisites that support change together with the external factors that condition change. When institutions are set up and delegated by the central state to manage and administer public goods and to support private action, they become an essential factor of change. Such institutions constitute a decisive distinction between the two cases under discussion here. In their latest research, North, Wallis and Weingast have described notions of "closed social orders" and "open access social orders" to distinguish between the two types of states. These are, on the one hand "natural states" whose underlying principle is control over access to resources (whatever they might be) by political elites, and on the other hand "open states", which are characterized by the rule of law, the permanence of institutions and the centralization of control over the army. The notions of "closed" and "open" (established on the basis of control over institutions by different groups who shape the law) might be further developed by analysis of the "weakness" and "strength" of the states. This is because these categories are used to highlight the ability of the states to control the internal and external dynamics present within them, and therefore to control the degree to which they are open or closed (North *et al.*, 2009).

---

[14] See Chapter 5.

2.2. Economic Dependency

For other scholars, the technological variable is much more important than the polity. A weak state is one that is unable to increase its research and development (R&D) budget and is unable, therefore, to launch coherent policies (Konstadakopulos, 2002). The degree of dependence on external powers provides a crucial variable in defining a state as weak or strong. In several Southeast Asian countries, the levels of R&D spending (as a percentage of gross domestic product (GDP)) is indeed weak (see Table 2.1): 0.2% in Malaysia and the Philippines, 0.3% in Thailand, 0.4% in Vietnam and 1.1% in Singapore (Intarakumnerd and Lecler, 2010) despite many technological and industrial plans concentrated in a few sectors and mainly supported by foreign direct investment (FDI). This major failure seems to mirror the incapacity of these particular Southeast Asian states to integrate foreign technologies. In Malaysia and the Philippines, where there are constitutional incentives for undertaking basic and applied research, the science and technology agenda has failed to encourage private firms to upgrade their technological level (Intarakumnerd and Lecler, 2010, p. 104). With regard to the automotive industry, "Thai industry has not been able to absorb foreign know-how and technology" (Konstadakopulos, 2002, p. 104). The technological variable is quite interesting for the purposes of comparison, because although the level of EU R&D expenditure is only about 2.6% of EU GDP, it is even less in ASEAN at less than 1%.[15]

The EU considers R&D expenditure to be a major lever towards realizing the European goal of making the EU the most highly developed "knowledge" society. Far from achieving this goal,[16] CEE

---

[15] The 5th Report. DG Regio, November 2010.

[16] The Lisbon Agenda sets up different targets, none of which were reached. Concerning R&D — despite a goal of 3% of EU GDP expenditures — the result was 2.6%. Concerning the employment rate, rather than the 70% EU target, only 67% was attained, with major differences seen between countries, with Demark at over 70% and Poland lower than 55%. Moreover, three quarters of R&D investment in the EU is concentrated in only three member states: Germany (34%); Great Britain (19%) and France (19%) (see Science, Technology and Innovation in Europe 2009, Eurostat Edition, Chapter 8, p. 176).

Table 2.1. S&T Indicators for selective Asian countries.

	Scientists and engineers in RD (1987–1997)	Scientific and technical journal articles (1997)	Expenditure in RD (1987–1997)	Patent applications filed	
				Residents 1998	Non-residents 1998
Indonesia	182	123	0.03	0	32,910
Malaysia	93	304	0.24	179	6,272
The Philippines	157	159	0.22	163	3,280
Singapore	2,318	1,164	1.13	311	44,637
Thailand	103	356	0.13	477	4,594
Vietnam	—	106	—	30	35,478
Cambodia	—	3	—	—	—
Laos PDR	—	2	—	—	—
Myanmar	—	3	—	—	—
South Korea	2,193	4,619	2.82	50,714	71,036

Source: World development indicators (2001), quoted in Konstadakopulos (2002, p. 105).

suffers greatly from the massive laying to waste of former R&D public potential over the past two decades. Furthermore, foreign investors have not transferred R&D to these countries making local development more fragile and more dependent on western FDI. Lepesant considers there to be a strong risk that the gap between developed EU countries and less developed ones (Southern and Eastern countries) will widen in the near future because of the very weak public structures supporting innovation. Worse still, although the new member states applied for 166 patents in 2006, that number was four times smaller than in Belgium and 4,300 times smaller than in Germany (Lepesant, 2012). Can it be inferred from these observations that CEE states are weak even though most of them have succeeded in implementing regionalization and privatization policies?

Mark Beeson adds a new perspective by stating that Southeast Asian states are weak because they are under the joint power of multinational actors, foreign banking systems, and a domestic coalition that has delegated part of their sovereignty to private actors (Beeson, 2003).[17] Intense state privatization (Hibou, 2004) is a major aspect of this kind of state that is characterized by asymmetric relations, rather than by norms or identity. Preferring to avoid the term "national sovereignty", Beeson instead highlights the weight of multinational enterprises, which are very few in number but which nonetheless manage to challenge or weaken states. In a similar vein, Phongpaichit and Baker consider that Thailand is a "weak state" due to the increasing importance of "big families" who used the Thai crisis of 1997 to reinforce their links with foreign investors and the ruling bureaucracy (Phongpaichit and Baker, 2008). A causal link can then be inferred from a weak state to a weak ASEAN defined as "a collocation of weak states" (Jones and Smith, 2007). Finally, in Southeast Asia the term

---

[17] The Thai crisis in 1997/1998 was an opportunity to reinforce the power of MNEs. "The principal players became the multinational firms that now owned much of the industry as well as the politicians who influenced decisions on excise taxes and governments budgets to support the auto industry through infrastructure development and technical training. Thai government ministers and industry leaders now fell captive to the multinational assemblers" (Niyomsilpa, 2008).

"weak state" refers to limited institutional state capacity, a lack of desire on the part of ASEAN members to improve this, too much bureaucracy and a "sluggish" decision-making process.

For their part, CEE states are strongly dependent on the West. The huge success they experienced from 2000–2008 can be linked to an increasing push from FDI that transformed CEE into one of its most successful locations (see Table 2.2).

The region's success can also be attributed to increasing public and private consumption fostered by an efficient banking system, which was almost completely in the hands of foreigners. Baltic states operated under the Swedish banking system while central European states operated under the Austrian system. Fully 70% of Hungarian banks are in foreign hands. Public investments supported by remarkable annual growth rates (over 6% in 2008) enabled extensive

Table 2.2. Eastern central monetary regimes and loans IMF after the 2008 crisis.

Countries	Monetary regimes	Economic risks	Loans IMF (€billions; %GDP)
Bulgaria	Fix changes ("currency board")	Monetary crisis and liquidities	
Estonia	Fix changes ("currency board")	Monetary crisis and liquidities	
Latvia	Fix changes ("peg")	Monetary crisis and liquidities	1.7 (10.6%)
Lithuania	Fix changes ("currency board")	Monetary crisis and liquidities	
Hungary	Floating changes ("forint")	Insolvability	11.8 (13.1%)
Poland	Floating change ("zloty")	Less value of zloty export decreasing	16 billions asked but avoided
Czech republic	Floating change ("courone")	Fall of exports	
Roumania	Floating changes ("new leu")	Insolvability	12.9 (13.4%)
Slovenia	euro Zone		
Slovakia	euro Zone	Fall of exports	

housing and transport programs to be implemented. However, from 2008 onwards, Sweden and Austria decided to limit operations in their eastern units in order to avoid a crisis in their own countries. The simultaneous effect of decreasing western demand, FDI withdrawal and a drop in production led to a sudden breakdown of these economies. Many firms went out of business, unemployment grew and private domestic demand decreased. Growth stopped, some states experienced huge negative growth, (Latvia in 2008 had a growth rate of 10% and one year later of minus 14%; Hungary respectively 7% and minus 5%), and the level of public debt rose to the extent that some states had to apply to the IMF for support (see Table 2.2). Bulgaria, which all the experts had praised for its financial discipline based on the adoption of a currency board was then strongly criticized for being unable to adapt to the new situation. Estonia experienced the same blame. For this reason, their situation, which was initially seen to be advantageous turned out to be a major disadvantage just one year later. Lack of flexibility was a positive sign of fiscal discipline but by the same token a negative sign heralding an inability to adapt. In other words, the very strong (greater than 70%) integration of Eastern and Central European trade into the European market was in some ways considered a fundamental success and in other ways a fatal dependency. This begs the question of how to define strong states.

2.3. Regionalism and Regionalization

The other dimension of "strong" versus "weak" states to merit discussion is what kind of supranational region emerges from strong states and what kind from weak states.[18] A causal link seems to unite weak states and weak regional ensembles so that strong states with "pooling sovereignty" lead to more institutionalized regions. However, this seeming causality is misleading if one interprets it to mean that: (1) Southeast Asian states are "weak"; and, (2) Regional development occurs only in the EU and not in Southeast Asia. Indeed, in both

---

[18] Even this word "Region" is misguiding because it also defines the subnational level.

areas, an interesting discussion opposes "regionalism" and "regionalization" wherein the term "regionalism" refers to a type of state-led dynamic, with a formal and institutional framework, while the term "regionalization" refers to a type of more informal business network. A sketch of both concepts will allow them to be clarified, which is necessary as they are polymorphic and will also pinpoint the links between institutions and identities. This is a object worthy of study in both regions.

Many scholars in Southeast Asia use both terms (Fort and Webber, 2008; Higgott, 1997, 2008; Katzenstein, 1999, 2005, 1996; Katzenstein and Shirah, 1997; Pempel, 2005; Telo, 2007). The term "regionalism" emphasizes the capacity of states and of multinational enterprises (MNEs) to build networks in the long term, thanks to institutions that provide social learning to the economic and political elites,[19] while "regionalization" stresses the capacity of certain players (Japan, China, ASEAN, and AFTA) to build systems of production/distribution in different worldwide regions (the EU, the US, Asia, etc) (Felker, 2003; Yeo, 2010). Higgott reformulates the two concepts: First, "regionalization" by stressing the process of integration resulting from the markets, and second "regionalism" by referring to state led projects resulting from the intergovernmental approach (Higgott, 2006).[20] "Regionalism" is more state driven and "regionalization" market driven. Therefore, the term regionalism is more appropriate to the EU which is highly regulated while regionalization is more appropriate to ASEAN which is more informally governed. However, several studies on EU actors have demonstrated the importance of interest groups at EU level where various lobbies exert strong pressure in Brussels. In both areas, economic networks are of

---

[19] "The expression of increased commercial and human transactions in a defined geographical space" versus "regionalization — the expression of the common sense of identity and destiny combined with the creation of institutions that express that identity and shape collective action" (Evans, 2005).

[20] Telo shares the same perspective when he writes, "By regionalization we understand the different public and private forms of societal and economic networking, association and cooperation within a region" (Telo, 2007).

great importance. They are part of the same reality — in short, the influence of business interest groups. In both areas they have an impact on the supranational levels. What Forst says about Asia, "to some extent, network theory might give the best explanation of the Asian integration process" (Eliassen and Arnesen, 2007) can be equally applied to the EU. Indeed, economic networks can be considered to provide the main support for EU rules. For Putnam, the Europeanization process is not a two-tier game but much more of a three-tier one, which can be explained by the capacities of domestic actors to weigh upon their national level, in order to use community resources for their own benefit (Putnam, 1988). In other words, EU rules reflect the influence of the domestic actors who can set up national rules at the national level. The stronger they are at the national level, the more influence they have in Brussels. Business actors from certain industrial sectors and agricultural lobbies are key players (Balme and Didier, 2008). Indeed EU interest groups and policy networks are of paramount importance in Brussels (Kohler-Koch, 1998). In Southeast Asia (and, more generally, in Eastern Asia), business networks are seen as the main driver of regional integration.[21] Japanese and Chinese networks support the huge dynamics of regionalization.

"Regionalism" is supported by institutional and formal official rules together with formal and informal relationships, while "regionalization" refers to the capacity to regionalize globalization by embedding production locally (Higgott, 2007). Both terms are equally important as each of them frames the concept of regional "identity". They do this by underlining the system of official relationships which ultimately lead to agreement and consensus and the strong networking capacity of Asian actors. By highlighting this great variety of formal and informal rules and networks, they contribute to the building of a Southeast Asian identity (just as such an identity exists in the EU), that Western states have constantly denied to the

---

[21] "By regionalization we understand the different public and private forms of societal and economic networking, association and cooperation within a region" (Telo, 2007; Borrus *et al.*, 2000).

region. Rather than define *a priori* a concept of identity that history seems to annihilate (Acharya, 2010; Duara, 2010; Hefner, 2010; Petman, 2010),[22] Southeast Asia observers defend the idea of a step-by-step construction that unites "bottom up" and "top down" approaches, by blending shared values and extended networks. To this extent, the constructivist approach is legitimate in that it stresses the importance of values and shared ideas. A region as such can be defined a "social construction" including identities, shared values and common rules which are developed through both top down and bottom up dynamics.[23]

In the EU, "regionalization" is used more often than "regionalism". With regard to the new member states, the term "regionalization" was used to describe the completion of the unified market by candidates once they had adopted the 21st chapter of the *Acquis Communautaire*. This 21st chapter tackles regionalization and is of particular importance on the subject. It forced EU candidates to implement regionalized organization, thus ending the centralistic administrative architecture put in place by the Communists, bringing citizens closer to their own institutions and making public administrations more efficient in the management of structural funds and the organization of public and private partnerships.[24] Therefore, by inviting future new members to reshape their own administrative map, the EU invited them to combine efficiency (efficient administrations and well-trained civil servants) and equity (institutions reflecting citizen identities). This is one of the EU's most distinctive features: The ability to target collective action by using efficiently run effective institutions. Economic development (regionalization) is supported by relevant formal rules (institutions) that forge and consolidate trust

---

[22] Acharya (2010) distinguishes at least five forms of Asian identities.

[23] For Jayasurija regionalism "is a set of cognitive practices shaped by language and political discourse, which through the creation of concepts, metaphors, analogies, determine how the region is defined: These serve to define the actors who are included (and excluded) within the region and thereby enable the emergence of a regional entity and identity" (Katzenstein, 1999).

[24] See Chapter 3.

between partners. In this regard, Frost is correct when he points out that "A key long-term lesson from Europe is that cooperation in specific, tangible areas of mutual benefits builds communication and trust and helps to manage change in regional power relationships, thus contributing substantially to regional peace, prosperity and security" (Frost, 2008).

Institutional identity is a core feature of the EU and it must be conceded that such a term is part of identity in CEE in that the process of adjustment was made possible because of the shared values of the candidates who clearly showed themselves to be in favor of shared rules (Schimmelfennig and Sedelmeier, 2005). Indeed, EU reunification was possible not only because a clear majority in both East and West were in favor of shared rules (Bafoil and Beichelt, 2008; Lippert and Umbach, 2005; Schimmelfennig and Sedelmeier, 2005; Schimmelfennig *et al.*, 2006), but also because the rule of law was an element, which the Central–Eastern states had in common (Winiecki, 2004). Because the process of differentiated development led to deeper territorial polarization, the meaning of the term changed slightly and came to define the capacity of EU rules to better organize EU development by jointly targeting efficiency (referring to areas of growth) and equity (referring to help for regions lagging behind). Regionalization has become more and more congruent with the term "integrated approach". This is used to designate a shared orientation of public policies achieved through the elaboration of cohesive development strategies, combining priorities and measures of development projects, and finally by achieving EU multilevel governance. This is what Haggard and Dauvergne refer to above albeit it in other but identical forms. However, there have been numerous failures in attempts to achieve these objectives and several reports have denounced wrongly implemented structural funds (Barca, 2009). EU conditionality has been insufficient and EU governance has failed to unify the different EU actors involved.

2.4. Conclusion

The current worldwide crisis clearly shows the return of the state as do the latest economic, social, and political developments in each regional area. This return has not led to a reinforcement of collective action or an affirmation of the emergence of supranational rules. Rather, it has restricted the emergence of supranational rules and has reasserted the unquestionable importance of national sovereignty. Far from leading the way to any old type of post-statism or federalism, the latest political dynamics in both regions have led to the consolidation of one central actor: The sovereign state. This has even occurred at the expense of collective action, as exemplified by enlargement. Moreover, during the last decade, policies of privatization and region-alization have fostered a recombination of state power thanks to the ability of the state to recombine internal and external assets.

Bureaucracy provides a core tool for the consolidation of this vertical and central position. Controlling bureaucracy means control-ling the potential centrifugal risks, which accompany the autonomy of certain components. Whether controlled by a tough but rational set of legal rules or by patrimonial domination, bureaucracy plays a part in reassessing national sovereignty by securing assets. The central position of the state backed by its own national bureaucracy is ana-lyzed in two chapters of this book which discuss the role of national sovereignty, regionalization and privatization policies implemented by all European and Asian states during the last few decades (Chapters 4 and 5).

From a historical viewpoint, and only if centralist aspects are con-sidered, in the aftermath of WWII both regions belonged to the cat-egory of "strong state", whether they were dependent on the Soviet-type or the Asian system. They shared a very similar economic structure backed by political dictatorships based on a single dominant party, a lack of organized opposition, and a highly controlled social system. In the absence of social control, resources were concentrated in the hands of a minority, either a political group or a few ruling families, and/or a patrimonial bureaucracy. Levels of corruption were high. Chapters 4, 5 and 6 will also illustrate this.

A comparison between Southeast Asian and CEE states is worth-while as it allows the conditions that can explain changes within highly centralized and corrupt organizations to be measured. External shocks provide a necessary explanation for transitory periods.

However, Chapters 5 and 6 show how it is possible to buffer these periods by recombining assets using military force to keep any alternative source of power at bay, or by creating new alliances with domestic forces and foreigners to secure funds. An analysis of CEE countries demonstrates that interest groups in favor of change must be present in candidate countries. New rules governing democracy and markets can only be adopted if a strong majority of interest groups favor change and believe that these changes are beneficial. There must also be a clear perception of the costs entailed by the process of adjustment. In other words, a cost-benefit analysis is legitimate because it makes the rational reasons for modifying long-term habits clear, provided the costs ensuing from the process of transformation are outweighed by benefits. In Europe, these benefits are both economic and political. However, such a cost-benefit approach only makes sense if it is closely connected to perceptions of the value of national sovereignty. Internal conditions for change must be backed by external ones, meaning EU conditionality or great power influence (US, Japan, and China). Only a recognized and admitted external actor or force likely to provide expected benefits can force states to implement or resist change as in the case of Southeast Asian states where more pooling of sovereignty is perceived to be a danger for non-democratic regimes. In Europe, in order to exert this conditionality, both partners — the principal and the agent (meaning the EU and the candidate) — must recognize their own limits by accepting reciprocal duties ("limited asymmetry"). The EU accepts the principle of integration as long as the candidates commit to guaranteeing collective security. The candidate adopts the whole *Acquis Communautaire* expecting to benefit from the structural funds and the political statutes associated with membership. To this extent, the common stakes can be defined as limited asymmetry because both principal and agent are constrained by reciprocal duties and rights (Schimmelfennig and Sedelmeier, 2005). Therefore, the "logic of consequences" is legitimate to analyze the process of eastern adjustment to EU norms (March and Olson, 1989). But because long-term history strongly impacts human behaviors, the "logic of appropriateness" is also legitimate to explain how actors adapt the external pressures of rules.

Such a process shows that rules cannot be transferred only from the top. This is the case for both the EU and ASEAN (Cowles *et al.*, 2001; Acharya, 2004). External rules are constantly adapted by the players in accordance with their own historical trajectories. Even in the extreme case of Central and East European adjustment, the individual states remained the main actors. Even if EU pressure was very strong indeed, the national states could have refused the deal and withdrawn from the game. Furthermore, they could have negotiated a memorandum. This provided the ultimate proof that states are free and could choose to become members and that the EU is likewise free to refuse any candidate if the conditions for accession are not met. This is also true for ASEAN members who may use ASEAN principles to their own advantage, while ASEAN itself may not force members to change.

PART I

CONCLUSION — CLUSTERS OF MODERNIZED STATES IN SOUTHEAST ASIA AND CEE

Rather than using the general terms, it would be more correct to say that this book focuses neither on the EU27 nor on the ASEAN as a whole, but more precisely on a sub-region within each regional ensemble: The CEE region concentrating on the 10 new members that joined the EU in 2004[1] and 2007[2] and the continental ASEAN area often referred to as the Greater Mekong sub-region[3] (and not the whole of ASEAN).[4] With the exception of Thailand in Southeast Asia, these new members from each region were Communist until recently or indeed continue to be so. Whatever the nature of their current political regimes, all of them have nonetheless launched the same policies of privatization, regionalization, and integration into regional ensembles. Moreover, this particular focus does not prevent reference being made to other "older" members especially when the politics of enlargement is addressed. Lastly, by using the terms "CEE" and "Southeast Asia", it is clear that the notion of unity is fallacious since CEE is actually a very uncertain category which

---

[1] Estonia, Latvia, Lithuania, Poland, the Czech Republic, Slovakia, Hungary, Slovenia (Cyprus and Malta joined also EU but they were not former soviet-type economies).
[2] Romania and Bulgaria.
[3] Myanmar, Thailand, Cambodia, Vietnam and Laos, although the GMS still involves two Chinese regions (Guangxi and Hunan).
[4] ASEAN was created in 1967 by Indonesia, Singapore, Malaysia, the Philippines (Brunei joined later).

includes very different states or groups of states,[5] and the same is true of Southeast Asia.[6]

1. Southeast Asia

Three clusters of states can be identified in Southeast Asia, depending on their position on private property (Owen, 1992). Even if on the whole, (as mentioned above), Mekong riparian states are more often studied than ASEAN states, examples can sometimes be drawn from other states, such as Singapore. The first cluster of states includes capitalist states committed to the preservation of private property in Thailand, Malaysia, the Philippines and Singapore.[7] The second cluster includes the communist states, which suppressed private property, Vietnam, Laos, Cambodia and Myanmar. Extreme cases include Cambodian agrarian communism (Democratic Kampuchea) (Chandler, 1983) and Burmese authoritarianism (since the 1960s) (Verbiest, 2012a), while Vietnam mostly experienced

---

[5] Eastern Europe historically refers to part of Russia. Central Europe comprises Poland, Hungary, the Czech Republic and Slovakia but also for some observers, Germany. The Baltic states include the three Northern states and the former USSR Republic. Romania and Bulgaria are said to belong to the Balkan, though many citizens refuse this idea. Geographers speak of "Median Europe", historians speak of Mitteleuropa including Germany. Below we use the term "Central and Eastern Europe", CEE.

[6] Tarling, N in his introduction underscores the fact that "'Southeast Asia' is still a useful category, though we should always be on our guard lest we are tempted to overemphasize either its cohesion or its diversity", Preface to the Paperbook edition, *The Cambridge History of Southeast Asia*, Vol. II, part 2, from World War II to the present, p. XII.

[7] This includes the particular cases of South Vietnam, which was a capitalist country up to 1975, Kampuchea from 1972 to 1975 (under Lon Nol's rule), and Indonesia after 1965. According to Owen, the capitalist regimes can be divided into three major periods: The postwar recovery period characterized by "reconstruction of a primary producing export economy based on the colonial model"; the 50s, when attempts were made to "develop the Import Substitution Model of Industrialization (often accompanied by economic nationalism)"; and, the 60s starting with Singapore and export-oriented industrialization.

Table 1. Main economic and social features of Southeast Asian Countries in 1930 and Post-'70s.

	Indonesia	Thailand	Singapore	Cambodia	Vietnam	Laos PDR	Myanmar	Philippines	Malaysia
Political economies in the 1930 minorities	Rural colonial dependency	Rural/Bangkok 1932, constitution 20% minorities	Rural colonial dependency	Rural colonial dependency 15% minorities	Rural Saigon colonial dependency 54% minorities	Rural colonial dependency between 60 and 129 minorities	rural colonial dependency various minorities Karen	Rural 110 ethnic groups and 170 languages (Balisican *et al.*, 2006)	Rural colonial dependency
Ex-colonial Independence	Dutch 1949	No	Malaysian GB, 1965	French 1953/54	French US 1954 and 1975	French 1953/54	British 1948	Spanish US 1945	British 1957
Communist	No (liquidated in 1949)	No	No (forbidden 1966)	1975–1978	Yes 1954; 1975	Yes 1975	No	No (liquidated in 1953)	No (forbidden)
Per capita (UNDP, 2008) GDP/$ (UNDP, 2003)	2940	6400 9667	22,680	1860 2727	2070 3071	1620 $2039	1027 —	3840	8750
Poverty ($1 a day) 1995 (Rigg, 2003). < national poverty line 1990 2004[8]	7.7% (1997)	10% 13.6%	<1%	35% 35%	42.2 28.9%	39% 38.6%	— —	25.5	<1%

(*Continued*)

[8] UNDP Human Development Report 2007–2008.

Table 1. (*Continued*)

	Indonesia	Thailand	Singapore	Cambodia	Vietnam	Laos PDR	Myanmar	Philippines	Malaysia
Regional inequalities 2000's	Jakarta Aceh	Bgkk > 80% FDI 1990 rural > 30%			$152 rural areas 200 cities 2,200$ Ho chi minh	Ventiane/ Northern region		3 regions (Manila Central and Southern Luzon > 55% GDP	
Urban/Rural From 1950 to 2010		From 83.5% to 66% Urban population from 16.5% to 34%.	—	From 89.8% to 77.2% Urban population from 10.2% to 22.8%.	From 88.4% in 1950 to 71.2% in 2010. Urban population from 11.6% to 28.8%.	From 92.8% to 66.8%. Urban population from 7.2% to 33.2%.	From 83.8% to 66.1%. Urban population from 16.2% to 33.9%		
Agriculture	> 60%	43%	—	70%	58%	85%	70%	> 60%	> 60%
Minorities 1990/2000's	250/300 (Dauvergne, 1998) ethnic groups		3 Chinese (75%); Malaysian 15% Indian 10%	< 10% minorities	60 minorities	<50% Lao sung > neighboring ethnic minorities (Grant Evans, 1999)	130 minorities registered and Bamar = 65% of Burma	The 1. input group: Tatalog 30%; the 2d = 25% 170 languages (Balisican et al., 2006)	Malaysian < 50 % Chinese 30%

a war economy up to 1975. After 10 years, the Soviet-type system implemented in 1975 gave way to the *Doi Moi*, in 1986 and to a step-by-step approach to liberalization under an unchanged communist rule (Balme and Sidel, 2007). Laos was similar to a Vietnamese province. The last cluster includes what Norman Owen calls the in-between "nationalistic socialist authoritarian" states, who professed a vague type of socialism, reinterpreted through local cultures.[9] Despite the differing profiles of each cluster from the other, all these countries have adopted the same ideology and a very similar power structure based on bureaucracy and strong links between the ruling class (Families/Nomenklatura), the military, and the government.

2. Central and Eastern Europe

In CEE, despite the institutional (systemic) similarities between all the countries due to their inclusion within the Soviet-type system for more than four decades, central-eastern states can be differentiated according to three pieces of criteria (Bafoil, 2009c).

The first criterion was the ability of some states to challenge the Communist Party through a national movement characterized by a national historical identity. The very few upheavals during the communist period were led by a civil society which represented political and sometimes economic alternatives. Poland, Czechoslovakia, and Hungary belong to this group with the German upheaval of June 17, 1953 being an exceptional case. Bulgaria and Romania are not part of this group. Their absence has been explained by the fact that both states were "latecomers" in history (Mantran, 1992). They emerged in the 1880s after several centuries of liquidation under Ottoman rule, with no traditional elites and no strong national civil society. Non-democratic regimes had prevailed during the interwar period when pro-Nazi leagues had flourished.

---

[9] The case of Burma under U Nu (1948–1962), Indonesia before 1965, Cambodia under Norodom Sihanouk, and perhaps Thailand under Nai Pridi Phanomyong (1945–1947).

Table 2. Main economic and social features of European countries in the 1930s and after the 1950s (excluding the Baltic countries).

	GDR	Czechoslovakia	Poland	Hungary	Romania	Bulgaria
1919–1939						
Ethnic Composition		51% Czech 23% German 16% Slovak 5% Hungarian	65% Polish 16% Ukrainian 10% Jewish 6% Bielorussian 2% German	87% Hungarian 6% German 5% Jewish	75%, Romanian 6% Jewish 4% German	87% Bulgarian 10% Turkish 1% Jewish
Per capita Ind GNP 1938 (Janos, 2000)		60%	23%	34%	11%	19%
FDI (Kaeser and Radice, 1985)		30%	40%	24%	59%	18%
Agric in 1930 (Kaeser and Radice, 1985; Wädekin, 1977)		35% 26.3%	68%	55%	70%	72%
		43.8%	30.3%	71.5%	52.1%	27.0%
< 2 has 2–5 hectares		29.0% 0.9%	33.4%	21.5%	22.9%	36.1%
			36.0%	15.1%	4.2%	36.8%
5–10 has > 100			0.3%	0.9%	0.8%	0.1%
1945–1989						
1945	Destroyed	Victorious	Victorious	Defeated	Defeated	Defeated
Upheavals	1953	1968	1956; 1968; 1970; 1976; 1980; 1981	1956	—	—

(*Continued*)

Table 2. (*Continued*)

	GDR	Czechoslovakia	Poland	Hungary	Romania	Bulgaria
Economic regime	Centralized reform in 1960, 1970	Centralized failed reform in 1968	Reformed in 1970, failed reform in 1981, and the 1980s	Reformed in 1968 'Neither plan nor market'	Centralized	Centralized reform in 1960, 1970, 1980
Agriculture 1990	12%	8%	22%	18%	25%	25%
Public sector percent to GNP (NMP)[10]	99%	91%	83%	93%	98%	99.3%
1989/1990	Round table	Low	Round table	Gradual (88)	High	High
Successor to the CP (Bozoki and Ishiyama, 2002)	PDS	CP	Reformed SDL	Reformed MSZP	Reformed	Reformed
Debt (Billions of $)	4.6	4.6	35.3	15.8	4	8
Minorities 1990	1% (Sorbian)	3% Hungarian Roma	0.8% Ukrain 0.8% Bielo 0.1% German	5.6% Roma	4.5% Roma 6.6% Hung.	3.7% Roma 9.5% Turkish

[10]Net material product. See Wild (2002).

The second criterion to distinguish these states relates to the economic reforms and links formed with foreign (West European) partners during the Communist period. Hungary is the only exception to this case because Janos Kadar, the First Secretary responsible for the bloody repression of the 1956 revolution, was the same ruler who launched the only economic reform in 1968 ("neither plan nor market"). However, all of the Soviet-type states launched economic reforms from the 1960s onward when extensive overuse of resources gave way to more urgently needed policies (Brus, 1985). Unlike in Asia, CEE countries have not adopted the same ideology. In Poland, Hungary and Czechoslovakia civil societies existed at certain periods and because of this the rule of law did also exist (Winiecki, 2004). The third criterion distinguishes this group on the basis of the strong continuity of certain social aspects associated with minorities and agriculture.

For these historical reasons, a distinction should be made between three groups of countries. The first one includes the former Soviet Baltic republics, Estonia, Latvia and Lithuania. The second one comprises more highly developed central states: Poland, Hungary and Czechoslovakia (that split in 1993 into the Czech Republic and Slovakia); the last group includes the so-called "Eastern Balkans", Romania and Bulgaria.

PART II
INTRODUCTION — COHERENCE OF THE PUBLIC POLICIES: PRIVATIZATION, REGIONALIZATION, INDUSTRIAL RELATIONS

Introduction

Changing the rules of the game with respect to either privatization or regionalization is a highly risky maneuver for any governing ruler. Such change presents a critical challenge from a political perspective as it introduces new players into the game. Tocqueville and Weber have clearly shown this: Tocqueville by asserting that absolutist states have a lot to lose when they begin a process of transformation as they release unstoppable and unexpected dynamics (de Tocqueville, 1856); and Weber by stressing the additional burden of having to support more clients on the periphery.

All countries emerging from Communism or authoritarian regimes — whether by a radical break as in some CEE countries, or by a "softer" transition as in Southeast Asia — had to implement the same policies. The first of these was privatization. Changing property rights in such precarious environments bereft of legal rules necessarily called for implementation from the top down, meaning from a highly centralized state. Without a strong central state guaranteeing coordination between different policies — financial, economic, and possibly social — privatization in such situations cannot succeed. This is why decentralization never takes precedence during a transition period. The central state has to be convinced that other central economic tasks have been securely put in place before any process of decentralization is launched. Privatizing state ownership demands a strong state, not a decentralized one, as major risks exist with possible rent capturing by independent local groups. Privatization dynamics seek to liberate economic activity from state rent capture rather than shift it from one type of rent capture to another. Decentralization policies can also be risky because they contribute to the emergence of counterweights that may compete against the central state. The emergence of regions deeply modifies polity. Regional competitors mean differently organized networks and resources. Moreover, decentralizing means equipping regions financially and in this regard contributes to the pumping dry of central resources. Indeed, decentralization leads to the devolution of more fiscal capacity to the benefit of local actors. For political economies based on a solid mix of public and private interests, this implies a direct loss. Financial loss in these countries often means loss of prestige and of legitimacy. Furthermore, it means loss of capacity to rule because the former dependent people look elsewhere for other resources that the former boss is no longer able to provide. Finally, in a transition period, many components of the previous system become disaggregated. Centrifugal forces thus threaten state unity and cohesion. For all these reasons, decentralization needs to be organized from the top down.

Another challenge results from the pressure exerted by the existing historical situation. In a transition period, urgency is all the more prevalent as people want to see all their expectations satisfied immediately. Because they felt powerless for such a very long time under the previous regime, they want to obtain immediately what only time itself can achieve. The simultaneous achievement of all goals is quite simply impossible. Distinguishing priorities and sequencing political timing is needed. In such a situation, the relationship between ordinary citizens and ruling elites whose temporalities are not identical, may very quickly become tense. For this reason, the coupling of justice and effectiveness (which can never be simultaneously satisfied) constitutes one of the main challenges for transition economies: Justice, because of the trauma experienced by a majority of citizens at the hands of unfair and arbitrary Communist institutions; effectiveness, because of the huge waste of resources leading to a deep lack of individual responsibility. From an abstract perspective, democratic institutions are effective and effective rule is fair. But in the reality of everyday life, both objectives — effectiveness and justice are rarely achievable together. Rules are the result of difficult conflicts and mirror a social average which cannot satisfy every player.

In CEE countries one of the most important public debates during the first post-Communist period focused on what forms of privatization were to be adopted (Balcerowicz, 1995; Aghion and Blanchard, 1998; Major, 1999). Should public firms be transferred to national workers or to foreigners? What final beneficiaries should be targeted and selected — domestic (*insiders*) or foreign actors (*outsiders*)? Was it sufficient to say that because workers (*insiders*) had built the firms but had no access to their profits during the Communist period, that they therefore should be granted the new property rights? Or was it better to target more effective players such as foreign investors? Although it was obviously fair to grant property rights to workers for the reasons just stated, it was not necessarily effective because self-autonomy was not *per se* proof of effective management. Many studies have focused on corruption in firms given to their employees (*Management Buy-Out:* MBO) not only because they are unable to make a profit, but also in particular because of mismanagement and the ability of former managers to use the new rules to their own profit (Frydman *et al.*, 1998). Indeed, former managers who acquired new property rights were frequently blamed for having taken advantage of the new rules to make a rapid profit — by selling the firm immediately after the transfer while laying workers off. This practice of management buy-out (MBO) therefore turned out to be a source of profit only for former managers, at the expense of the legal owners, the workers.[1]

---

[1] Almost all observers have concluded that the productivity of CEE firms has depended strictly on the process of privatization. However, the comparison between the different types of firms is more complicated. Frydman and Alii consider that the superiority of privatized forms depends on the presence of outsiders. Konings considers that state-owned enterprises (SOEs) do not perform less well than others, and Amess and Robert conclude the same about co-ops. The great advantage of FDI is the role of conditionality, incentives and less corruption. Concerning MBOs compared with FDI their advantage lies in the less conflicting situation in enterprises managed by employees, a higher rate of satisfaction, a lower level of threat and less risk of free riders. (Frydman *et al.*, 1999; Koning, 1997; Amess and Roberts, 2007).

On the other hand, foreign investors were expected to introduce clearer rules of governance, create access to new markets, implement new technologies and improve training and career prospects. Effectiveness was rarely synonymous with fairness because the necessary changes required by the new legal framework paved the way to massive lay-offs, which in turn led to major discontent. Furthermore, very often during the first decade at least, former managers were kept in their jobs by the new owners because they were familiar with the local situation, even if it was well-known that under the previous regime the former managers were the very people that had mismanaged the firms and undermined workers. The lack of job rotation at the top levels of new firms gave rise to a huge wave of frustration and despair during the implementation of "effectiveness" in restructured firms. This frustration was also fueled by white collar workers that often saw technical projects they had developed under the previous regime simply put aside due to radical changes in technology. Many alternative and clever restructuring plans designed by technicians and engineers who were never able to implement them under the former Communist regime, became obsolete in the subsequent period because newly created technologies required different skills. Lastly, many social plans, such as severance packages were sources of disillusionment among workers, even though firms were initially sold to foreigners under the strict condition that the employment level would be respected for a specific period of time, which was usually of three to four years. However, resolute in their decision to reduce over-employment, new owners gave out "severance packages" consisting of an offer of a large lump sum of money in exchange for rapid worker departures from the firm. Trade unions were not opposed to such a policy because of the large amount of money offered and because they themselves were given job security by the new owners (Bafoil, 1999; Hibou, 2004).

Taking the three policies just mentioned (privatization, regionalization and industrial relations) into consideration the comparison is useful in that it looks at whether the ways chosen to rebuild societal balance are coherent or not. Societal balance can be rebuilt either by changing the rules of the game in economic, political and social terms or by merely adapting them so that the dominant political economies remain unchanged. Comparison allows the "strength" and/or "weakness" of the states to be better understood. One of the common features between these states is that they became fertile grounds for the extension of the least regulated type of capitalism as a result of the social and fiscal policies they put in place which are extremely loose.

3 TRANSFORMING ECONOMIES: FROM PLANNED ECONOMIES TO MORE LEGAL RULES OR TOWARDS NOMENKLATURA CAPITALISM?

Privatization policy is an important component of the redistribution of balance of power. In any analysis concerning the nature of the state, an evaluation of how property rights have evolved and why they have changed is essential. One of the key features of a strong state is its capacity to master its centrifugal forces. In this sense, privatization can be considered to be a major threat in that it allows various counterweights to emerge. In order to understand this major policy, the exact nature of the changes, how they are perceived and the results produced by these changes need to be analyzed. Another issue is to identify who the beneficiaries and who the losers are under such a policy.

Changes in economic regimes always occur under tough constraints. Without strong pressure, there is no need to change. New economic (and political) frameworks are adopted only when the ruling actors are compelled to usher them in.[1] When economic (and political) changes occur, they create the expectation that whatever was missing or not available before can now be acquired. This includes markets, technologies, financial assets, and qualifications. All of these are made available by various actors with whom it is essential to set up links and networks. In the European Union (EU) and Southeast Asia, most of these are foreigners, which means that foreign direct investment (FDI) is seen to be a basic form of aid

---

[1] The realist approach stresses the concept of self-interest to explain the emergence of common rules and supranational regulations. This approach can only be explained by the existence of a feeling of threat or by imperative economic need.

to support change. However, in both regions, at least during the transitory period when the former political order was in a state of flux, the main objective of the elites was to acquire new assets in order to secure their own interests. For this reason, they needed to pay particular attention to emerging competitors. Consolidating the state and its ruling elites by using new channels — among them privatization — was a way of exerting control over all sources of competition. Private actors were tolerated, as long as they cooperated with the initial political objective. In such circumstances, corruption is a major factor in all processes of privatization. The objective of this chapter is to go beyond this portrayal of corruption in order to understand it as a component of both centralized and decentralized systems. Corruption is not a cultural attribute proper to the Southeast Asian region and unknown in Europe as a result of some innate sense of virtue there. The legal uncertainty during transitory periods, the amount of money at the disposal of elites, and the resources inherited from previous regimes together explain the broad scope of corruption in all political regimes.

After 1989, the sequencing of transformation in the Central and Eastern Europe (CEE) was based on the adoption of democratic rules designed to exert joint control over privatization policy by public and non-public actors. In the final stages, this control was exerted by public administrative powers to encourage the adoption of the *Acquis Communautaire*. Institutions played the major role but the pace of transformation depended on the initial circumstances in each state and the adoption of democratic rules did not immediately lead to democratic exchange. Privatization can lead to widespread corruption and the adoption of the *Acquis Communautaire* has been uneven and often conflictual. In Southeast Asia, privatization simultaneously implied an openness to trade and the implementation of new institutions. For some domestic elites, regionalism was seen to be a good political opportunity to strengthen their own power through strong alliances with foreigners. As Jayasurija writes, "in short, open regionalism went hand in hand with the domestic developmentalist political projects of East Asian governments" (Jayasurija, 2003). To this extent, privatization in both regions was a fundamental means used to reassess the state as the driving force of change, with corruption as an important lever. In one case, this meant a progressive opening up through the creation of institutions which were gradually made autonomous; in the other case, it implied the reinforcement of control over intermediary institutions.

This chapter explains the step-by-step construction and implementation of privatization policy. Corruption is referred to the former political economies in both systems facing urgent pressure of change. It does not deal with forms of firm privatization. The first part insists on the initial uncertainty which dominates all the transition periods, privileging ruling elites who know the rules of the game. The second part analyzes corruption in CEE while the third part-focuses on the links between "open regionalism" and "nomenklatura capitalism". Lastly, Singapore is analyzed as a strong authoritarian regime based on rule by law and wide liberalism. From a systemic perspective, CEE and Southeast Asia are very similar, even if their dissimilarities were more in evidence during the transition period, when the rule of law prevailed in a few CEE countries only.

3.1. The Theoretical Framework

The way in which privatization was carried out can only be understood in reference to the type of organization, which prevailed in the immediately preceding regimes and the type of behavior expected from citizens. To use Max Weber's terms, every type can be distinguished by means of a form of rationality. In the case of CEE (formerly under Soviet type rule), everything was centrally organized and dominated by the Communist Party which enacted and implemented all laws. Systematic corruption can only be understood through the primacy granted to the Communist Party with no possibility of scrutiny. This type of organization reflected value-based rationality.[2] In

---

[2] The final objective of any economic activity in Communist organizations (according to ideology in any case) was the promotion of fraternity and equal sharing among all producers. The aim was never the search for profit as is the case in (capitalist) market organizations.

the case of Southeast Asia, the cultural dimension of dependence on bosses explains this type of corruption. In this case, rationality can be defined by feelings.[3]

3.1.1. *Political and economic dimensions of corruption*

In former Communist European and Southeast Asian countries, the political aspect of corruption includes the fact that certain elites are accountable to and controlled by no one. Communist regimes and non-Communist dictatorships usually emerged from *coup d'états* and other types of violence that imposed silence on any protesting voices, at least in CEE. In all circumstances, rulers used the pretext of social unrest to impose martial law. Generally, such a situation results from the unquestionable political domination of a charismatic leader whose personal qualities are not open to discussion. Charisma is an obvious quality and the charismatic leader is said to hold his indubitable prestige from God or from the People assimilated to God. In Indonesia, for example, the "Pancacilla principles" removed all protest that was suspected of being a sign of antisocial behavior, by imposing respect for God and Indonesian state unity.[4] Complete faith in the leader is

---

[3] Using a Weberian approach, it is neither the search for profit — as a formal finality — nor the objective of sharing-value-oriented finality — but rather the familial matrix which accounts for this third type of economic policy which Weber called rationality according to feelings. See Pye (1985).

[4] Indonesian "Pancacilla" principles were constitutionalized when Indonesia was declared independent in 1949, see Osborne (2010). The Pancacilla principles consisted in a set of rules fundamentally based on the strong and unquestioned adherence of people to the central directives: Belief in God, in a humanized society and in Indonesian unity, were the main pillars that supported the conviction of the pursuit of social justice and democracy through consultation of all parties concerned. Concerning industrial relations, it meant mutuality of consensus and interests embodied in tripartite organizations. Within this ideology, Suharto was considered to be the Father of the Nation and the people were his children. A strong and asymmetric dependency linked the parties, similar to the bonds between members of a family. The populace is considered to be immature and infantile, rewarded when it satisfies the father by respecting the principles of social harmony and punished when it causes troubles.

required together with the absolute conviction that the nature of his charisma will not be questioned and blind loyalty will be expressed. Any demand for another source of control is interpreted as a sign of mistrust. "The party is always right" is the indispensable Communist slogan. Corruption, in this regard, can be defined as the obvious excess of unlimited power.

Furthermore, the economic dimension of corruption is inherent in the centralized power of such regimes. In his fundamental work, the *Economics of Shortage*, the Hungarian economist Janos Kornai (1980) has shown how central planning brings about self-corruption. A centralized planning process defines all needs to be used in the process of production from the top down thus aiming to deal with all expectations emerging from the bottom up. However, this approach fails because it is quite simply impossible to make a comprehensive assessment of everything that is required to feed an entire economy and therefore sooner or later shortages at different levels of the production process become apparent. Such shortages impede economic exchanges. Furthermore, in such a political regime, the central authorities must be complied with as anyone who fails to do so would run the risk of being thrown in jail or even of incurring the death penalty. Because it is crucial to produce what the top has decreed must be produced and because managers and workers strive to make up any shortages, everyone involved in the system must find ways to adapt. The ability to identify substitute products or components is essential. Firms therefore produce not only what they are officially committed to producing but also other products that each manager will exchange in order to obtain whatever is needed to function effectively. In Soviet firms, a special worker — the *tolkasc* — was employed to find whatever component was needed and to exchange this with other managers who were also experiencing shortages (Nove, 1961). Dissimilation of components entering into the composition of a product becomes common place as does the manipulation of accounts. Lying becomes normal. Everyone from the local manager to the regional officer and up to the Ministry has a vested interest in lying in order to be believed and, as a result, everyone lies more and more. As a direct result of this shortage economics, a "secondary" mentality and a "second" economy flourish. Both depend on central planning but in the end, because the hierarchy expects its plan to be fulfilled, the opposite causality results: That is, the central economy depends on the "second" economy. And this second economy appears to be the only system capable of providing the goods requested.

To conclude, corruption can be defined as a "functional" component of a "dysfunctional" central economy. It provides the social "glue" that allows the whole system to function. Corruption is therefore considered to be socially "normal" because everyone benefits from it and needs it to survive. From the bottom to the top of society, everybody tolerates corruption because there is no other way to obtain what is expected. Campaigns against corruption are never launched to make the economic machine more accountable, but only to reassess political legitimacy. When social tensions become too strong because goods are not available in collective shops, the upper elites eliminate signs of obvious excess. Such campaigns are indicators of political sensitivity as much as corruption is an indicator of social tolerance.

3.1.2. *Infant, father, client and boss: Patronage and neo-patrimonialism*

In Southeast Asia, the organizational system is not the point of departure. Society is organized through the fundamental link between people as illustrated by the language of "kinship". In his seminal book, *Asian Power and Politics, the Cultural Dimension of Authority*, Lucian Pye (1985) asserts the importance of a basic human dynamic by highlighting the primitive need for protection manifested by children towards their father. He also stresses the intertwined link between need, dependence and protection. Far from being mono-dimensional, this involves an infinitely more complex relationship in which asymmetric duties and rights are exchanged between children and fathers. Children must respect and love their father, and by extension, their ancestors. By fulfilling these duties they get protection. Aside from their natural features, which automatically define them as charismatic leaders, the Father, the Boss and the Lord are loved because they fulfill their duties by protecting the weak and needy (Bertrand, 1999;

Kimchoeun *et al.*, 2007). The fundamental link of patronage, symbolized by the tutelary figure of the father and anchored in the familial milieu, corresponds to the same pattern seen in more complex social and political arenas. The patrimonial relationship is the basis of the neo-patrimonial order found in social organizations.

In fact, the basic relationship between father and child is used to explain the progression in ties from the family within the closed village to larger private organizations such as firms and even further to political and international systems. The link between boss and client is of the same nature. The firm becomes an enlarged family. 'Patrimonial bureaucracy' involves a complex mix of personal relationships and informal rules on the one hand, and strict hierarchy and complex administrative tasks on the other. Two "orders" are blended: The patrimonial order related to the figure of the father, and the rational order related to modern organizations.[5] The same pattern of dependency and protection supporting the relationship between vassal and lord is repeated at the international level between a small nation and a regional power. Cambodia's ambiguous relations with Vietnam and Thailand can be explained in this way.[6] The same was true for Laos (Evans, 2002).

What unifies patronage, patrimonialism and neo-patrimonialism within more complex units such as bureaucracies is the nature of rule:

---

[5] Pye, "One can describe the bureaucratization of Southeast Asian systems of governance as the rationalization of the administration. A rationalized bureaucracy is characterized by its hierarchical and linear nature, stretching uniformly across the state's domain, a "machinery" of government was envisaged that could regularize and homogenize power and authority into individuals departments and functions. This utilitarian system replaced the more elaborate and ramshackle mosaic of patron–client relationships that characterized monarchical rule, except in pre-colonial Vietnam, where the Confucian Mandarinate had many of the characteristics of a rationalized bureaucracy. But while the Confucian scholar official was examined for literary skills, the skills demanded by the new forms of bureaucracy introduced by colonialism often demanded new forms of education" (pp. 204 / 205).

[6] Chandler (1983): "Cambodian history since WWII and probably for a much longer period can be characterized in part as a chronic failure of contending groups — patrons and their clients — to compromise, cooperate or share power".

Not formal and rational rule, which can be explained clearly by means of its origins and transparent supporting contracts, but informal rule, unquestioned in its origin, accepted as such and leading to the exchange of personal services. This Weberian view of the major features of two typical ideal systems is useful in understanding the role of time in both types of relationships. On the one hand, a formal contract is signed between two supposedly free people linked by formal commitment and for a limited period of time. On the other hand, the informal relationship is set up between legally unequal people who are linked by personal duties for an unlimited period. The notion of "unlimited duties" is key to understanding how continuity is maintained from the village to the city and the fact that former relationships are not undone by migration. They are simply transferred into more complex living and working environments, such as big cities or industrial plants. The debt of duty can never be repaid. As Norman Owen says in discussing "kinship", "it acts as confirmation. Kinship may have persisted simply because it was the only constant in an otherwise kaleidoscopic world" (Owen, 1992). In these circumstances, corruption is not a sign of moral failure. It is rather the consequence of a fundamental social link that secures deprived people or deprived states through time.

3.2. The European Transition Period

In any transition period, when former rules are no longer valid and when new regulation is not yet in place, corruption tends to be widespread. This is not because people feel they can do whatever they want. On the contrary, in such a situation it is more usual for important moral voices to emerge accusing the previous rulers of corruption and of maintaining the "double standards" that have forced people to lie and to develop immoral attitudes. If corruption is so prevalent, it is because the former leaders remain in place and use their position to pass laws that benefit themselves. CEE was the theater of such pervasive corruption in the period immediately preceding the fall of Communism. It is now well known that long before the end of Communism in 1989, Communist elites were well aware of the catastrophic economic situation of their own countries (Pirker *et al.*, 1995). It was widely known that in Moscow, as a result of Gorbachev's Perestroika policy, several Communist elites had transformed state property rights into private assets. These assets were managed in new firms set up for the purpose which they themselves became the directors of. In 1988, during the last year of Communism in CEE, a whole series of "privatization" laws were also passed. These laws started by extending special judicial rights to firms in charge of trade. Subsequently, joint ventures with foreign firms were permitted. This was considered normal because at the end of the decade, a number of decisions were taken within firms allowing certain sectors to function as private ones. Private contracts were signed between managers and directors of departments, who legally used public equipment to work overtime to finish public or private contracts. During this period a whole "private" economy was developed within the public economy, and for this reason, nobody was really surprised by the new "big" wave of "privatization". Private companies and even banks were thus created entirely legally. They were in a position to siphon off incoming funds, particularly those that came in later from the European Community, which supplied money in order to secure the first stages of the transition process.

3.2.1. *"Red privatization"*

Prior to the end of Communism, the whole of the CEE was characterized by a fully legal system of "red privatization" (Hankis, 1990). This primarily concerned the banking system and military supplies.[7] When Communist regulation was being shaken everywhere in the CEE, space was left for disoriented parliaments to pass unfair laws. The German Democratic Republic was a typical case. Since the fall of the Berlin wall on November 7, 1989, its institutions had been

---

[7] For instance, in January 1989, Bulgarian decree 89 cleared the way for the beginning of privatization. By September of the same year, there were already 5,520 private firms. The 1990 decrees N°74 and N°129 completed the process, permitting the leasing or even sale of goods that were to be replaced and thus no longer required. Lastly, Decree N°111 of November 14, 1990, authorized the transformation, lease-sale, or transfer of a number of state concerns largely in the metallurgical, oil or food sector that were formerly managed by external trade agencies.

completely disorientated. While waiting for the election of the new parliament on March 18, 1990 — the first free election to be held in this part of Germany since 1933 — the still ruling Communist parliament decided to create an office which would be in charge of GDR public assets, the *Treuhandanstalt*. One of its obvious objectives was to provide jobs to former Communists who had lost their positions.[8] It is claimed that 62,000 instances of economic crime were registered during the transition period in this vanishing state — 21,000 for the city of Berlin alone. About 10,000 individuals were accused of being involved.[9] However, corruption was not only a prominent feature in periods of extrication from Communism. More generally, it accompanied the entire process of transition during the 1990s. Countless elites were charged with corruption, while at the macro-level, corruption was a fundamental component of privatization policy.[10]

---

[8] One of the first decisions of the next president — from the Western side — was to fire all the members of the first *Treuhandanstalt*, except the person in charge of human resources.

[9] The period of German monetary unification saw an astonishing level of generalized corruption. When it was known that on July 1, 1990 a monetary union would unify both German sides and that the DM would be extended to Eastern Germany, a considerable amount of misappropriation occurred. The official exchange rate made 1 DM equivalent to 4 Ost Marks. In the street, it was exchanged at 13 OM. Worst of all, the former Deputy Minister for External Trade, Alexander Schalck Golodkowski, was arrested while leaving his office carrying a suitcase full of DM. The total amount of embezzlement by his ministry has been estimated at 26 billion DM.

[10] In the Czech Republic, scandals led directly to the fall of Prime Minister Václav Klaus in 1996. In Romania, the entire political class was mixed up in the Rosa Montana goldmine scandal. After being closed down because it destroyed the fauna and flora of the Tisza Basin, the mine was very quickly re-opened under the auspices of a Romanian/Canadian company. In Hungary, Viktor Orban, the Prime Minister from 1996–2001, was criticized for acquiring a vineyard in the Tokay, listed among the best of Hungarian wines, for a nominal sum. He also enabled several members of his family to make illegal fortunes, including his own father, who acquired a state-owned mine without any public tendering process taking place. There was more of the same in Poland where just before EU integration the ruling elites were accused of setting up corrupt agreements with private media businessmen in order to pass laws for their own benefit. Multiple other examples can be found in all of the newly independent states.

3.2.2. *Domestic transformation in CEE: Privatization policy*

In Central and Eastern Europe, liberal economic rules were not immediately accepted by each new state. In 1990, some of them were very reluctant to open trade and state structures to foreigners, and even to domestic competitors. In Poland, most of the political elites belonging to Solidarity were initially against radical privatization (Baltowki and Mickiewicz, 2000). Moreover, important interest groups in heavy industry were strongly opposed to any transformation of property rights resulting from the law adopted in September 1981, which gave them important shared economic powers with the factory directors (Shields, 2004, Hunter and Ryan, 2008). In Romania and Bulgaria, new rulers strongly resisted the liberal wind that blew through Europe by violently suppressing nascent civil societies, by trafficking elections, and by transforming privatization laws for the good of their own cliques and inner circles. Former managers kept their positions by not laying off workers and avoiding emerging competition (Gallagher, 2009). In both countries, for the major part of the first post-Communist decade, privatization policy was limited to strictly formal changes with regard to property rights, meaning that public property rights were scripturally transformed into private ones that were then sold to the same managers as before (Ragaru, 2005). In other newly independent states, mainly those in Central Europe privatization was accepted but within certain narrow limits, meaning that privatization would be accepted as long as it did not threaten the newly found national sovereignty.

In Czechoslovakia,[11] strong "economic patriotism" developed a very original way of organizing privatization that turned citizens into capitalists by making them the new owners of public property, at the expense of the West which was suspected of attempting to "buy" the Czechoslovakian industrial patrimony in its entirety (Martin, 2003b;

---

[11] Czechoslovakia disappeared between the end of 1992 and January 1, 1993. In 1993, two new states emerged, the Czech Republic and Slovakia. Each of these countries followed completely different economic and political paths.

Smith, 2003). In the first stage, the "mass privatization" design adopted allowed all citizens to become "petty capitalists". This was because they were legally entitled to buy vouchers equal to a certain amount of shares in national firms at a very low price. At the same time, the large national banks remained under state control and were not privatized. However, because capitalism cannot work within a dispersed environment, it became necessary to concentrate shares in secure hands and the banks took on this role. The second stage of privatization consisted of securing all of the scattered shares by setting up a National Investments Fund comprising different investors, including the centrally controlled banks (Bornstein, 1999). This very popular mass privatization policy, which transformed each citizen into a private owner of national property, strongly contributed to the legitimization of the leading party, the ODS, led by Vaclav Klaus, which would rule the government until the end of 1996. This legitimacy was strengthened by the fact that Czechoslovakia was the only country in CEE at that time, to boast an unemployment rate lower than 5%, while in neighboring countries unemployment was more than double that amount. Such a situation could be explained by a remarkable social consensus based not only on "mass privatization" but also on two very strong and dynamic sectors: Tourism and the Automobile industry. The Czech car-maker Skoda was supported by Volkswagen, and its business represented more than 10% of GDP. Czech authorities could impose a moderate wage policy in exchange for high levels of employment. These political and economic policies were a source of profound satisfaction for national sentiment. Nonetheless, this period ended in 1996 when a World Bank report indicated that privatized firms were backed by a non-privatized and highly corrupt banking system (Lavigne, 1999). Moreover, although political elites were quickly fired and replaced by newly elected rulers, this was not the case within the private sector. Several analyses have shown that Klaus preferred to leave former Communist managers in place rather than sell firms to foreigners, even at the expense of financial benefits (Pavlinek, 2002). The Czech political economy was secured by recombining domestic alliances, which rarely involved foreigners, who were perceived as more of a threat than a benefit as regards national sovereignty. For these reasons, Czech elites can be counted among the most reluctant actors in terms of any further "sovereignty pooling".

Poland provides another example of privatization (Balcerowicz, 1995; Orenstein, 2000). It is often presented as liberal due to the so-called "shock therapy", which the new Minister of Finances, Leszek Balcerowicz, launched in 1990. However, although the first stage of his plan based on the stabilization of the exchange rate and on the devaluation of the zloty fully succeeded, the other stage failed in part. Obviously, the implementation of a new fully-fledged market economy required the end of state subsidies, which was quickly effected. But what was unexpected was the capacity of many big firms to resist this new regulation by reorganizing their assets. Reorganization was conducted either legally by reducing working hours rather than making people redundant, so that wages would continue to be paid and workers would benefit from the firms' social assets or illegally through a type of "privatization" that benefited the former managers (Zecchini, 1997). Moreover, previous worker groups, which supported *Solidarnosc*, were still very strong in heavy industry including the coal and steel sectors, mechanics, chemistry and raw materials. They were in a position to force the first governments to limit privatization by fostering the alternative model of "commercialization" without privatization which allowed state-owned firms to be financially supported by the Ministry of the Treasury (Shields, 2004). In other cases, they could limit sales to foreigners by opting for sales to employees through Management Buy-Outs (MBO). These MBOs were frequent until the middle of the 1990s (Bornstein, 1999). Corruption was widespread and it was only in 1995 that the National Investments Funds, which brought together 517 of the top firms, could launch privatization. This is when FDI came to Poland, albeit very slowly. Apart from Hungary, state property remained significant till the end of the first post-Communist decade (see Table 3.1).

These examples of privatization in the CEE in the aftermath of 1990 allow four conclusions to be drawn. First, from a theoretical viewpoint it appears that a systemic transition tends to strengthen actors who can use general uncertainty to their own benefit thanks to

Table 3.1.   Distribution of enterprise assets as a percentage of privatization methods in selected CEECs up to 1997 (%).

	Sales to foreign investors	Sales to domestic investors	Equal access voucher	Insider	Other	Still state property
Czech Rep	10	10	40	5	5	30
Hungary	45	12	—	3	20	20
Lithuania	12	2	43	9	—	43
Poland	10	—	6	—	44	40
Romania	5	5	20	10	—	60
Slovakia	7	3	25	30	5	30
Slovenia	1	8	18	27	21	25

Source: Based on UNCTAD; Djankov (1998); adjusted by data drawn from EBRD (1998).

their former position within the system. They can manipulate new rules at the expense of other actors who have no assets available to them. In this sense, the "conversion" of resources from the political to "economic" sphere is a common feature of transition periods (Szelenyi and Szelenyi, 1995).

The second empirical conclusion shows that the new elites had no model available to them. In the 1980s, the privatization policies led by Reagan and Thatcher concerned only 1,500 firms. In 1990, more than 8,400 firms awaited privatization in Eastern Germany, almost 9,000 in Poland, 6,000 in Czechoslovakia, etc. However, it was not only the model that was missing. Tools and skills were also unavailable. Nobody knew where to begin producing goods for which market values had never been established. Hence the dilemma concerning the speed of privatization.[12] These deficiencies resulted in the setting in place of secret procedures which led to a huge waste of public resources. Stock exchanges were non-existent and personal

---

[12] "The slower the pace of privatization, the more time to exercise non-transparent administrative discretion to arrange corrupt transactions" (Bornstein, 1999).

"face-to-face" procedures were the order of the day. Corruption was widespread (Kaufmann and Siegelbaum, 1997).

Third, private firms did not immediately get the lion's share of direct foreign investments. Because of the unclear and uncertain rules, foreigners mistrusted Central and Eastern Europe. Prices changed frequently and personal commitments did not guarantee that a contract would be concluded. On the contrary, during the entire first post-Communist decade, important transfers favored domestic buyers. Personal links favored such procedures. This led to widespread public debate between those who defended FDI on the grounds of effectiveness, and those who pleaded for equity and therefore wanted to favor domestic actors. The former were liberals, mainly located in Hungary and although some were in Poland where they shared power with the Sovereigntists. The latter were represented by all groups who argued that national sovereignty was a better tool to defend national industrial policies aiming at limiting foreign capital. However, if equity was beneficial to workers it was at the cost of pervasive corruption, and if efficiency was clearly related to procedures, it was at the cost of large-scale redundancies. Finally, privatization really took hold when obstacles to the arrival of foreign investors were removed. In Poland, this happened in 1995 when the 1981 law which granted significant powers to the workers' councils in large companies was overturned. In the Czech Republic, it took hold in 1996 when the public banks were transformed. In Romania and Bulgaria, it took hold in 1997 when the former elites were expelled from government. On every occasion, it was a question of dismantling former interest groups and notably those belonging to the working class. As Stuart Shields writes: "One of the main tasks of the transition to capitalism has been to break the resistance of the working class" (Shields, 2004). Once this objective was achieved, the sale of firms to foreigners was speeded up.

3.2.3. *The role of the EU in extending corruption*

Corruption was not limited to internal procedures; it was also closely linked to the EU adjustment process. Many scholars have highlighted the overwhelming complexity and bureaucratization of adjustment procedures which were not accompanied by EU expertise. Membership candidates were completely ignorant of how to use these new rules. The overstretched and hasty liberalization of economics resulted in the establishment of strong undemocratic domestic interest groups. Furthermore, there was little coordination between different Directorates General (DGs), which resulted in a lack of leadership within the Commission.[13] Added to this, the EU Commission was prone to acting ambiguously by accusing certain national and regional administrations of not having prepared adequately but then finally sending out positive signals with regard to their integration into the EU. This was particularly the case with the Balkan states. As mentioned previously, the obstacles were enormous because the EU transferred rules without first considering local situations in CEE. There was a huge waste of resources because of the lack of appropriate institutions and the skills required to do the job. Gallagher has shown how the adoption of the *Acquis communautaire,* led to the expulsion of civil societies from public debates and nurtured the causes of existing interest groups, that had already bent the rules to suit their purposes in 1989. Moreover, these are the same interest groups that in the 1990s would play around with privatization policies by taking control of public acquisitions and delivery of property rights.[14] Once again in the 2000s, these are the same people who could turn structural funds[15] to their own profit and engage in a much greater level of corruption than before 1989 precisely because the amount of money to be played for was incomparably bigger. The major failure of the EU was that it was too bound to its formal rules and too concerned with formal compliance alone from the candidates. EU experts considered that it was not their job to define the content of the

---

[13] The main conflicts occurred between the Enlargement DG which pushed for rapid enlargement and the DG Regio which remained reluctant because of the lack of guarantees on the institutional capacities of the candidate countries.

[14] "The roadmap for entry, known as the *Acquis communautaire* did not make a dent on the problems of underdevelopment, bad administration and post-Communist misuse", (Gallagher, 2009, p. 7).

[15] Concerning the structural funds, See Chapter 6.

formal procedures and rules adopted by candidates. They believed that the rule of subsidiarity highlighted the preeminence of states. This respect of legal principle was in fact a huge mistake. It resulted in the ruling elites presenting formal rules to the EU Commission while simultaneously deciding not to apply them to themselves.

What these examples tell us is that corruption is a feature of uncertain situations and not a national feature that differentiates countries. Corruption cannot simply be linked to cultural tradition.[16] Furthermore, it is not just because market and democratic rules change that fully compliant behaviors emerge. Independent people need to exert control over players to get them to respect rules. But, then again, it takes time to build institutions which implies that a steady and in-depth accompaniment is needed for this to happen. Shifting from corruption to rule of law often requires external controls that only binding rules and strong agencies can provide. A final important lesson drawn from 20 years of transformation in CEE countries is connected to the process of Europeanization, starting with the adoption process of the *Acquis communautaire*. EU rules were produced by EU15 members and not by CEE candidates. For this reason, some of these rules were inappropriate to them. They are relevant for a certain level of democratic and economic development but EU candidates were characterized by very particular features and many democratic and liberal

---

[16] If we consider the main types of corruption present in Romania, listed by a legal adviser at the Romanian Ministry of Justice in 2008, there seems little to distinguish certain CEE and Southeast Asian countries: "giving or taking bribes; trafficking of influence on which someone induces a public official to show favor towards his client; receiving a gift in return for showing favor to a supplicant; manipulating rules in order to give an advantage to a party such as when competitive tendering is involved; fraud, usually involving the falsification of data; blackmail, usually involving securing an advantage through pressure or force; favoritism in which a public official assists friends or associates to progress in the bureaucracy or the justice system by unfair means; favoritism involving nepotism whereby personal relatives benefit from access to public goods or appointments in a manner, which contravenes the law; embezzlement; the use of confidential information to obtain advantage in public transactions; reciprocal commissions or kickbacks in which someone commits an illegal act on behalf of another who returns the favor by different means, also illegal" (Gallagher, 2009).

components were not in place. Civil societies which bear witness to strong levels of social development were absent (Zimmer and Priller, 2004). If EU rule cannot be effective without being supported by civil societies, it is difficult to know how to proceed. If this happens from the bottom up, there is a risk of fostering undemocratic interest groups. If it happens from the top down there is a risk of being seen to be proceeding exactly like the previously hated regime. Far from producing positive effects in favor of the majority of citizens, adopted rules have very often produced unexpected effects by reinforcing the bureaucratization of activities. Nadège Ragarau has shown how the transformations that occurred among different DGs sharply impacted the different ways of tackling issues in CEE. Far from solving issues, EU classifications more often contributed to creating them, as was obvious in the case of the "Roms". They were "ethnicized" even though they were not a unified population, nor did they even exist as such on the western side of the EU (Ragaru, 2008). Other examples of the inappropriate adaptation of EU rules by local CEE actors led to distortions as in the case of trade unions or political parties responsible for tasks they were unable to fulfill because they lacked the know-how and skills to do so as this was not part of their traditional role (Kutter and Trappmann, 2006; Sedelmeier, 2010) (see Chapter 7).

3.3. Southeast Asian Political Economies, Liberalized Economies and Open Regionalism

In order to understand the logic of transforming economic regimes in Southeast Asia, the impact of change should be considered. This will allow the concept of developmentalism analyzed by some authors in terms of "nomenklatura capitalism" and exemplified by the case of Singapore to be clarified.

3.3.1. *A theory of change*

In the article referenced below, Doner, Ritchie and Slater describe three major constraints that force political authorities to adopt new public policies (Doner *et al.*, 2005). These constraints concern external security, public budgetary balance and social peace. During a crisis, public authorities have to make "side payments" to satisfy the leading groups — military, social and administrative bodies — rather than respond to a rational choice that would involve a calculation of costs and benefits. By using March and Olson's terms, one can say that these actors have to develop a "logic of appropriateness" and not a "logic of consequences". In other words, they have to pay compensation to groups so that they would support their action and legitimize them. They have to decide how to go about this and how to select these supportive groups and public policies. That is the basis of what several scholars have called "developmental states" the forms of which vary greatly from one country to another. Political economy refers to different national "assemblages" or domestic "arrangements" between political, social and economic actors. Taken together, they guarantee national consensus and the stability of the ruling elites.

"Developmental institutions" respond to adaptive pressures (budgetary constraints, scarcity of resources and security). Leaders are forced to build coalitions, mainly with a military power that consumes a giant portion of the national budget. Because protective policies lead to clear failures and to the (potential) massive withdrawal of foreign aid the only option is to adopt a completely different policy.[17] Export-oriented industrialization policy (EOI) responds to this pressure and need, forcing the adoption of radically different priorities (Barret and Chin, 1987). The idea is to adjust the market to international tendencies by finding a niche in certain industrial sectors. Education and high wages appear to be the best tools to achieve this policy. Because it is impossible to continue with strict market options by producing low added-value products, the transition can be brutal. There is a need to attract skilled people and pay them appropriately. Education, housing, transport and infrastructures are all part of the "side payments" that necessarily accompany this paradigm shift, which simultaneously leads to the exclusion of many people. This type

---

[17] "Developmental states have arisen from political leaders' recognition that — under conditions of systemic vulnerability — only coherent bureaucracies and broad public –private linkages could produce the resources necessary to sustain coalitions, secure State survival, and thereby maximize their time in office" (Doner *et al.*, 2005).

of shift brings about radical change in leading bureaucracies, which henceforth are governed by clearer rules and skilled civil servants.

3.3.2. *"Nomenklatura capitalism"*[18]

When using the term "nomenklatura capitalism" Kanishka Jayasurija also refers to "embedded mercantilism" to highlight the social background supporting the economic transformation process of each nation state that complies with globalization. Complying means adapting national resources in accordance with the state's own configuration shaped by the ruling elites.[19] The major challenge for ruling elites is to be able to pass privatization laws which work to their own benefit. The nature of property rights may change, but not necessarily result in empowering new managers who might be better able to incite more rational economic behaviors. By changing economic regimes, political elites must find a solution to the very pressing question of their own survival. They need to decide how to maintain their domination while implementing new policies, which imply new rules and new actors. They also need to involve new players without allowing them to take power for themselves and to decide how they can evolve from one kind of political consensus to another without risking a loss of power (Nesadurai, 2003). In all cases a predominating authoritative power is necessarily backed by a single party, which monopolizes the situation. This party becomes the only actor to lead the transformation process, proclaim the national cause of privatization, pass laws and select relevant partners. For instance, in Malaysia the UMNO proclaimed its wish to re-nationalize the Malay economy, which was accused of having been perverted by Chinese business.[20] Privatization

---

[18] "The term 'Nomenklatura capitalism' is used to highlight the close connection between political elites and insulated domestic cartels" (Jayasurija, 2003).

[19] "From this perspective, regional integration needs to be explained in terms of the political projects undertaken by domestic coalitions rather than deriving from the kind of external pressures identified by the market model" (Jayasurija, 2003).

[20] "This privatization resulted in a shift of ownership from the public to the private sector, but control over the newly privatized assets were still dependent on linkages to the dominant political party, the UMNO. Therefore in Malaysia, ownership of key strategic enterprises shifted from state to party" (Jayasurija, 2003).

was thus seen to satisfy nationalist expectations by reallocating national property to those who had once been deprived by "corrupt" people. In Indonesia, the transformation process was strongly supported by the oil boom that boosted growth. New domestic cartels in cement, paper and fertilizer emerged, led by a middle class linked to the ruling political elites. The opening up of industrial sectors was carried in strict accordance with the idea that the Nomenklatura would benefit from this policy. Deregulation to this extent meant a reinforcement of Suharto's clan.[21] This was also the case for the Singaporean ruling party, as shall be seen below.

Privatization policy fortifies the political elites by reinforcing their involvement in the economy through new economic links with foreign partners and by rejuvenating their nationalist profile. As Jayasurija (2003) writes: "These examples illustrate that contrary to much of the prevailing economic orthodoxy, trade liberalization or open economic policies have served to consolidate a particular economic and political bargain between a politically connected non-tradable sector and an open-orientated export sector. From the late 80's the state-led developmental projects gave way to a system of nomenklatura capitalism: Powerful domestic cartels connected to the ruling apparatus of political power". Southeast Asian countries are characterized by a very strong system of family ownership: In Singapore, 10 families control 25% of the corporate sector, in Thailand 10 families control 50%; in Indonesia, 15 families control 62% of market share capitalization; and in the Philippines, five families control 42% (Tipton, 2009). Conglomerate structures are similar and resemble Korean *chaebols*.[22] Banks are either in the hands of a few families or nationalized, which means more or less the same thing since the ruling authorities are made up of a limited number of families. Finally, the central state is strongly involved in economics as the rate of state ownership reveals:

---

[21] "In essence, the market reforms that were at the heart of the kind of open economic strategies pursued by Indonesia served to entrench a segmented political economy composed of a foreign-owned tradable sector and domestic-owned non-tradable sector, comprising politically connected cartels" (Jayasurija, 2003).
[22] See definition in the introduction of this book.

The Singaporean state is involved in most of the top 500 companies, the Indonesian state controls over 40% of national assets and Philippine state ownership is huge with 179 state-owned enterprises (SOEs).[23]

The concept of developmental state refers to a political economy in which one political party has a high level of control over society and the economy. In Northeast Asia, Japan is the best example of such a political economy, followed by the "Asian dragons". In Southeast Asia, Singapore can be considered a unique example of a "developmental state" because it has successfully combined a political dictatorship, based on strong personal authoritarianism, with a highly liberal economy and a lack of an organized opposition. Bryan Ritchie speaks of a "coordinate — state, liberal market economy (SLE)" (Ritchie, 2009a), in other words a mix of the categories isolated by Hall and Soskice to define two distinguished forms of capitalism.[24] With regard to the city-state, "hybridation" does not designate a corrupt and arbitrary system, rather a mix of rule by law associated and a fight against any form of deviance. Meritocracy here intertwines with deep authoritarianism. For Stephanie Lawson, Singapore is a strong State combining legal order with clear rules regarding the regime's succession and liquidation of any opposition. It provides security for the people and is legitimized by the people, who acquiesce to a regime that delivers the goods (Lawson, 1998). Compared to other Southeastern Asian states, Singapore is remarkable because it has successfully combated corruption. According to international rankings, the former "British colonial *entrepôt*" (Deyo, 1989) is in first place for fighting corruption, well ahead of western democracies.[25] Nevertheless, as King has pointed out, the criteria for corruption used by international organizations such as Transparency

---

[23] See Chapter 2.
[24] Hall and Soskice consider unlikely this mix of both types of regulation because of the incapacity of employers and workers association to be able to combate an economy, due to their strong dependence on the State. (Hall and Soskice, 2001). See the General Conclusion.
[25] Transparency International (2007).

International are strictly limited to business affairs (King, 2008). Singapore has proved very skillful at limiting the scope of international screening to bureaucracies, leaving the political decision-making process unscrutinized. This process is under the strict control of Lee Kuan Yew's family and close associates.

3.3.3. *Singapore, the exceptional case: Rule by law and nomenklatura capitalism*

In Singapore, a single political party, the PAP, still dominates the whole system, even though since 2010 it has been seriously contested internally. Its authority is based on several ingredients: A middle class and domestic bourgeoisie allied with foreign investors,[26] a strong domestic bureaucracy facilitating trade, and lastly, strong neo-corporatist and redistributive policies which are financed by high revenues, thanks to the State's channeling of FDI through its own banking system. As Rosan *et al.* write, "The question of the direction of Singapore's development strategy is inherently a political one" (Rodan, 2001). Forced to adopt a new policy and only able to count on its own resources Singaporean authorities borrowed from the models of South Korea, Hong Kong and Taiwan (although unlike them Singapore did not benefit from any US support). To survive after the split from Malaysia in 1965, the city-state was forced to fully open its economy and take advantage of a cheap labor force. The export-oriented industrialization (EOI) strategy, involving the strategy of coupling its sectors with world-wide sectors, was perceived as the only possible way to survive. With "strategic coupling" firms were simultaneously linked to Global Production Networks (GPN) and public authorities (Yeung, 2009). Successful local firms were those able to be independent manufacturers while

---

[26] PAP could prevail as the single organization able to manage Singapore because the leading figures had not compromised with the bourgeoisie that had cooperated with colonialism. Lee Kuan Yew was able to put aside their representatives and be free from any business links. He was backed by a very nationalist middle class and a young and well-educated generation to whom he offered leading roles in the state.

remaining connected to the dynamic of GPN outsourcing linked to transnational corporations and brand names. On the other hand, there was no privatization. It was more a case of "corporatization", meaning the transformation of SOEs into Joint Stock Companies. The vast majority of Singaporean companies remain SOEs, or so-called Government-linked companies.[27] These companies are placed under the responsibility of a minister — very often the Finance Minister — and are part of a holding company. There are between 600 and 700 of these GLC in existence within four enormous holding companies, which are inspired by the Korean chaebols and Japanese Kaimatsu. These GLC are frequently headed by individuals from outside the civil service, and their managers are often retired military or government personnel. As Jayasuriya and Rosser say, "the powerful domestic enterprises are the core components of Singapore's dominant coalition" (Jayasuriya and Rosser, 2001). As we will see in Chapter 7, special economic zones were to become a useful tool for lowering certain taxes, such as revenue or excise taxes.[28] After the crisis of the 1980s, the time was ripe to strengthen the coupling with the GPN by supporting labor-intensive manufacturing and upgrading labor, as seen with the wide-scale policy aimed at attracting Singaporean elites from abroad by offering them high-level posts, high wages, social facilities and privileges.

Compared to other Southeastern neighbors, Singapore's outstanding success has been to have created "markets (that) are embedded in systems of power and interests" (Jayasuriya and Rosser, 2001) without having become a dependent state. Singaporean elites devised a "nomenklatura capitalism" that still exerts control over firms and governmental companies, who are completely dependent

---

[27] "There is an almost incestuous relationship between the governement and the bureaucracy as top civil servants have gone into politics to reach ministerial posts under the practice of meritocracy and elitism", in Low Linda "State entrepreneurship" (King, 2008).

[28] "In the context of regional development, strategic coupling refers to the dynamic processes through which actors in regions coordinate, mediate, and arbitrate strategic interests between local actors and their counterparts in the global economy" (see Yeung, 2009).

on the PAP.[29] The state has considerable fiscal resources that allow it to intervene rapidly. Its fiscal institution is one of its best performing institutions. In 1992, reform introduced self assessment by taxpayers and imposed high tax compliance on civil servants and taxpayers. Thanks to close links between the state bureaucracy and ruling families, allied with foreign capital that controls its tradable sector, Singapore benefits from a strong legitimacy abroad.[30] For several observers, the key to Singapore's success in introducing reform in the 1990s, is threefold: (1) Employer domination of collective agreements that limits conflicts,[31] (2) The institutional coherence that has allowed the social agenda to converge with new challenges, and finally (3) The redistribution of power in favor of young well-educated people (as opposed to nationalists, who were previously the PAP's main supporters[32]).

Neo-corporatism refers to the strong social control exerted by the PAP upon social movements. After the ethnic riots of 1964, trade unions were banned. They were then unified within a confederation (NTUC) and placed under firm state and management control. Heads

---

[29] Henri Ghesquires sees in the proximity of political and bureaucratic elites a key factor in Singapore's success: "Top officials in the government and civil service work closely together and are on the board of directors of GLCs and statutory boards, making for an integrated and hierarchical approach" (Ghesquière, 2007).

[30] "In fact of all the economies of Southeast Asia, the Singaporean State is the most deeply permeated by an internationalist ethos" (Ghesquière, 2007).

[31] "Cooperation between workers and employers meant that strikes were rare, thereby creating a pro-business environment conducive to investments and productivity enhancement" (Gesquieres, *op. cit.*, p. 106).

[32] The economic development board (EDB) created in 1961 is staffed with qualified and well-paid young people and was a major tool for setting up strategies of development, in addition to other public institutions like the banking system which made Singapore a central financial hub. All these institutions — among them the customs service — have proven Singaporean bureaucracy to be very efficient and professional, based on meritocratic principles, high wages, and tough performance indicators. Jean-Louis Margolin rightly speaks of an "enlightened despotism", in Jean-Louis Margolin's (2010, Chapter 21).

of trade unions always follow Lee Kuan Yew's lead (Barr, 2000). Strikes are legal in theory but in practice they are not allowed, and the number of work stoppages rapidly declined from 116 and 88 in 1961 and 1962 respectively, to five in 1979 and to none in 1980 and 1986 (Palat, 2004). Tripartism was created in order to facilitate the transition from a low-cost labor market period to a medium and highly skilled one (Barr, 2000). Heads of trade unions are appointed by the President himself and all of them are MPs or members of ministries.[33] Following the Leninist model, trade unions can be considered as the "transmission belt" of state orders to labor (Sing, 2004). Neo-corporatism, which binds labor movement leaders to the state, can be successful because opponents are prosecuted, civil society is weak and employment relations are harmonious. Good treatment for workers is confined to Singaporean citizens, and migrant workers have no employment rights. In fact, the lack of labor disputes is based on almost full employment, due to global firms investing in Singapore, as well as high investment in housing, health care and education for Singaporean citizens.[34] Combined with high wages, it offers an important social package capable of satisfying social expectations, although it should be noted that there is serious discrimination in favor of the ethnic Chinese majority, and against the Malay workforce (Barr, 2000).

3.4. Comparing CEE with Southeast Asia: From the Corruption to the Rule

There are two closely linked dimensions to the main difference between Southeast Asian and CEE states. The first of these is the

---

[33] "To avoid … unnecessary misunderstanding and the risk of collision, the PAP and the NTUC have adopted a strategy of cross-fertilization … Able union leaders have been co-opted into the PAP leadership, fielded as Members of Parliament, and when found able, appointed to office. PAP MPs have been made to work in the unions" (see Lee Kuan Yew address to NTUC seminar "Progress into the 80s", November 6, 1979, quoted in Barr (2000).

[34] Palat mentions that Lee Kuan Yew launched one of the biggest housing programs in the world building some half million units in 25 years and 15 fully-equipped satellite towns to house 85% of the population (Palat, 2004).

purely endogenous and intense institutionalization of the process of change in central countries (not the Balkans). The creation of institutions responsible for both privatization and employment reflect this. And yet, although this dimension is purely national it could not have existed without the support of the EU. The Copenhagen criteria[35] immediately imposed the adoption of the rules of democracy, of the market (and therefore of privatization) and the respect of minorities on countries seeking to achieve EU integration. During the process of EU integration, Central European states were placed under a tough conditionality, and to that extent could not manipulate EU rules. In many circumstances EU rules have exerted a "moral pressure", limiting opportunistic behaviors from Eastern candidates. In 1994, Hungary was forced to limit its budget expenditures after being threatened with being placed on the top of the risky states list. The impact was immediate. Under supervision Hungary reformulated its budget and managed to regain the trust of FDI. In 1997, the EU was one of the major actors supporting the establishment of the Bulgarian currency board, which was supposed to be the major tool for reducing corruption and currency manipulation. More obviously the imposition of the *Acquis communautaire* from 1997 onward, like the final series of constraints to be achieved in order to join the EU, has had a decisive impact upon candidates. By imposing the series of changes to be made it has limited risks of defection. Obviously certain local adjustments of EU rules in accordance with some national particularities were accepted.[36] But such modifications were limited in scope. National parliaments all voted through the *Acquis communautaire* in its entirety. This was an absolutely necessary step to guarantee collective security and development. Each enlargement requires

---

[35] They were formulated in 1993 but were backdated for all EU candidacies. Any country wishing to belong to the EU could only do so on condition that these criteria were respected. A second stage also has to be completed for integration to be achieved. This is the adoption of the *Acquis Communautaire*, which makes up the legislative arsenal used to regulate the Community.

[36] The moratorium on the land in 2004. Some countries have been allowed not to fully liberalize their land markets in order to protect themselves against more powerful purchasers from EU15, mainly the former German and Austrian occupants.

candidate nations to pass into domestic law the whole of pre-existing European legislation. It is the fundamental component of the EU contract, which is based on collective and reciprocal rights and duties.

This, at least, is the theory. What actually happens in practice can be rather different. The acceptance of EU rule does not necessarily lead to the adoption of "good practice". Indeed, as noted in the last chapter, the acceptance of rules and their passage into legislation does not guarantee compliance. One of the major lessons of 20 years of transforming CEE states is the difference between adopting a rule and implementing it. Implementation requires both firm control from the top and a strong willingness to comply. Rules can be easily ignored by the people in charge of applying them. Adopting the *Acquis communautaire* does not automatically mean that rules and procedures will actually be respected. EU conditionality is efficient only if it leads to the setting up of independent state agencies able to sanction state and market failures. In 2009, the EU Commission concluded that the Bulgarian State mismanaged structural funds and refused to pay a bill of 260 million euros. In short, supranational rule has a positive impact only if national agencies and domestic forces respect the rules. If this is not the case, the EU has very little means at its disposal to enforce respect for rules once the enlargement has been achieved.[37] This is what we saw with regard to new members in Chapter 7, and is also the EU's major problem concerning foreign policy (ENP) with its peripheries, which we will examine in the last chapter.

3.4.1. *Rule of law, rule by law*

The lesson delivered by the Singaporean example is that an efficient fight against corruption requires political will, backed by a strong corps of well-paid civil servants and a strong police. Political

---

[37] This is also the main concern about Greece since 2010.

authorities must give their absolute assurance that crime and corruption will lead to criminal proceedings. Under Lee's strong leadership, the state bureaucracies of trade, police, and justice were cleaned up. The death penalty is still used. Those who are accused of receiving bribes lose not only their jobs but also pension benefits and also run the risk of not being re-employed in the private sector. The strictness of the judicial system is accompanied by good pay for civil servants, whose salaries are in line with similar posts in the private sector.

Rule by law is crucial to both creating commitment to the state and establishing citizen trust in the state's ability to protect property rights. As Lee Kuan Yew proclaimed in 2000, "You can have a free market only if there is a government to manage the rules and enforce them" (Rodan, 2001). Managing rules is the most important public objective. It is supposed to reflect a private duty to conduct public affairs properly, to do nothing that exceeds what the rules permit and to only do what the rules allow. Rule by law means guaranteeing an honest bureaucracy focused only on adherence to the law. In doing so, rules are predictable not only for the public authorities who make them, but also for people who have knowledge of the law. Quite different from the communist claim "the communist party is always right", "rule by law" under Lee Kuan Yee's leadership is framed by a public bureaucracy which secures stability for all and enables citizens to confidently plan ahead.

Rather than defending a rule of law model, based on the clear distinction between a limited state and a fundamentally free citizen as the Western liberal tradition postulates, Lee Kuan Yew defends a system of rule by law where the state itself sets legal limits on what the citizen is allowed to do. Where does the difference lie? For Yew, democracy is not necessary. Western values are not useful. Respect of Confucian virtues still represents the right way for Lee Kuan Yew to avoid any "potentially disintegrative pulls of Chinese", as Katzenstein (1999) says. By emphasizing the importance of family and respect for ancestors, they can both dismiss democratic claims from different social groups and distinguish themselves from the Western model (Dauvergne, 1998). They can claim to create a kind of new Asian model freed from colonial and post-colonial influences,[38] which are still steeped in Western values (Tipton, 2009). Finally, following Katzenstein (1999), "Lacking a distinct identity, Asian values offer Singapore's political elites a plausible ideology for building a new state". Having said that, it should not be forgotten that the state can be neither questioned nor controlled. External control only applies to the state bureaucracy, not the leaders of the regime. Lee Kwan Yew's decisions are above criticism, strikes are forbidden and opposing views are strongly discouraged. To this extent, the rhetoric of Asian values can be seen as no more than a device used to silence the opposition within a system where democracy has only a very limited role.

There is clearly a major difference with Cambodia, where the lack of political will to impose clear rules allows Cambodian authorities to perpetuate a vertical system of patronage, from the village level right up to the top of the system, headed by Hun Sen's clique. Hun Sen is at the head of a corrupt system — based on appropriation of funds from "donors" and foreigners (to whom he gave important tin, timber and forest concessions) — which left civil servants to organize their own wage payment by allowing them to exploit local people (Hughes and Un, 2011). He took 15 years to yield to pressure from the International Community and pass an anti-corruption law. During that time, he organized meetings twice a year between civil servants, lawyers and foreign exporters, and paid for by "donors", which in the end produced a three page draft.

---

[38] "To some extent, this expression of an 'Asian' identity is viewed as a reaction to the way in which the US treats the region. The notion of an Asian identity is an exercise in invention, seen by leaders who advance such notions as a way of stemming the intrusion of Western cultural and moral value systems without rejecting the dynamic aspects of Western economic and technological modernization" (Higgott, 1997).

Table 3.2. Legal bases of social consensus in both regions.

Rule of law	Rule by law
Reference to the philosophical background that in Western world since the 17th century supports: The citizen and the property rights as basis of law.	Reference to the governance allowing respect of rules, confidence in the legal framework and in its capacity to guarantee and sustain growth on the long term, social consensus based on search for legality both from state and citizen. The reinforcement of the confidence implies:
Contract between citizen (property rights, individual freedom) and State (power versus security).	A clear commitment from the country's leadership about the long-term role for the private sector in economic development.
Separation of powers: Mainly the judiciary and police, state and law.	Fundamental change in thinking at all levels of society reflected in the processes of recent regulatory reform (Enterprise Law).
Intermediary bodies between citizen and state. Civil society independent from state. Public opinion.	Commitment to the private sector from the political authorities.
State limits on overcoming or penetrating the individual sphere.	Simplified procedures that have reduced opportunities and incentives for corruption.

3.5. Conclusion

The major difference between the EU and Southeast Asia can be found in the ways of negotiating a new social consensus (see Table 3.2). In Southeast Asia, political economies are rarely transformed as radically as CEE ones were in the years after 1990. Southeast Asian systemic crises are an opportunity to recombine preexisting ruling alliances, meanwhile in CEE the crises at the end of the 1980s opened the door to a profound redistribution of political and economic opportunities. Traditions and history can partially explain this: The rule of law had existed previously in CEE, at least in certain states, namely the central ones (Winiecki, 2004). This had never been the case in Southeast Asia. The nature of supranational rules is of great importance and, in fact, the EU and ASEAN play a major role in these processes. They guarantee a path of economic development and enlarge markets which allow increasing rates of growth thanks to different internal agreements, even though the EU activities go far beyond just trade agreements. Indeed, the EU participates in the consolidation of democracy and the rule of law, by exerting strong pressure and by supporting public agencies that financially accompany the entire process. In the end it offers the final benefits of integration in return for adopting EU legislation in its entirety.

As we have seen in this chapter, corruption can fill a functional role in a highly centralized system because of the inability of central authorities to provide the required input at the intermediary and local levels. It can be defined as a kind of "social glue" enabling the entire economic and social system to work. But what our analysis also shows is that corruption does not disappear when communist or highly authoritarian regimes are replaced. During a period of transition there is lack of traditions, institutions, appropriate rules and a stable regulatory framework, which leads to corruption being rife at all levels of the social and economic architecture.

To this extent, one of the key factors likely to explain the transition from a corrupt system to a more regulated system is the existence of free agents a pluralist civil society, implying a capacity to avoid violence and force, independent agencies in charge of controlling ruling elites, and strongly regulated social sub-systems as in the field of industrial relations. This will be covered in the next chapter. Another requirement is the existence of enforceable supranational rules to ensure compliance from member states. The most important issues are those related to conditionality, as we shall see in Chapters 6 and 7.

4 TRANSFORMING POLITIES: STATES, REGIONS AND ADMINISTRATIONS

The regionalization process has been a core policy in both the European Union (EU) and Association of Southeast Asian Nations (ASEAN). By strongly encouraging EU candidates to implement regionalization laws and to create sub-state levels (Chapter 21 of the *Acquis Communautaire*), the EU has aimed to foster both democracy and effectiveness. However, in many fields it failed to do this, as shall be explained below. In some Southeast Asian states, the aim of the regionalization process was mostly to control peripheral regions. This was the case in the Island States, the Philippines and Indonesia, and to a lesser degree in Malaysia and Thailand. Such an aim was in contrast to the riparian Mekong States that remained highly centralized. As already mentioned, national sovereignty was a priority for states in both areas given that they had been deprived of it for long periods of time. For this reason, it is easy to see how even a minor transformation of each polity could adversely affect these new states and entail strong political reactions. The regionalization process, understood as decentralization, implies a redistribution of power — particularly in the areas of finance and taxation. It can lead to tension between the central level and the regions. In contrast with de-concentration that refers to the central authority and its sub-state levels — which probably best describes the situation in Southeast Asia — decentralization implies not only limited self-governing rules in the area of fiscal measures for example, but also the legitimization of authorities and regional bodies likely to develop their own strategies.

Because of the competition between the center and the regions to secure their own resources, there is a need to decide on the optimal design of the state and the optimal polity capable of strengthening effectiveness and combating corruption. By focusing on state capacity to manage bureaucracy and centrifugal forces coherently, these questions concern issues relative to strong and weak states as mentioned in Chapter 2. Because post-Communist and post-colonialist periods were characterized by an intense promotion of national sovereignty, it is easy to see why states did their best to buffer the impact of pressures exerted both by the forces of globalization and the EU, in the case of Central and Eastern Europe (CEE) states. In general terms, national interests prevailed over other objectives thanks to the recombination of domestic alliances. These alliances have been all the more successful as they were set up in accordance with the national trajectory of each state. For these reasons, transforming these states has been a long and conflictual process that mirrors the importance of liberal or illiberal actors at the domestic level. The transformation process also mirrors these actors' ability to share representations, values and rules with foreign actors, and to redesign political coalitions in order to reshape polities.

A large variety of regionalization models can be identified in the EU. They reflect the importance of historical legacies, minorities, state capacities and finally EU rules. These historical, domestic and geopolitical constraints allow a better identification of constraints specific to Southeast Asian cases to be made by indicating the factors that are specific to one region to another. This chapter uses European regionalization models as a useful framework for Southeast Asia to better identify variables which are absent or lacking in both regions (CEE and Southeast Asia). Finally, a study of the situation in each area enriches the concept of strong and weak state by highlighting different ways of managing internal tensions. The first part of this chapter presents different theoretical models of regionalization that distinguish Western Europe from CEE (the lack of civil societies) and from Southeast Asia (ethnic minorities). The second part offers a comparison of CEE and Southeast Asian examples based on three types of organization: Administrative regionalization, regional decentralization and regionalization through existing territorial communities.

4.1. Regionalization from a Comparative Perspective: Conditions for Reform and a Comparison of CEE and Southeast Asia

Pasquier and Perron have developed an interesting comparison of both East and West European trajectories which provides a useful basis for comparison between these two regions (Pasquier and Perron, 2008). It highlights seven variables that foster regionalization: National political and institutional pathways; the territorialization of capitalism; the politicization of territorial identities; European integration; national political agendas; regional policies and institutions; and the territorialization of political parties. These variables can be considered as either strong or weak factors that constitute the path of dependency and that either are or are not conducive to decentralization (see Table 4.1). From this perspective, a strong state can depend on either of these two options: A weak state, in contrast, is one that cannot manage its centrifugal forces and finds itself unable to impose either strong centralization or coherent and efficient channels between center and periphery.

4.1.1. *Varieties of EU regionalization*

In the case of CEE, neither regional autonomy recognizing ethnic particularity nor a federalist approach has ever been adopted. Everywhere, regionalization has been granted to citizens from the top down and not as a final consequence of social mobilization, with the single exception of Poland. Because of the importance of "path dependency",[1] a large variety of designs exist. It is all the more the case

---

[1] The "path dependency" concept is central in the neo-institutionalist approach. It indicates the capacity of institutions and rules to "lock in" the made choices by eliminating alternatives, shaping preferences and making the selected rule effectives (Pierson, 2000; North, 1990). In transitional countries where the choice of new rules and new institutions was a fundamental and urgent goal, people selected relevant references from their own past but also from existing Western models, and combined them with new constraints (Pierson, 1996). Based on this approach, Stark (1996) insisted on the process of reconstructing institutions, and spoke of "recombinant" property.

Table 4.1. Strong and weak factors influencing regional decentralization.

Factors unfavorable or not conducive to regional decentralization	Factors conducive to regional decentralization
(1) Political and institutional pathways. Old centralizing traditions. Legacies of Communist rule.	(1) Indispensable reform of state administration after Communism. Legacies of ideas of dissidence (importance of pluralism, diversity and subsidiarity). Desire for diffusion of power.
(2) Legacies of Communist paradigms of economic development.	(2) Obsolescence and de-legitimization of instruments of economic development inherited from the former regime (sectoral policies).
(3) Fear of irredentism, of possible centrifugal effects of minority demands. Lack of politicized territorial identities.	(3) Absence of strong minorities.
(4) Recentralization of programming and implementation of structural funds. Increase in control mechanisms.	(4) Structural funding reglementation.
(5) Existence of strong illiberal political forces. Dominance of national issues on the political agenda (privatization).	(5) Existence of pro-European parties/coalitions.
(6) Difficulty of local actors to act at different levels and to become part of European networks.	(6) Existence of institutionalized (elected) bodies at the regional level.
(7) Dominance of weakly territorialized, governmental political parties.	(7) Existence of regionalist political parties.

Source: Pasquier and Perron (2008).

that in the EU, there is no one single model of regionalization. The lack of a "one-size-fits-all-model" is due to the fact that the EU is a union of rules. This principle of "subsidiarity" compels each state to comply to the formal aspects of EU rules, while simultaneously leaving each of them free to define the content of their own laws. Consequently, a tremendous amount of variety in function of the different historical paths and choices can be found nationally. This means that regions vary greatly from each other within the EU (see Table 4.2). Some of them have fewer than one million inhabitants and others such as Bavaria or Rheine-North Westphalia have more than 10 million. Finally, as previously mentioned, most new European states had to contend with important critical issues surrounding their minorities. For all these reasons, the administrative architecture of newly independent Eastern states remained untouched during the first decade of 1990, whether they were ruled by new elites or by "Gorbachevian" wings of the former Communist parties transformed into "new-social-democrat" parties in Balkan states (Bozoki and Ishiyama, 2002; Orenstein, 2000). All of these parties were highly centralized and none of them had a regional basis. In fact, regional political parties did not exist — apart from in Silesia or Romania where they were few in number. Indeed, the major task during this period was to reassess national sovereignty rather than to contribute to its "deconstruction".[2]

---

[2] Once Communism had disappeared in 1990, it was believed that administrative freedom would be immediately transferred to municipalities. However, certain geopolitical events crushed that hope. The German Chancellor, Helmut Kohl refused to admit the permanence of the border between newly unified Germany and his new neighbors Poland and Czechoslovakia. Such a position enflamed nationalist passions in both new states and destabilized all of Europe. It led CEE authorities to accuse local traders in border regions of wanting to destabilize newly centralized authorities and put a halt to trade. Almost simultaneously, the Soviet empire broke into different regionalist conflicts that paved the way to violent nationalist uprisings which very quickly led to the collapse of the whole Soviet empire in 1991. Finally, in Europe, a bloody conflict erupted in Yugoslavia in the name of regionalist demands. Using these numerous sources of conflict as a pretext, central authorities in Central Europe halted the dynamics of regionalization, arguing that it was too dangerous and costly for states that valued national sovereignty so highly. As a result, regionalist debate shut down throughout central Europe. It was only under pressure from the European Union that it was possible a few years later to re-launch the process, but under a very strong EU conditionality. At that time — in 1998 — the EU commission imposed a regionalization process as a condition for joining the EU. It was described in the 21st chapter of the *Acquis Communautaire*, which each EU candidate had to fully incorporate in order to become a EU member (see Bafoil, 1999).

Table 4.2. EU regional levels, departments and municipalities.

Regional levels + department + municipalities	Regional average population	Regional average area (Km²)
Countries with three sub-national levels		
Germany 16 federated states + 323 rural districts + 12,312 municipalities	5,152,000	21,010
Italy 20 regions (of which 5 with a special status) + 103 provinces + 8,101 municipalities	2,938,000	1,060
Spain 17 autonomous communities with different status + 50 provinces + 8,111 municipalities	2,585,000	29,710
France 26 regions of which 5 with special status + 100 departments + 36, 683 municipalities	2,416,100	22,100
Poland 16 regions + 314 countries + 2,478 municipalities (307 urban, 1,587 rural, 583 mixed)	2,385,100	19,540
Belgium 6 communities and regions + 10 provinces + 589 municipalities		
Countries with two sub-national levels		
The Netherlands 12 provinces + 443 municipalities	1,35,700	3,460
Denmark 5 regions + 98 municipalities	1,083,000	8,620
Austria 9 federated states + 2,357 municipalities	914,800	9,320
Czech Rep 14 regions + 6,249 municipalities	731,000	5,630
Slovakia 8 regions + 2,891 municipalities	673,000	6,130
Hungary 19 counties + 3,175 municipalities	530,900	4,900
Romania 42 counties + 3,173 municipalities	514,900	5,680
Ireland 8 regional authorities + 114 local councils	518,600	8,720

(*Continued*)

Table 4.2. (*Continued*)

Regional levels + department + municipalities		Regional average population	Regional average area (Km²)
Sweden	18 county councils and 2 regions + 290 municipalities	45,500	22,500
Greece	50 departments + 1,034 local governments	221,700	2,640
Latvia	26 districts + 527 municipalities	88,500	2,480
Portugal	2 autonomous regions + 308 municipalities		
Countries with one level of sub-national government			
Bulgaria	264 municipalities		
Cyprus	524 local governments		
Estonia	227 municipalities		
Finland	416 municipalities		
Lithuania	60 municipalities		
Luxemburg	116 municipalities		
Malta	68 local councils		
Slovenia	210 municipalities		

Source: (Dexia, 2008, p. 19).

From this perspective, the French experience offers an interesting model as it is a blend of highly centralized and partially decentralized governing entities. Indeed, in each region the prefect who represents the central state shares powers on regional development with the regional council whose members are elected by the citizens of the region. The prefect is responsible for the ex-post assessment of the use of funds and the regional assembly (with its president) is in charge of regional strategy and its implementation. This model was widely preferred to that of the federalist state of Germany which requires much experience in decentralized negotiations and sharing of responsibilities by different actors. Within this framework, the state (the *Bund*) as such, is not an appropriate partner compared with the regions (the

Länder), which are in charge of regional affairs.[3] Similarly, while in France social partnership is based on the solid centralization of collective bargaining, in Germany professional players are the only source of social regulation at the regional level to the exclusion of the state.

This German administrative model could not be shared by Central and Eastern Europe (CEE) countries in 1990 as they had no tradition of that type and were above all concerned with assessing their own national sovereignty (Wollmann, 1997). Negotiation was not thought of as a way to balance power.[4] The state had no regional counterweights and the central parties had no regional partners. Civil societies were almost completely absent from the landscape. At regional and local levels, many actors such as the Church were strongly opposed to the most minor modifications of their administrative units, which would necessarily have led to a reduction of their local assets. To this extent, the regionalization process, far from reducing the role of the state actually strengthened it. In summary, there has been a hybrid process of mixing top down processes and local, regional adaptations which can be defined as bottom up in all CEE countries. This explains why the process of regionalization in CEE was so different from the Western experience.[5]

---

[3] The Bundesrat (assembly of regions) is a very important political actor.

[4] This is the same reason that explains the non-reproduction of the German model of industrial relations in Eastern Europe. Its very strong efficiency lies/lay in the long negotiations between trade unions and employer organizations within each sector, and at the regional level the setting up of agreements that were extended to all the firms of the given sector.

[5] In their convincing article, Pasquier and Perron try to identify the major differences between both parts of the EU. For them, "regionalism" is key because in Western Europe, the regionalization dynamic has very often been spurred by local actors. This bottom up perspective emphasizes the role of regional identities, local ethnic groups and the numerous constant conflicts between state and sub-state levels. Regionalization, therefore, is understood as being the product of collective social mobilization. In Western Europe the "ethno-territorial approach" underlines the emergence of new phenomena that Keating (1998) has called "post-sovereignty", based on the regional examples of the Catalonian and Scottish experiences. In the 1990s, another wave of analysis highlighted the impact of EU rule in order to better define what "Europeanization" is. This analysis focused on the ability of member states to

To put it briefly, civil societies are rather rare in CEE for reasons that strongly differentiate these countries from Western ones, and make them unable to develop counter models *vis-à-vis* the state (Hann and Dunn, 1994; Howard, 2003; Mansfeldová *et al.*, 2004; Bafoil, 2010b). The lack of interest in collective action can be explained by the obligation imposed on everyone during the Communist period to become a member of a number of social organizations. For instance, being a trade union member was not a signal of subjective support for the regime. In reality, it was the only way to have access to benefits which could not be obtained from a market that did not exist. This included social benefits. Moreover, the strong mistrust of all types of state affairs was extended to local public authorities, which, in any case were deprived of all responsibility in this very highly centralized system. This explains why after 1990, individual freedom was vastly preferred to any form of collective action. Micro-local networks, friendship and kinship took precedence over membership of professional or civil organizations. Moreover, dissident and social groups that flourished in the 1980s and which were strongly opposed to the Communist Party's moral and private values, had not developed a strong vision of administrative or civic decentralization within their

---

negotiate with their own sub-state partners in accordance with their own institutional capacities and "power of veto" (Hooghe, 2006; Börzel and Risse, 2003). While other scholars were asserting the importance of these major domestic actors and their capacity to shape EU rule, the institutionalization of regions led to a great deal of reflection on "multilevel governance" everywhere (Hooghe and Marks, 2001). Finally, an extension of the first ethno-territorial approach, the "neo-regionalist approach" considered European integration to be only one factor among many. It pointed to cultural and political forces at play, as illustrated by certain "self-governing" provinces and even more so by "autonomous" movements. Certain authors, who are convinced of the validity of this approach, have highlighted the role of social conflict (Baisnée and Pasquier, 2007). By emphasizing the variety and differentiated importance of institutions, interest and values from different actors located at different levels of the EU ensemble, they use "Europeanization" as a sub-discipline appropriate for the analysis of a variety of global, regional and local changes. From this perspective, CEE was seen under a different and particular light, characterized by the shortcomings and deficiencies that define what a systemic transition is (Hall, 1997; Heclo,1994; Palier and Surel, 2005).

own democratic programs. The only exception was Poland where the social movement *Solidarnosc* promoted an independent self-ruled republic based on self-ruled industrial and regional organization. That is why a few Polish democratic activists, who felt frustrated by the way public debate was evolving in the 1990s, decided to intervene at the local level only. However, they were rather isolated and most of them saw their legitimacy fade away with the disappearance of Communism. They considered the new rules of democratic consensus to be morally unacceptable (Rupnik, 2008). To this extent, it is argued that the modernization process that characterized the 1990s destroyed the social mobilization that defined the 1980s. The deep historical and social break between the two periods — before and after 1989 — forced former players to adopt new profiles and new codes, which were sometimes in complete opposition to former codes adopted in the fight against Communist regimes. The fact is that some CEE societies emerged without a basis of strong democratic values or European legacies (Winiecki, 2004). Jowit has emphasized the weight of the "Leninist legacies" in underlining the difficulties of democratic transformation (Jowit, 1992 pp. 284–305). Lastly, if civil society mirrors the level of economic and social development of a society, it is clear that CEE societies lagged far behind Western ones. Indeed, Western societies are characterized by a high level of citizen participation that reflects the importance of the "third sector", which offers social care and assistance to the poorest and most excluded populations (Kubik, 2005). In CEE countries, this sector has not been decentralized to social actors and remains highly centralized or even non-existent. All these reasons, and particularly the fact that civil societies were non-existent under socialism, not only explain why regionalization in CEE was imposed from the top — meaning from the EU — but also why it failed to produce citizen participation and why bureaucratic designs prevailed (Börzel and Buzogany, 2010). As shall be seen below, true decentralization really only occurred in Poland. This also offers an explanation for the fact that the implementation of the *Acquis Communautaire* provoked the emergence of many obstacles and blockades to the adjustment process to EU integration (Kutter and Trappmann, 2006).

4.1.2. *Southeast Asia*

In the case of Southeast Asia, it is interesting to note that most of the factors (1st, 2nd, 3rd, 5th and 7th — indicated in Table 4.1) do not apply to them. Indeed, "dissidence" is quite negligible or even non-existent when compared to CEE. There is no equivalent to the social movement in Poland but there are many more minority groups fighting against the central state, which more often suspects them of seeking self-government rather than decentralization. For this reason, public development policies are very often combined with armed warfare. Examples of this include the Achese in the northern part of Indonesia, Mindanao and the militant Catholic Luzon in the Philippines, or Muslims in the southern part of Thailand where, the Malay Muslim minority, which represents 80% of the local population, is conspicuously under-represented in public office. In 2007, this part of Thailand witnessed 6.78 violent events every day (Askew, 2010). As shall be seen further below, this minority is widely seen as a threat to "Thai-ness",[6] in the same way external enemies are exemplified by the conflict surrounding the Preah Vihar Temple. Both perceived threats — internal and external — stress the fact that Thai-ness is based on territorial and sanctified integrity.[7]

Second, the de-legitimization of instruments of economic development inherited from the previous regime did not lead to more decentralized management, as shall be seen in the next chapter. It led, rather, to a more de-concentrated form of management equal to a delegation of power to regional actors who nonetheless remained

---

[6] "Thai-ness" is praised by all central parties to distinguish the national Buddhist Thai majority from the "non-Thai" who threaten social peace and national territorial integrity. In the past, this perspective addressed non-native Thai Chinese; currently, it concerns Muslims (Connors, 2003). Benedict Anderson refers to Thai-ness as the "endless affirmation of the identity of the dynasties and of the nation".

[7] "Thai nationhood, defined by the sacredness and vulnerability of Thai territorial integrity, is one that is permanently threatened by enemies, both inside and outside Thailand's borders. All this has been carried out in the name of Thai patriotism" (Cachavalpongpun, 2010).

intertwined with the central authorities to some degree. In the example of the Vietnamese *Doi Moi* reform (Balme and Sidel, 2007; Gillepsie, 1999), the central authorities gradually delegated more room to maneuver to the regions and the management of regional SOEs while simultaneously reinforcing links with the central government. To a certain extent, Vietnamese reformers succeeded in doing this without undermining the domination of the Communist Party, as opposed to Gorbatchev's reform that failed to foster more local initiatives within a less constraining central framework.

The third factor addresses the fact that apart from the strong minorities mentioned above, most Southeast Asian minorities are not well organized despite their numbers. Most of them are generally among the poorest of the population, scattered throughout the whole territory or along by inaccessible borders. No matter where they are, they are discriminated against. This is especially the case in Burma, but it is also true in Laos where the Mgong living in the northern mountains (Lao Sung) are openly considered as inferior to the other Lao — Lao Lum from the plains, and the Lao Theung from the slopes — for the sole reason that they resisted the Communist armies in the 1970s (Pholsena, 2006a). The fifth and seventh factor referring to organized political parties are not present within authoritarian regimes and likewise do not exist in Thailand. The fourth factor is irrelevant for Southeast Asia. The sixth factor mentions the existence of regional bodies. They are indeed present but as mentioned earlier, they represent the extent of the de-concentration of central power, and nothing more.

4.2. Cultural, Political and Economic Regionalism: Further Comparison of EU and Asian Peculiarities

In several significant papers, the German sociologist Artur Benz has identified three types of regionalization (Benz *et al.*, 2005; Benz, 2007). The first type, cultural regionalism refers to the delicate

Table 4.3. Different types of regionalization.

Type	Basic aims	People treated as	Conflicts	Main problems
Cultural regionalism	Preservation of culture and protection of the minority rights.	Ethnos	Inter-regional tensions	Separatism
Political administrative/ regionalization	Access to authorities. Balance of power.	Demos	Inter-governmental tensions	Blockade
Economic regionalism	Increasing wealth.	Bourgeois	Economic competition	Unbalanced growth

Source: Benz (2007).

balance between majority and minority, the second to the "balance of power" and the third to decentralization (see Table 4.3). Each of them can be characterized by four features: First, the basic economic aims that highlight the role of culture, politics and economics; second, each type is led by a core group: the ethnic group, the *demos*, the bourgeois; third, each of them is facing particular tensions created by opposition between the center and the periphery, between different governments and, in the third case, between economic forces: fourth, the inherent risk in each type is linked to separatism, blockade and social and territorial inequalities.

This approach is of obvious importance as it allows two considerations stressed in the theoretical framework about strong and weak states to be emphasized: (i) The role of social conflicts between emerging social groups fighting for respect of their own identity and cultural features denied them in the past by foreigners and/or domestic rulers; and (ii) The very fragile balance between these different social actors competing against each other, and consequently, the very precarious social consensus. These variables shall now be used to compare the CEE and Southeast Asian cases.

4.2.1. *The minorities: A delicate balance*

The first type — (cultural regionalism), refers to the existence of minorities within a country to whom the state accords the same powers it accords to the majority. Peaceful co-existence depends on effective power-sharing, supported by shared values and institutions. In this category, the minority is patently understood as an ethnic category and there is a risk of separatist aspirations. The huge challenge is to maintain a delicate balance between the different regional components that can be centrifugal forces. In Western Europe, Great Britain exemplifies such a case, having accorded important rights to Scottish and Welsh minorities, and later to the Northern Irish.[8] On each occasion, such a balance was only reached after long and sometimes bloody conflicts in Scotland and Wales that justified the vision of common rules as a "social armistice", to use Perroux's words (Perroux, 1980). It must be recognized that cultural regionalism would not have worked in a majority of cases in CEE and Southeast Asia. In fact, many minorities were never accepted by the majority for some of the reasons mentioned earlier. Moreover, all these minorities are located in certain territorial areas, are politically marginalized, and are separated from their economic assets.

In CEE, cultural regionalism was widely rejected for fear of irredentism from minorities that previously had important economic and even political powers (see Table 4.4). In the Baltic States, it was unacceptable for the local population to silently accept that former Russian occupants were taking over the economy and jobs and were therefore demanding identical political rights. In some countries, in the 1990s, Russian minorities represented more than 30% of the

---

[8] It should be stressed of course that Northern Ireland is a particular case as the island of Ireland was divided after 1922 when Britain withdrew from 26 counties of the island but continued to govern the remaining six counties known today as Northern Ireland. Although Catholics are a minority in Northern Ireland, they form part of the majority in the island of Ireland. The Protestant population in Northern Ireland is a minority in the island of Ireland but a majority in Northern Ireland. Thanks to Chantal Barry for this precision.

Table 4.4. Selective examples of minorities in CEE countries, 1930–1990.

	Czechoslovakia	Poland	Hungary	Romania	Bulgaria
1930	51% Czech, 23% German, 16% Slovak 5% Hungarian	65% Polish 16% Ukrainian 10% Jews 6% Belarusian 2% German	87% Hungarian 6% German 5% Jews	75% Romanian 6% Jews 5% German	87% Bulgarian 10% Turks 1% Jews
1990	3% Hungarian/ 1.4% Roms	0.8% Belarusian, 0.8% Ukrainian, 1% German	5.6% Roms	4.5% Roms 6.6% Hungarian	3.5% Roms 9.5% Turks

population and were strongly concentrated in the capital cities. After 1991, the newly sovereign Baltic States who found this unacceptable, adopted very unjust laws exclusively favoring the native Baltic populations and therefore deeply undermining the native Russian populations. Altogether 140,000 native Russians were given permission to become Estonian citizens after having successfully passed a language exam. Another 120,000 native Russians either failed the exam or refused to take it. For the moment, they are stateless as they are considered to be neither Russian nor Estonian. In 2010, Slovakia also used the linguistic method of discrimination against the Hungarian minority.

As stated earlier, similar dynamics can be identified in Southeast Asian countries (see Table 4.5) and may be observed in the three conflicts in Ache, Mindanao, and southern Thailand (Dosch, 2007). The conflicts in these areas share similar legacies linked to the colonial and even pre-colonial period. All of them involve ethnic and religious minorities, for whom religion is a main feature of their struggle. They are also the poorest regions, although Ache has plenty of natural resources that benefit the central power alone. Conflicts that are anchored deeply in history result directly from the nation-building that the central state used to oppose local demands and aspirations that were systematically destroyed. A huge level of antagonism exists between the Thai people, ("Thai-ness" expressing the essence of Thai citizenship), and the ethnic Muslim Malays. Thailand is a

Table 4.5. Selective examples of minorities in SEA, 2010.

The Philippines	Indonesia	Thailand	Singapore	Cambodia	Vietnam	Laos	Myanmar	Malaysia
The first important group: Tatalog 30%; the 2nd = 25%; 87 recognized languages	250 ethnic groups	80% Thai + 15 minorities	Chinese 75%; Malaysian 15% Indian 10%	85.4% Khmers 12 minorities Viet 7.4% Cham 3.5% Chinese 3.2%	60 minorities	Lao 48 ethno linguistic groups	130 minorities registered and Bamar = 65% of Birma	Malaysian < 50% Chinese 30%

highly centralized state and not even the 1932 revolution modified the verticality of its central power. The dictators, Phibun and Sarit, who were both marshals reinforced this historical dynamic (Phongpaikchit and Baker, 2005), they being more closely linked to the "religion, state, monarchy" ethos (Handley, 2006). By stressing the fact that Thailand remains highly centralized despite having 76 provinces, Marc Askew mentions that the administrative model implemented by King Chulalungkorn at the end of the 1890s remains important for ruling elites. It is based on the creation of a provincial administration having its own elected assembly and chief ministers, but placed under the authority of a superintendent who is appointed by Bangkok as are all the commissioners (Askew, 2010). This is an original example of "regionalization", mixing features of both de-centralization and de-concentration.

The clash between local ethnic peculiarities and national central states is equally evident in the case of the Philippines, characterized by a strong Catholic central state opposed to about 5 million Moro people, who are an ethnic Muslim minority. Indonesia also reflects the same pattern of a secularized and religious pluralist central state versus the Aceh region which is marginalized in its poverty despite having considerable natural resources. Central states everywhere replaced local authorities with their own people. This was accompanied by military force and "Thai-zation" or "Java-nization" and eventually led to an infernal cycle of violence and zero local economic growth.

4.2.2. The "administrative reform": The Asian and Balkan examples

Benz's second type of regionalization includes the notion of "balance of power". Within CEE, the Baltic and Balkan States have argued that the presence of strong minorities within their territory entitles them to refuse to implement regional reform. Instead, they have chosen to apply a formal EU design known as the Nomenclature of Territorial Units (NUTS). This design allows the central level to remain the most important actor. The regions are designated from the top–down and are provided with appropriate institutions. Rather than promoting an inexistent process from the bottom–up, the EU frees central and local actors as long as administrative rules are respected. This type can be understood as "administrative regionalization" or "political regionalization". The expectation is that inhabitants will become accustomed to such a top–down policy. The EU hopes that through economic development and the passage of time the citizens of each region will appropriate these regional units and develop a sense of ownership of them. The reasoning is that collective identity results from a shared institutional framework and a number of case studies in Western Europe have proven this to be true.[9] This framework is perfectly adapted to the case of Turkey, which is not an EU member. It is a highly centralized state with densely located minorities and a coherent sense of central identity with the center (republicanism) (Massicar, 2010). In this case, 'deconcentrated regionalization' is a more appropriate term than decentralization. The leading regional figure in Turkey is the governor who is appointed by the central authorities. There is no regional assembly and regional development is decided at the central level. Certain Southeast Asian states resemble this last figure and have adopted a similar administrative model.[10] During the 1980s, some states launched important administrative reforms which were widely inspired by the Weberian model based on accountability, neutrality, civil servant qualifications and career management. The case of Cambodia can be mentioned here as a counter example.

---

[9] The Rhône-Alpes region in France is a completely bureaucratic construction, which includes historically opposed cities (Lyon and Grenoble). Whatever the conflict between local populations covers, this region benefits from a strong identification from its citizens.

[10] Reforming the administration is not new in Southeast Asia. The Thai king Chulalungkorn based his politics on state reform at the end of the 19th century, coupling it with educational reform. The Philippines under American rule did the same by reinforcing centralization and reforming administrative structures. After independence in 1957, Malaysia had a crucial agenda to modernize its civil service. Indochina experienced regionalization under French rule, albeit in a very formal and bureaucratic form. Idem the Dutch with the Dutch Indies.

4.2.3. *Cambodia*

To some extent Cambodia is a case of *trompe l'oeil* in that it upholds the positive role of international organizations, but without producing any concrete and effective results. In Cambodia, international organizations are called "donors" and are the main initiators of forces behind "decentralization". Several competing models are present, including the French and the German one. However, none of them can prevail as the conditions needed to implement a French or German system, such as a spirit of cooperation and regional institutions, are lacking. However, more importantly, there is often a political reluctance to invest substantial powers in the regions. Hun Sen's authority is characterized by a strong personalization of power reflected in a highly centralized system and based on a few clans who are closely linked to the boss. The Cambodian People's Party has ruled Cambodia since 1993 and introduced even tighter rule after the Cambodian Coup in 1997 under the rigid authority of Hun Sen. In 2002, the party won the legislative election in 1,600 municipalities out of a total of 1,621, meaning a victory of 99%. This was officially depicted as "a great success". Despite the presence of democratic debate, violence and threats are the usual means of public action. Nobody has forgotten that Hun Sen blocked peaceful international intervention several times after 1991, going so far as to deny the results of the 1997 elections when he overthrew Prime Minister Norodom Ranariddh. He then forced the king into a partnership with him that he later used to become the sole ruler (Acharya, 2009). Within such a framework, there is no constitutional limit on central activity.

Finally, where regional institutions in Cambodia do exist, they are irrelevant either because they are "distributed" to Hun Sen's own family, or because they simply have no real power. In 2004, the central state allocated 2.5% of its total budget to the municipalities (double the amount allocated in 2002) and even if they get an average of USD 8,000 yearly they cannot get by on their own. They have no choice but to accept orders imposed from the top (Dosch, 2007). Moreover, conditions in Cambodia have made decentralization difficult. In the 1990s, "pockets of war" still existed because the Khmer

Rouge only ceased fighting in 1997. Because of this, centralization was absolutely critical in light of the sheer size and scale of the effort required to reconstruct and redistribute funds to poor people spread all over the territory. One characteristic unique to Cambodia is the fact that poverty is not an ethnic feature but concerns the entire population, as opposed to Thailand or Indonesia where poverty strongly impacts ethnic minorities. Social misery is not territorialized in Cambodia. Lastly, because of the immense destruction caused by the Khmer Rouge and the length of the Vietnamese occupation, the sub-national public administration system is very poorly equipped and its performance quite weak.

Finally, it can be argued that decentralization has no support in Cambodia other than from international "donors", which are the only institutions committed to democracy in the country. The combined effect of the predominance of the Cambodian People's Party, the absence of civil society and the lack of independent Cambodian NGOs has led to the permanence of patronage links (Dosch, 2007, p. 161). For all these reasons, even if the constitution adopted in 1993 postulates decentralization, there has been no real implementation and no legal framework shapes decentralization policy. This is the difference with the Philippines, Indonesia or Thailand where work has already begun on shaping the national framework and decentralization policies. In Cambodia, only international "donors" intervene (see Table 4.6), but their financial support is directed towards specific public policies — irrigation, agriculture, etc. — that

Table 4.6. Development assistance to four post-crisis states in 2000.

	Contribution in USD per capita	Contribution as percentage of GDP	Contribution as percentage of state budget
Angola	21.0	2.8	n/a
Cambodia	30.3	12.0	63.8
Ethiopia	16.1	17.3	49.7
Guatemala	19.2	1.1	7.4

Source: Dosch (2007, p. 150).

are strictly controlled by ministers. In this sense, donor funds are massively embezzled by public authorities under the control of Hun Sen's clan. A plan launched by the United Nations can be called a success by them even though in fact it supports corruption (Dosch, 2007, p. 160). Moreover, the Chinese donors who are becoming the most important donors in Cambodia have no interest at all in such a policy (Sullivan, 2011).

4.2.4. The "decentralization reform": A rare EU reform

The third type is "decentralization" based on the emergence of new regional institutions in charge of regional development and whose representatives are regionally elected. From the European perspective, this type of institutionalization aims at simultaneously reinforcing and creating efficient and democratic institutions. With this approach, justice and economics are thought to reinforce one another. This is a type of democracy based on participation from most of the social groups likely to support effective cooperation, while effectiveness is perceived as a result of collective action. For these reasons, and because the Baltic and Balkan states are concerned by the two other types of regionalization, only Central Europe corresponds to this third type. In fact, Poland is the only case of true decentralization, with strong democratically elected regional authorities (Ferry, 2003, 2007).

4.2.5. Poland

The Polish reform law was adopted in July 1998 and implemented on January 1, 1999. It was the first law to address true regionalization in the former Soviet bloc. After lengthy public debates, a design of 16 regions (*voivodship*) was endorsed, including 324 districts (*powiats*), all of which would have their own elected bodies and their own prerogatives. They replaced the administrative system created in 1975 which consisted of 49 *voivodships*. This is also when intermediary sub-regional levels — the departments (*powiat*) — were suppressed in order to eliminate any intermediary between sub-state level and municipalities, which were left without any room to maneuver. By restoring the *powiat* and by creating 16 regions at the end of the 1990s, the Polish parliament re-embedded Polish polity design within long-term tradition and simultaneously adapted it to modern EU requirements for effective and democratic regional administrations (Bafoil, 2009a). French administrative design played a major role in this not only because it distinguishes between state and regional institutions, but also by inspiring "regional contracts" signed between the regions and the state. This organization completely reshaped the Polish polity by placing the regions at the heart of political life. In managing nearly 30% of the entire amount of structural funds (60 billion euros for the period 2007–2013), they have become the major actors of regional development.

The other central countries have also adopted decentralization models but have been more reluctant to do so. Despite its "velvet revolution", the Czech Republic has remained highly centralistic and never agreed to delegate power to its regions, which have always been considered peripheral. Such a situation can be explained by the high level of power concentrated within the center-right ODS party (Martin, 2003a; Perron, 2003). The party has been under the strong leadership of its co-founder, Vaclav Klaus, for a long period of time starting when he was Prime Minister and continuing when he became President of the Czech Republic. The intense centralization of the political landscape drained the local levels and made it difficult for the ruling elites to be legitimized locally. Slovakia has likewise remained deeply centralized, due largely to the centrality of Bratislava where the majority of its economic assets are concentrated and despite its decision to set up seven regions. Hungary was also very reluctant to adopt the EU scheme, arguing that regional design is not part of Hungarian history, where the *county* level has prevailed. Such a scenario does not exist in Southeast Asia.

4.3. Conclusion: Comparing Both Areas

Finally, Gérard Marcou's classification is a useful tool to provide coherence to this huge diversity and to allow a better comparison of

Table 4.7. Distribution of EU and SEA countries in accordance with the institutional framework.

Countries	Institutional architecture	Territorial dynamics
Bulgaria and Baltic countries Vietnam, Cambodia	Administrative regionalization	Centralism
Czech Republic, Slovakia Poland	Regional decentralization	
Hungary Philippines, Indonesia, Thailand	Regionalization though existing territorial communities	Regionalization

both regions to be made. The French professor of Law identifies three types of organization (Marcou, 2004): Administrative regionalization, regional decentralization and regionalization through existing territorial communities (see Table 4.7).

The first type of organization is known as "administrative", and concerns the state's ability to organize regions under its own responsibility and to mobilize them to achieve the goals it has defined in cooperation with regional partners. This configuration is seen in Bulgaria, Estonia, Lithuania, Slovenia (and outside the EU, in Turkey (Massicar, 2010) and Croatia). In Southeast Asia, it is widely used by Thailand (Arghiros, 2000), Vietnam, Cambodia and the Philippines,[11] even if there is no equivalent there to the "NUTs". As seen above, all these countries are home to many significant minorities, concentrated in particular regions. This first administrative category can be implemented either by democratic regimes or by authoritative ones. Finally, it should be noted that this type of organization is currently experiencing huge social and political tensions in both regions.

The second type of organization is known as "decentralization through existing local units" in which local units implement the

---

[11] The Philippines consists of 7,100 islands divided into 17 administrative regions. In 2005, 80 provinces were created, 114 cities, 1,496 municipalities and 41,945 sub-municipal levels.

different priorities of their regional strategy by themselves. Hungary, Latvia and Romania are included in this second category as are Singapore and Indonesia.

The last type of organization is "regional decentralization", which is based on the creation of new territorial units and is characterized by its new institutions within the state unitary form. Poland, and to a lesser extent the Czech Republic and Slovakia are the main representatives of this last category. There is no equivalent to this in Southeast Asia.

To conclude, both regions can be contrasted by considering state and supranational competencies. EU decentralization is made possible by the delegation of regional policies to the regional level, where funds are managed. Whatever the characteristics of the region are, e.g., number of inhabitants or strategic capacity, they are necessarily designed from the top–down or from the bottom–up. The EU uses incentives to reinforce the bottom–up perspective, as it considers that only local levels guarantee effectiveness and equality, although it respects state prerogative to address national strategies. Among these prerogatives, spatial planning remains strictly a state matter. Therefore, because of the strong alchemy of shared powers, there is a great difference between EU and ASEAN approaches to regionalization (see Table 4.8). Neither supranational authority nor local powers are to be found in Southeast Asia. States remain the only arbiter of public policies and inter-governmentalism is the only way for exchange to occur at the ASEAN level.

The final design of such important reforms does not reflect a homogeneous model. Diversity prevails. Classic models of regionalization based on strong fiscal devolution and Weberian administration have not been adopted by the vast majority of CEE countries or in Southeast Asia, often for the same reasons. EU intervention in CEE countries has been characterized by a pragmatic approach.[12] In

---

[12] As Artur Benz (2007, p. 326) writes, "In all European countries, successful regionalization has been achieved by a pragmatic approach of policy making, whereas policies determined to implement idealistic aims of regional autonomy have failed. The European commission promotes such an incremental policy, in particular by avoiding regulative policies and by applying soft patterns of governance in regional policy".

Table 4.8. Comparison of types of decentralization in both regions.

European Union	ASEAN
• Mix of delegation and devolution; higher level of decentralization. • EU principle of subsidiarity allows for territorialization of development planning. • Lack of inter-ministerial cooperation and cooperation across all government levels. • Problem of policy coherence: Cohesion Policy versus CAP. • No overall arbiter in regional development strategy. • Weak monitoring and performance assessment. • Low level of local capacity in undertaking spatial planning.	• De-concentration; lower level of decentralization. • Central planning, local level has little autonomy; no territorialization of development planning. • National Committees to improve inter-ministerial and inter-agency coordination. • But, there are still problems of coordination, especially regional inter-agency cooperation. • No arbiter in the National Committees. • Weak monitoring and performance assessment. • Low level of local capacity in understanding the agreement. • Low level of participation from the private sector.

Southeast Asia, ASEAN is indifferent to regionalization because it is strictly based on national principles. In sum, full decentralization has never occurred either in CEE or in Southeast Asia. Central states are still the main actors, which means that weak civil societies and ineffective public debates still prevail. This shall be discussed further in the next chapter, which deals with state corruptions by industrial relations.

5 MANAGING FIRMS BY FLEXIBILITY: THE LACK OF INDUSTRIAL RELATIONS

As seen in the two previous chapters, privatization policies occurred within a world-wide dynamic which, from the 1980s onwards, challenged the preeminence of large state bureaucracies, public niches, as well as the limitations on the freedom of private actors. Privatization was introduced at the same time as a certain form of decentralization which left managers able to introduce flexibility within organizations now considered to be too rigid and centralized. New, more horizontal and diverse forms of governance were introduced. Loosely coupled networks and decentralization became the watchwords of the new management. It is therefore worth analyzing industrial relations, in order to assess whether the opening of economies led to new forms of governance, and greater worker participation in collective action. Participation means more collective rights, particularly for people deprived of them by authoritarian regimes. These rights include freedom of association, the right to organize strikes and even, to a certain extent, the right to co-manage firms. Making economies more open was possible because of social movements which demanded rights that the previous regimes had denied them. In other words, in both Central and Eastern Europe (CEE) and Southeast Asia social movements were of pivotal importance in the evolution of different regimes. But did they go on to influence social participation in the period which followed? Did workers obtain more rights? By providing so many things the former economies lacked — like funds, technologies and markets — did FDI also help to improve the quality of industrial relations? In other words, does more globalization imply more social benchmarking and does greater political democracy necessarily lead to more industrial democracy? When foreign investors arrive from the Western world (including Japan), where industrial democracy is more developed, do they transfer their industrial relations model to firms who are doing the outsourced work? It is known that domestic trade unions in some large Western European firms only accepted their firms' moves into CEE after 1990 under the strict condition that employment regulations in force in the West would be adopted in full in the East. VW was the most prominent example of this. In imposing this policy, Western trade unions hoped to limit the negative effect of deregulation because foreign investors were in the habit of applying the most flexible management models, including some that had previously failed in Western units. Some analysts of Southeast Asia have also mentioned the fact that foreign companies like Toyota and Mitsubishi transferred Human Resources departments to the Philippines (Erikson *et al.*, 2003).

Furthermore, questioning the reality of industrial democracy raises a set of issues, which concern the legacies of the transition process from authoritarian regimes to more open ones. In theory, more freedom should lead to more protest, if only because margins of maneuver are much wider and because people's feelings of privation can be expressed in public demonstrations of dissatisfaction. Examination of the period since the fall of authoritarian regimes shows, however, that this has not been the case. How can we explain that in more democratic regimes there has not been more industrial action? Is it to do with the way companies are managed? Is real democracy lacking, or is the lack of protest due to the fact that basic social needs have been satisfied? The thesis developed in this chapter postulates that privatization in the firms examined above paved the way for the extension of globalized capitalism accompanied by social deregulation and "management by flexibility". The first part of this chapter intends to draw conclusions from the fact that transition periods were followed by little collective action. Furthermore, everywhere fewer collective agreements were made. This hit female workers particularly hard, deepening the gender division of labor.

5.1. Globalization and Flexibility

Openness to globalization and privatization has led in both regions to a "race to the bottom" concerning wages. In order to obtain FDI, which is attracted by low costs, all private and public actors prize low wages. Special Economic Zones, which we will examine in the last chapter, are based on fiscal advantages and low wages. Besides market size and labor costs, what made CEE so attractive to FDI was the fact that these low labor costs came with a qualified workforce and a lot of industrial experience. This already existing industrial culture facilitated rapid development of several leading sectors, such as the automotive, electronics and pharmaceutical industries, whereas in Southeast Asia populations with low levels of education provided the workforce for labor intensive sectors, like garments, footwear, jewelry and clothes sectors. Singapore was the exception: It developed a unique strategy based on high added value industrial segments coupled with large investment in education (seen Chapter 3).[1]

Development strategy has therefore been different in each case. In Southeast Asia there was massive FDI, firstly in South Korea and Taiwan, Hong Kong and Singapore, then, in a second wave, in Indonesia and Malaysia, forcing other Southeastern States (mainly in the Mekong region) to set up short term strategies which involved steady reduction of costs and of immobilizations, outsourcing and implementation of a supplier system. These changes have not resulted in increased purchasing power. Indeed, people are poor and wages remain low, and they will remain so as long as states do not develop their own niches. This, however, is becoming increasingly difficult, due to fierce competition led by the more advanced economies. As Deyo (1989) says "Asian industrialization is associated with a continuing stagnation in the power and effectiveness of organized labor".

---

[1] In 2009, the average monthly wages for manufacturing workers was $2,832 in Singapore, $666.10 in Malaysia, $412 in China, $245 in Thailand, $169 in the Philippines, $136 in Vietnam, $128 in Indonésie and finally $62 in Cambodia, see JP Morgan, CEIC, International organization.

Moreover, Asia is characterized by huge unskilled workforces that lead the world in the number of hours worked and rates of female employment, as well as interregional differences.

Even if the gap between the 20% highest revenues and the 20% lowest ones is smaller than in Latin America (where in Brazil in 1972 incomes in these brackets differed by a multiple of 32) (see Table 5.1).

In this context, unions are not welcome. In the Philippines, the electronics industry has only 2,200 unionized workers, and the garment industry, about 4,000 (McKey, 2006).

In CEE, such a radical "race to the bottom" was impossible to implement, due to the joint effect of Western and EU rules, which converge to impose some European minimum standards. Therefore, strategies were more long term. Moreover, wages dramatically increased during this period, although at the start of the transition the gap between the two European sides was 1: 7 or 8. Lastly, Western trade unions paid a great deal of attention to unionization in the delocalized firms in order to limit any knock-on effect which would lead to reduced employment rights in western companies.

Table 5.1. Percentage shares of household incomes by country, year and percentile group.

	Year	Bottom 20%	Top 20%	Ratio of income share of top/bottom 20%	Gini coefficient
South Korea	1976	5.7	45.3	7.9	0.38
Hong Kong	1980	5.4	47	8.7	0.45
Taiwan	1982	9.2	51.5	5.6	0.30
Singapore	1980				0.46
Brazil	1972	2.0	66.6	33.3	
Argentina	1970	4.4	50.3	11.4	
Mexico	1977	2.9	57.7	19.9	0.58
US	1980	5.3	39.9	7.5	

Source: Deyo (1989).

Liberalization opened the door to more individualization and sub-contracting, which was likely to undermine collective action. A new form of employment contract was widely developed in CEE from the 1990s onward, in which the workers have self-employed status. In line with British legislation, this form of contract limits the duties on both parties, and employers does not pay social costs, thus penalizing the employee. On the other hand, the employee can leave their job when they want to, without giving notice. Levels of self-employment rose in Poland and in the Baltic states (Portet, 2005). Such individualization, linked to more sub-contracting, self-employment and various forms of tripartism, was not extended to Southeast Asia, where highly informal rules prevail. In Singapore, however, tripartism has been mentioned as one major tool for imposing strict social control (see previous chapter). Flexibility of working conditions was widely used in Southeast Asia, as we will see. Self-employment and short term contracts are the norm and very few workers are able to benefit from long term contracts.

Nevertheless, a similar type of management prevailed in both regions, giving more power to employers and less power to trade unions, which were expelled from many firms. It has led to an increasing deregulation of the working conditions, generally associated with the terms "informality" and "flexibility" (Vaughan-Whitehead, 2003). Deyo speaks of state labor policies, which have encouraged an "autocratic flexibility" that functions "by excluding from collective bargaining such matters as job assignments and work transfers, which are an important element of "labor flexibility" (Deyo, 2001). For Caraway, "the most common flexibilization measure adopted in the region was the expansion of flexible working hour arrangement" (Caraway, 2009). In the last decade a lot of Southeast Asian states like Malaysia, Singapore, Taiwan and Vietnam, following the Taiwanese model, increased the number of annual working hours. Southeast Asian industrialization was based on compliance to assemblage norms, and the exclusion of any social progress. Moreover, MNEs requested much more adaptability from local firms. That is the major difference from CEE.

5.1.1. *Management through flexibility*

In both areas under consideration, a particular type of management called "management through flexibility" emerged. Enmeshed in the globalization dynamic, its principles were largely inspired by the Japanese experience. Transferred to the Western world in the 1980s, it brought with it various tools like "quality circles", "team objectives", the nurturing of "company spirit" and the development of "company identity". All these tools were coupled with technical measures, aimed at reducing transaction costs within various departments, from production to sales, and to the supply chain where suppliers and subcontracts were also obliged to reduce their costs. In general, all the participants to the value chain were invited, even forced, to reduce their costs and embrace the slogan "0 defaults, 0 stock, 0 waiting time". An important book published at the beginning of the 1990s popularized these methods (Womack *et al.*, 1990). In CEE, management through flexibility allowed managers to use disciplinary methods already criticized in the West, like Kaizen, making CEE a remarkable field for experiments in liberalization, with workers' rights kept to a minimum (Bafoil, 2009a). In Southeast Asia Japanese methods were an inspiration, but only for disciplining the workforce. The positive aspects of the Japanese model, including long term employment and highly regulated industrial relations, were not adopted. Furthermore, these tools were accompanied by both material and symbolic rewards which ironically replicated methods already implemented in Soviet-type economies, where the "best" workers were identified in motivational campaigns in departments, enterprises and even regions. But the quantitative results of these campaigns were totally manipulated, and final decisions were decided in advance by the top management in collusion with trade unions.

In Southeast Asia, individual incentives are linked to individual performance in relation to monthly, quarterly or annual targets; the best performers are singled out for praise by the use of "honor tables", photos displayed in the workplace, and such like. Donella Casperz mentions that in Malaysia the best performers are presented with a coat in the firm's colors. Elsewhere they might be rewarded with a trip to Japan (Caspersz, 2006). Wages that are attractive at the start of the working life quickly become meager. Based on 55 interviews carried out between 1994 and 1996, the author concludes that there is a deep double divide: The first is the wide gender gap: As we will see below, the best paid jobs tend to be allocated to men and the less well-paid work to women. The second addresses ethnic differentiation, Chinese and Indian workers being better treated than members of other ethnic groups. Men and members of the favored ethnic groups are the only ones to receive material and symbolic incentives. This type of management, based on massive use of flexibility, does not concern itself with improving working conditions, but fights hard against any union activity and seeks to increase the number of hours employees work. Casperz mentions 8 hour, sometimes 8.5 hour shifts, with a maximum of 45 to 60 minutes for meal breaks per shift and the implementation of a three shift system to enable factories to operate around the clock. A common pattern involves two shifts being worked a day for 12 days followed by two days off (only rest day per week is allowed). Regular overtime of at least four hours a day is made compulsory, using tactics such as the delaying of company-provided transport which ferries workers to and from the workplace. Production continues on holidays. These new methods of management provoke resistance: Some workers refuse to do the gymnastic exercises which they are supposed to do at the beginning of the working day.

Organization of work is often based on a supplier system, in which a boss indicates a volume of work to be done in a limited time for a fixed payment, the supplier being free to employ whoever he wants. Teams of five to seven, most of whom are children, are led by an adult who is paid ten times what a child is paid. Although the contract between the boss and the supplier may be a legal one, the agreement between the supplier and his workers is an informal one. Moreover, the boss often delivers machines and dormitories to the supplier who organizes how they are used himself (Rigg, 2003). Complaints frequently mention the lack of security, particularly in the coal mining, construction and transport sectors (see Table 5.2).

Table 5.2. Accidents at work (per 1,000 workers) are said to be most frequent in Thailand.

	1988	1992
Thailand	36/1000	43
Malaysia	23	22
South Korea	24	15

Source: Charoenloet (2000).

The worst conditions seem to be in dormitories where workers not only pay high rates for a bed, but also sleep in unsafe conditions.[2] Thailand is said to have one of the least effective labor law systems in Asia. Private sector workers have no way of setting up collective agreements, which are actually forbidden in state-owned enterprises. Workers typically work between 55 and 60 hours a week, and 77 hour weeks are not unheard of. The minimum wage is set by a tripartite council which does not take workers' family situations into consideration. This minimum wage is a thousand baht. A total of 1,200 baht is considered the minimum necessary to cover basic needs. A lot of workers, many of whom are migrants, women and children, are paid less than this minimum. A study published in the 1990s reported that in 1990 44% of the workers did not receive the minimum wage; this figure rose to 55% in 1992. Finally, work inspectors have very little power and the welfare system is practically non-existent, due to the lack of unemployment benefits and pensions. Insurance only covers sickness, death and pregnancy. Very bad social conditions, particularly those linked to dormitories, have been regularly denounced (Riggs, 2003; McKey, 2006).

---

[2] There have been many cases of fires breaking out in these buildings, which are packed with mainly female and child workers. On May 10, 1993, the premises of a Thai firm was burned down: 174 women and children, and 14 men were burnt alive. The court found against the owner, but it later became clear that no compensation had been paid (Charoenloet, 2000).

The history and traditions of CEE are completely different. It could be expected that workers who had actively participated to the end of communism would be able to organize effectively. Many scholars have explained the lack of collective action in this part of Europe by contrasting the new freedom gained after 1989 with the lack of freedom before that date (Howard, 2003). People were forced to join a trade union not only because it was stipulated within their employment contracts, but because trade unions replaced missing market institutions by selling what was rare, even unobtainable, outside the firms. Social security services depended on trade unions, and thanks to them it was sometimes possible to procure a very rare good, like a flat, a "small garden", or even a car. There were long waiting lists for such goods, and to obtain them you had to be a trade union member. Trade unions under communism were further discredited because they played the role of a "transmission belt" for communist parties by organizing "socialist competition" between workplaces, departments and enterprises. Moreover, in the aftermath of 1990, unions did little to defend collective rights when unemployment rose steeply (to upto 20% in Poland, Slovakia and Bulgaria). Finally, the post-Communist period has brought a culture of individualism, which is not conducive to collective action. What was said in the last chapter concerning the lack of a civil society is worthy restating here. In CEE forced membership before 1990, which led to membership rates of nearly 100%, was followed in the 1990s by a massive layoffs of workers and dramatically reduced union membership. Unskilled workers were particularly hard hit during the restructuring processes.[3] With the exception of the public sector — and among them, mainly those working in health, education and transport — unionization rates are very low.[4]

---

[3] The Polish sociologist Adamski speaks of reduction of 20% of unskilled workers (see Adamski *et al.*, 1999).

[4] "In the majority of the EU-12 (27) collective bargaining is characterized by mixed industry and firm-level bargaining as well as a weak enforceability of industry agreements. The average score for the EU-12 is 2.7 compared with 3.3 for the EU-15". (2008 Industrial Relations Report, European Commission Directorate-General for Employment, Social Affairs and Equal Opportunities Unit F.1 Manuscript completed in September, p. 70).

Southeast Asia also suffered from high unemployment and low wages. As previously discussed, poor conditions do not favor collective action. Interestingly, documentation exists which shows that strikes in Vietnam had several common features with strikes in CEE before 1989 (Clarke, 2006), which tended to be "wild strikes" (although from 1995 to 2005, 978 strikes were registered (Clarke, 2006, p. 345)). These strikes were numerous, and generally wage related: They were often caused by anger over unpaid overtime or low pay. Workers mistrust trade unions because of their strong links with the management and political authorities are afraid that strikes in foreign firms will spill over into domestic firms. From one period to another, structural features remain the same as under communist rule.

5.1.2. *Gender issues*

In both areas, a very deep gender divide exists.[5] High, skilled sectors seem to be male dominated, while domestic firms, starved of investment and without any capacity to expand beyond local markets, are usually staffed by low-skilled female workers.[6] Owen mentions that,

---

[5] Korean provides a good case study of the gender division of labor. During the transition from the ISI to EOI, millions of workers migrated from rural area to emerging industrial cities. Low cost and intensive labor was mainly done by women and girls. During the 1970's, 30% of female workers were employed in industry. About 80% of textile workers were female. All were strictly managed in collective housing while trade unions helped to keep the work force under strict control. Trade unions were forbidden to organize strikes and their leaders were appointed by the government. As Cumings (2005) said, "working conditions in the 1960's were as old as textile production in Korea, going back to the turn of the century". Intimidation, massive use of lays off, threats against workers, unemployment and huge poverty contributed to silence a massively feminized working class. "All combined to weaken unions, intimidate many workers, and account for the flocks of docile, discipline, low — cost laborers in Korea's light industries in the 1960's" (*idem.*, p. 374). The suffering of women and girls has been well-documented.

[6] "If recent industrialization in East Asia is associated with the expansion of occupational sectors regulated by bureaucratic and communal paternalism, it is generally male workers who receive the education, training, and preferential recruitment to enter these new sectors" (Deyo, 1989).

regarding rural employment, men have been harvesting jobs whereas women (Tarling, 2006) are engaged in subsistence activities and tend to be allocated the more dangerous tasks (Tarling, 2006, p. 182). As well as this gender differentiation, there is another huge division: Between men who benefit from protection guaranteed by collective agreements granted by Western firms, under pressure from trade unions, and those who are employed by domestic firms, where there are no collective agreements.

A Hungarian sociologist has distinguished two paths of development taken in the 1990s: a high path and a low path, where collective capacities correlate strongly with gender (Neumann, 2000). The high path of development includes high technology sectors, where workers are skilled and unionized. There are strong collective bargaining rules and most of the employees are men. On the other hand, there is a low path, taken by low-tech light industry — including textiles, leather goods, clothing, etc. — in which there is minimal collective bargaining, and the vast majority of workers are female. In Thailand, Charoenloet identifies a similar pattern: Work is divided between formal, protected jobs, massively occupied by men, and non-protected, sub-contract and informal work, which is mainly done by children and women (Charoenloet, 2000). Deyo mentions the same gender division[7] and, like Deyo (see Table 5.3), Rigg indicates which sectors are the most "feminized".[8]

In Southeast Asia, it is considered "normal" to pay low wages to women. For some observers however, "although factory work organization and discipline are strict and often brutal, female workers perceive factory employment as a progressive change in their lives, not as a gaping, un-healed wound" (Rigg, 2003, p. 275). Because a lot of

---

[7] "A general observation is that occupations characterized by low skill, low wages, job insecurity, and lack of career mobility tend to attract young, female, minority or immigrant workers who are disadvantaged in the labor market" (Deyo, 1989, p. 194).

[8] "In garment factories, sewing, cutting, button-holing, sorting and packing are all dominated by women, while men are employed as technicians, warehouse staff, drivers and security guards" (Rigg, 2003).

Table 5.3. Female workers as a percentage of total workers in selected light industry by country.

	Korea (1980)	Singapore (1985) non-managerial workers only	Hong Kong (1981)	Taiwan (1986)
Textiles	69	73	49	63
Apparel and footwear	78	93	68	74
Plastics	57	58	50	50
Electrical equipment	56	65 (85 electronics only)	63	61
Professional and scientific equipment	49	76	56	61

Source: Deyo (1989, p. 184).

people want a job where the workforce is huge meaning that a person who is dismissed is easily replaced. For many workers the focus is therefore on keeping their job. According to the same author, many young women want to avoid a rural life and enjoy an urban one. Rigg has depicted their trajectories and indicated that during the first seven years, girls are totally dependent on their family for everything. Then between the age of 8 and 15, they become family helpers. During the next 15 years up to the age of 30, they are usually employed in large scale manufacturing, often geared towards export. These women are often unmarried with no responsibilities and are hard-working thus finding favor with employers. Between the ages of 31 and 40, they work in smaller enterprises or at home, so that they can take care of their children. Between 40 and 50, they work as subcontractors at home, under highly flexible conditions that remain attractive to mothers with two or more children. After 51, they do more work at home where they are self-employed and in charge of labor within the family. Older women find it hardest to secure employment and often have to accept the lowest paying option. Added to an almost complete lack of organization and the fact that these societies are male dominated, this prevailing fatalistic attitude means women rarely protest (see Table 5.4).

Table 5.4. Level (%) of organization of social partners and rate of collective agreements (% employees).

	Trade unions	Employers	Coverage of collective agreements	Betriebsrat firm council
Slovenia	42	50	98	Yes (broad)
Slovakia	35	50	48	Yes (weak)
Hungary	25	40	42	Yes (average)
Czech Republic	30	30	35	Exceptionally
Poland	18	19	30	Only in the SOEs
Latvia	19	30	20	Rare
Estonia	15	30	20	No
Lithuania	14	20	13	Planned

Source: Kohl (2005).

5.2. International Rules and Legal Obstacles

Despite the general adoption of ILO rules in the 1990s, (some countries such as Poland and the Philippines had adopted them in the previous decades) injuries are part of daily life. Although freedom of association, the protection of representatives and collective agreements guaranteed by Article 68 and Article 98 were agreed by all states, the reality is very different from these regulations. Informal rules play a much more important role than formal ones and more generally, the reality is in contradiction with the legal texts on the subject. There is a huge gap between official recognition of trade rights and their implementation.

Generally speaking, Southeast Asian trade unions were destroyed under authoritarian rule (with the exception of Malaysia and the Philippines for historical reasons[9]) although a significant worker protection system did exist as a result of employment guarantees. A

---

[9] In Indonesia, the right to organize and bargain freely through trade unions was granted to workers under the 1945 Constitution (Article 28) even if other laws and legal regulations severely limited these rights subsequently (Gall, 1998).

minimum level of health care also existed. However, in the middle of the 1990s, very few workers belonged to trade unions. In Malaysia, around 15% did, in Singapore, 14%, in the Philippines 10% and in Thailand 1.6% because of the Marshall law in 1991 (Deyo, 2001). Generally speaking, there was no unionization in the private sector. The Thai state enterprise Labor Relations Act enacted on April 19, 1991 allows state enterprise trade unions to function as associations without having trade union rights or collective bargaining power. On July 1, 1992, 707 trade unions were registered. Only 5% of membership was drawn from the private sector and 57% from the state sector. There were few collective agreements and those that did exist covered very few people: Around 5% in Thailand, Malaysia and the Philippines. In Thailand and Malaysia, only 11 collective agreements out of 120 have been ratified (Deyo, 2001, p. 272).

In many cases trade unions were forbidden and are still very limited in number. According to Caraway, although Singapore has the smallest gap between formal and real rights, this is because of the huge flexibility within the labor market (see Table 5.5). In Cambodia, Vietnam and the Philippines, formal rights are strong and enforcement is defined as average, as opposed to Laos and Malaysia where the discrepancy between the two is the highest (in China also). In Thailand, both formal and real rights are assessed as average. Indonesia and Cambodia are the countries which best comply with ILO regulations[10] although civil servants do not fall under the scope of the labor code and generally, in both countries trade unions encounter many difficulties. They do not have the right to bargain collectively. In Cambodia collective agreement is almost non-existent: In 2005, five agreements were signed within the clothing trade which is the largest industrial sector, (where most of the employees are members of the trade union). Caraway concludes "…labor laws are poorly enforced in many countries of the region, so actual levels of flexibility are higher than indicated by law" (Caraway, 2009). The same author adds that Cambodia

---

[10] Steven C McKey (2006) mentions that in the mid-1980s there were 10 National Labor centers, 171 federations and 1,672 unions representing 1.5 million members (10% of employees) but only 550,000 were covered by collective agreements.

Table 5.5.   Unionization and collective agreements in Southeast Asia, 1995–2000.

	1995 (As a percentage of non agricultural workforce)	2000 (As a percentage of the total workforce)	Legal right to form unions	Collective bargaining	Coverage of collective agreements (9)
Democracies					
Indonesia	2.6	1.2% (Caraway, 2004) (1995–1999)	High	Closest compliance with ILO (5)	
The Philippines	22.8	12.3	High	Average level (7)	weak: 16% 2%[10]
South Korea	9.0	11.8	Medium	Compliance with ILO (6)	7.3%
Taiwan	27.9	—	Low (1)	Compliance with ILO (6)	
Thailand	3.1	—	Low (1)	Compliance with ILO (6)	
Semi Democracies					
Cambodia	—	1.0	High	Closest compliance with ILO (5)	5 in 2005[10] (Caraway, 2009)
Malaysia	11.7	8.3	Low (4)		3.3%
Singapore	13.5	15.7	Low (3)	Average level (7)	12%
Authoritarian					
China	54.7	—	Medium		
Vietnam	—	10.0	High	Average level (7)	
Laos	—	—			

Source: Caraway (2009, p. 167).

and the Philippines have the worst record as in both countries it is not infrequent for activists and protestors to be assassinated (Caraway, 2009, p. 172).

The fact that ILO regulations were immediately adopted in 1990 and that all the fundamental rights were recognized by new regimes was proof of a decision to reassess what the formal constitution had admitted but never respected. Everyday practice provided another picture because apart from in large firms, workers in Southeast Asia are unlikely to see their rights being recognized. Moreover, the labor courts are practically non-operational and there is no state control of labor conditions. Generally, in both areas and from a legal perspective, contracts tend to cover state employees only and individual contracts prevail over collective rights. This implies a style of management that has been summarized as "management by flexibility".

In Southeast Asia, the "the boss rules" style of management covers a huge dependency relationship that impoverishes employees who are submitted to informal and arbitrary rules. For many observers, the situation in Southeast Asia is one of the worst as recourse to a legal complaints procedure is almost impossible. The courts are insufficiently staffed, corruption of the judicial system is omnipresent and legal professionals are not always competent.[11] Following Suharto's fall, two reasons can explain the decline of Indonesian trade unions that were successful in the period immediately following 1997.[12]

---

[11] As Caraway (2009) says, "although the right to bargain collectively fares relatively well compared to other collective rights, in practice collective bargaining is poorly institutionalized in the region. Most bargaining takes place at the enterprise level".

[12] Some oppositional trade unions such as Solidarity emerged in 1991. They were opposed to SPSI and were accused of being submissive to the government. They claimed to have 50,000, then 100,000 members in the Jakarta region but proved unable to maintain this level of membership. Internal conflicts and strong opposition led to their disappearance. In 1998, a new trade union, the SBSI emerged (a welfare labor union) which was supported by NGOs and civil rights groups. It initially had 100,000 members, then 250,000 and 500,000 in 1998. Faced with this social opposition, Suharto reacted by making trade unions legally impossible. In order to be legally recognized, they needed to be present in at least 100 firms, spread out in five districts, and at least five provinces. Militancy was hugely repressed (Caraway, 2008).

Firstly, unemployment affected 17 million people (from an Indonesian workforce of 70 million). Added to this, the sector-based unions were unable to overcome the informality that characterized the last years of Suhartism (Hadiz, 2002). Moreover, the trade unions had no links with the ruling parties. Politicians who tried to cooperate with the unions lost their seat at elections. For this reason, students were the only ones who endeavored to support the unions but their connection with the working class was limited. The period of *reformasi* was partially successful, as witnessed by the adoption of Article 84 of the ILO and the official recognition of the right to trade unionism. A law passed in 2000 stipulated that dismissed workers had a right to be paid, even when they left the firm. However, the strong emerging employer union forced the government to put an end to the law, which was overturned.

Finally, all of the countries have multiplied legal obstacles to break trade union initiatives (Caraway, 2009). As Caraway (2009) says "the right to strike is the most weakly protected right in the region. Not a single country is in full compliance with international labor standards". In Malaysia, the Philippines, Singapore, Taiwan, Thailand and Vietnam, the trade unions need 2/3 of the workers to declare a strike before it can take place. In Indonesia, Thailand and Vietnam, time consuming conciliation procedures before a strike can be declared effectively prevent them from taking place.[13] In the Philippines, a long strike notification period is imposed while in Cambodia a minimum level of service is guaranteed during a strike and some categories are forbidden from striking. In Thailand, this is the case for workers in state enterprises including education; in Malaysia and Thailand, transport; in Malaysia, Indonesia, and Thailand, oil refineries; in Cambodia, the Philippines and Malaysia, no civil servant is allowed to strike. Vietnam allows the state to ban strikes in a list of industries that the government deems to be important for the national economy. In Thailand, in order to be registered within a firm, a trade union has to recruit at least 25% of the employees. However, in Thailand as in South Korea, teachers, civil servants and SOE employees within can

---

[13] "Strikes are to be, at best, prevented, at worst controlled" (Gall, 1998).

be unionized. In South Korea, wages are not fixed by collective agreements and the state alone decides them with the trade unions playing a consultative role only. Singapore limits the number of trade unions and trade union participation in political events is forbidden, while the state can have a say in how the union functions internally. For instance an employer can refuse to recognize a trade union if it does not represent a majority of workers. Moreover, the law excludes promotions, transfers, hiring, etc. from collective bargaining and limits wages supplements. The state has the authority to amend the provisions of collective bargaining agreements. Finally, in Malaysia, trade unions must be recognized by the employers before they are allowed to negotiate.

In CEE countries, the 1990s privatization process was not based on a strong vision of worker participation, but rather the exact opposite. However, the paradox was that the most important social regulations were observed in foreign firms where Western trade unions were in a position to export social rules. In other firms unionization was rather poor and in many SMEs it was even absent. Furthermore, although the EU called for the involvement of trade unions in the new public life and the management of structural funds, it never provided them with the means to play such a role (Ferge and Juhasz 2004). Although the EU claimed that structural funds were effectively managed by wide horizontal governance, this lack of commitment to strong union participation was considered as one of its major failures. Between the two basic pillars of community objectives — growth and solidarity — the EU commission was much more in favor of the first at the cost of the second. This approach was strongly supported by those who considered that the first objective in an economic recovery period is to guarantee sustainable growth and consequently that in a safe economy social redistribution has to be closely connected to economic results. Finally, trade unions tend to be characterized by ideological features rather than by the defense of the economic interests of their members. This is particularly the case in Poland with *Solidarnosc* and in Bulgaria with *Podkrepa* where these "new" trade unions did battle with the former "old" unions which supported the Communist regime. In both cases at the very start of the systemic transition, they defended more liberal and more "rightist" options and wanted to represent the interests of not just the working class but of the whole of society. Therefore, both quickly transformed themselves into political parties but these failed very quickly (Ost, 2000).

5.3. Conclusion: Comparing Both Areas

For some analysts, the main difference between both areas seems to be the higher level of violence and the density of family links, which are proper to Asia.[14] Rather than drawing conclusions on these apparent cultural differences, some similarities might be considered. In both regimes, the state has remained the central actor by setting up fixed wages and industrial policy. Under these conditions trade unions are dependent on state authority and function as "transmission belts".[15] The fact is that in low wages countries, labor rights are less likely to be implemented than in high wage countries and in countries with the highest wages such as Singapore there are fewer protective laws but they are more likely to be implemented. Secondly, a decrease in collective forms of protest has been observed in recent decades in both regions. This raises issues about the nature of modernization that followed the fall of authoritarian regimes. Although civil societies and social movements played a major role in the overthrowing of dictatorships they tended to be sidelined in the ensuing period. For some analysts, this was even the most urgent priority of those who took power during the transition process (Shields, 2004).

What is particular to CEE countries is that strong protective (often even formal) social regimes under Communist rule provided no protection from liberalization to workers in the 1990s. Indeed, throughout CEE, rights have become less effective. Caraway considers

---

[14] "Non-formal systems may involve reproduction of customary practices, political organizations, clientelist arrangements, family and community networks and networks based on corruption and violence" (Cooney, 2006).

[15] This expression is used by Gregor Gall to define the SPSI in 1998.

that Indonesians who enjoyed social protective rights under Suharto's regime[16] were less docile and less likely to suffer the consequences of flexibility. However, in both Indonesia and Poland where workers were at the forefront of the fight against dictatorship their importance declined dramatically in the following period and this requires some explanation.[17] The number of state-owned enterprises decreased and more generally the importance of the state also decreased during this period while privatization increased and was accompanied by considerable numbers of layoffs. Moreover, in Indonesia trade unions had little political support and in Poland, they have none. Finally, in Indonesia, NGOs are more interested in human rights issues and the private system is dominated by a "jungle of bosses" (Caraway, 2004).

Within the framework of export oriented economies, industrial relations have become a kind of "poor relation" of economic and social development. Globalization has led to huge transformations within the private sector and the number of state-owned enterprises has rapidly declined while FDI was multiplied and SMEs mushroomed. This joint dynamic has led to an intense deregulation of organizations and to an individualization of working contracts. Collective rules have become much less important as much more individual dimensions have blossomed. Wages have been linked either to strict measurements of individual performance, to no rules at all or indeed to purely arbitrary ones.

Under these conditions, tripartism which was implemented everywhere, was not very effective. However, it allowed states to continue to manage remaining important public enterprises, control trade unions and master nascent social expectations. In these difficult

---

[16] Teri L Caraway uses the term "protective repression" when describing Suharto's regime (2004). This term "protective repression" describes Soviet type economies as well.

[17] "Todays, workers do not play a vital role in defending and developing the infant democracy, despite the undermining of former authoritarian structures and the new space for action", in "Labour and Democracy? Reflections on the Indonesian Impasse", *Journal of Contemporary Asia*, 2004, Vol. 34, 3, p. 386. On Poland and the rather negative attitude towards social rights and the increasing individualization of tasks during the recent period, see Gardawski *et al.* (2010).

transitory periods when economic crises needed to be tackled by measures reducing wages and public expenditure, states needed to involve trade unions in dealing with unpopular measures so that the social costs could be shared. For their part, trade unions needed to be part of public life to regain legitimacy. Tripartite commissions therefore dealt with social measures such as minima rights and social wages but they failed very rapidly. Like foreign investors, new employers did not play the game ignoring tripartism and demanding that there be no social disturbances. Subsequently, privatization was organized by the states themselves who were less interested in such policies.

Finally, "management by flexibility" has often implied a reduction of protective rules for workers, particularly for those who were better protected under repressive regimes. For this reason, Caraway is right to emphasize that "All of the countries (in SEA) that are democracies today were protective and repressive under authoritarianism" (Caraway, 2009). This remark can be extended to include the former Soviet type economies where a vast amount of legislation offered lifetime protection to workers guaranteeing them wages and social benefits (even at low levels of quality).

Lastly, because Southeast Asian economies are export oriented they need many more high quality and innovative competitive products than before. As Deyo (1989) remarks, "diversification into new, higher value-added industries is accompanied by expanded vocational and technical education and by growth in occupational sectors wherein better educated workers are employed for less routinized tasks demanding higher skills and greater autonomy". Such change is likely to significantly modify the former style of relationship, which was characterized by patron–client dependence and has now shifted to more individualized relations. Addressing labor force development in the Philippines, some analysts share the same view about the shift from traditional paternalism to more professional management, adding that labor management councils similar to those in the EU are in progress there (Erikson *et al.*, 2003). Pursuing his reflection, Deyo adds about Singapore: "In these new occupations and industries, bureaucratic paternalistic labor systems increasingly supplant proletariat market controls. Paternalism is further encouraged by a government policy, initiated in the late 1970's of shifting many welfare programs from unions and state bureaucracies to firms themselves" (*Idem.*, p. 199). However, these changes have not only affected qualified members of the labor force. The low-skilled labor force has also been deeply affected by globalization and the transformation of work practices. For Hadiz, a much more ethnic and religious awareness has begun to appear leading to an emerging class consciousness irrigated by strong feelings of deprivation and a questioning of the legitimacy of the ruling order (Hadiz, 2002).

PART II

CONCLUSION

In Europe, in the 1980s, and even more so during the following decade, the generalization of exchanges led to a huge decentralization of decision-making (see Table 1). The reasons for this were not only because the former centralized states were known to have failed. It was also because the local level was seen to be the only place where the worldwide dynamic of exchanges was likely to be embedded. The same was true for Southeast Asia.

From the very start, the rhetoric of globalization has been supported by earnest and erudite discourse on the need for freedom for economic actors, on their capacity for initiative and on the need to destroy barriers inhibiting development. In this context, local levels were seen as being free from protectionist limits. Such a vision also sees intermediary institutions as unnecessary; the state was considered superfluous. Similarly, civil societies, associations, trade unions, and all the so-called intermediate bodies were rejected as unnecessary barriers. Furthermore, market transformation played an important role in shaping public institutions. Bringing the manager closer to the decision-making process and the worker closer to the product were assimilated to bringing the customer closer to the market and citizens to their institutions. Modernization of the state was based on the model of economic transformation, anchored in two dynamics. At the theoretical level, the idea of the individual actor prevailed, free from all limitations, capable of moving where demand emerged and of rationally organizing the combination of different means to achieve goals as long as barriers were removed. At the local level, the concept of "lean production" and "lean state" originated from the same

147

source. In the 1980s, Womak and John's study of "lean production" greatly influenced all managerial modes of thinking. The buzz terms were "zero stock", "zero default", and "just in time" (Womack *et al.*, 1990). Various approaches to managerial organization flourished in the implementation of these flagships. These included "Toyota-ism", and more concretely, the "Kaizen" method modeled on "team-based organization", "quality circles", etc.

Whether they were democratic or not, the newly emerging states in Asia and in Europe made this discourse together with the discourse on public management their own. Under this strong economic impact, "New Public Management" schools emphasized the role of business schools that were supported by strong epistemic communities and that propagated the same ideological models based on competition (with performance indicators) and disaggregation of hierarchies and incentives — with reinforcement of motivation and output control (Lane, 2000). The globalization of management methods drew its strength from "market-based public administration" and "entrepreneurial government" based on the model of the economic firm and on the performance criteria of accountability, efficiency and incorruptibility. This was the only approach to the modernization of state administrations deemed to be capable of achieving the Weberian ideal-type of bureaucracy based on the neutrality of civil servants. This means, in other words a type of civil service designed to implement a non-particular rule and recruit employees based on merit. Freed from any personal links, the civil servant would be well-equipped to combat corruption. Against such a background, democracy was initially not explicitly called for or even needed.

Hence, the immense success of the approach in both regions for having led a reform which simultaneously linked the privatization (or "corporatization") of state-owned enterprises (SOEs), reform of bureaucratic administrations, and the training of civil servants. Rule by law is based on such a model which Singapore exemplifies as seen in Chapter 3.

Deregulation supported by public policies of privatization and regionalization was given a huge push forward by the process of integration into supranational regional ensembles. This is dealt with in the next section.

Table 1. Decentralization processes and features in private enterprises and administrations in the 1980s/1990s.

Enterprises	Administration
Decentralization	De-concentration/decentralization
Local initiative (incentive to increase productivity and tailor-made tasks Individualization)	of administrative units WITS (work improvement teams
Team work, Quality circles (Toyota-ism)	
Zero stock, zero defaults	No client waiting
Training qualification	Life-long learning, training qualifications
Accountability	Accountability

PART III
INTRODUCTION — EU AND ASEAN ENLARGED
AND GLOBALIZED REGIONS

Having analyzed in previous chapters the various transforming processes under state control, the final three chapters will consider how states manage their relationships with the supranational (regional) entity within which they are embedded.

By pursuing our initial reflection about strong and weak states we question firstly what the distinction strong versus weak means at the supranational level. What type of links exist between supranational and state levels and what do these links mean for each level? To what extent are strong rules capable of forcing states to comply and to be more cohesive? The introduction of this book identified a defining characteristic of a strong state: The capacity to make policies coherent, in order to achieve optimal efficiency and equity by redistributing the fruits of growth. We question, first, the ability of a strongly institutionalized supranational entity to develop coherent regional policies and, second, the expected lack of coherence from a weak supranational level. What are the EU rules of conditionality which impose compliance on EU member states? Is it right to claim a correlation between weak states and weak regional ensembles? By focusing on regional policies the three chapters aim to show states' abilities to manage regional policies.

This exploration of the nature of the state leads in turn to an exploration of the forms of economic development adopted by each state. It goes without saying that the forms of development adopted necessarily reflect the particular regulations which characterize the regions the state belongs to. The same is true for the forms of capitalism favored and set up by each of the different states. It may well be that a particular form corresponds to a region whose ability to constrain its members is weak. Or on the contrary, that a highly regulated region promotes a type of capitalism bordered by restrictive rules. Or indeed that the two regions can then be distinguished according to the types of capitalism adopted. These and other questions are developed in the third part of this book.

The first thesis is drawn from empirical observations. It postulates that both regions — the EU and ASEAN — are mapping their territories by developing integrated interventions, but from different starting points. The EU organizes its interventions by setting up a grand scheme — the cohesion policy articulated in the current "Strategy 2020" (previously the "Lisbon Strategy") which consists of objectives that are supported by tools and rules which aim to foster growth and employment, and reduce territorial inequalities. Regional policies take shape within the cohesion policy and, as we shall see, represent the second largest expenditure item in the EU budget. The ASEAN is much more engaged in facilitating trade in order to foster export-oriented activities. Regional policies are not organized from the top but are much more concerned with networking business activities. In the end, both regions construct their spatial territories, but each is supported by different dynamics.

Our second thesis concludes that EU development can be identified with regionalism, which implies more institutions-driven development, while ASEAN development can be more associated with regionalization, which relies more on informal networks.[1] In fact, the reality is more complex. EU institutions also facilitate a deep regionalization process by framing business activities, and Asian business networks cooperate in order to set up more shared rules.

The third thesis insists on the opposed dynamics of states in the two regions. Although the EU can be defined as a very strong region, it often fails to ensure member states comply with regional policies. Policy is still made by the individual states. Although ASEAN had been defined as "a collection of weak states" (Jones and Smith,

---

[1] For Asia, see Deyo (1989). For Eastern Europe, see Kaeser and Radice (1977).

2007), these weak states can actually use this weakness in order to reinforce their own positions.

The fourth thesis explores the idea that the new members in each region have provided fertile ground for the extension of less regulated forms of capitalism because of the fact that they had fallen behind both in older and in more modern times in comparison to older members whose development has been swifter and more autonomous. In order to catch up economically, less regulation and indeed an unbridled opening up to foreign investors has clearly been considered as more advantageous than strict regulation in the minds of those in power.

6 THE EU AND ASEAN: COHESION POLICY AND EXPORT-ORIENTED AGREEMENTS

The European Union (EU) is a work in progress, which has developed in stages. Regarding regional policies, which have the second largest EU budget, the EU continually defines its whole territory, first by statistically distinguishing developed and less developed regions and, second, by mapping local territories from the most local — the Euro-regions — to the broadest areas. Each region is supported by an objective, a particular financial fund and specific rules of management. A region is said to be underdeveloped or "backward" if its level of development is less than 75% of EU averages. Almost 80% of EU structural funds are devoted to "lagging regions", mainly located at the Southern and Eastern European peripheries.[1] Apart from these regions, one finds different territorial areas — Euro-regions, meso or macro regions, even non-EU-bordering areas[2] — supported by special programs[3] and funds. All these step-by-step spatial planning schemes define concentric territorial areas that deepen the integrated approach and diversify multilevel governance.

In contrast to the European territory's constructive approach, which features enlargement mapping, the ASEAN strategy is based on both facilitating trade through agreements and developing regional

---

[1] Beside these Eastern and Southern regions, one can mention islands which are part of France: Like Réunion, Guadeloupe and Martinique.

[2] The European Neighborhood Policy (ENP)

[3] INTERREG involves different spatially limited programs: INTERREG A refers to trans-national cooperation; INTERRG B concerns trans-regional cooperation; INTERREG C concerns trans-border cooperation.

Though several authors stress its weakness (Beeson, 2009).

geographical areas. From a broader perspective, the ASEAN economic community (AEC) may be seen as the best framework for integrating national economies, supported at the national level by a considerable number of foreign trade agreements (FTAs) and taken over at the regional and local levels by cross-border trade agreements (CBTAs) (Banomyong, 2005; Brooks and David, 2009). However, while the ASEAN trade facilitation supports significant development of regional integration, it also concentrates on some less integrated areas. It is based on the model developed by the Chinese at the end of the 1970s which started with special economic zones, was extended to state cooperation (e.g., IBMT, SIJORI) and ended with the economic corridors of the Greater Mekong Sub-region (GMS).

Finally, both processes of regionalization mirror a dynamic between an on-going integrative approach involving a step-by-step construction of regional areas, and a cooperative approach between different partners at different administrative and institutional levels. To this extent, governance is a shared value. Moreover, in both regions, between supranational policies of regional development that address each region as a whole, and local policies targeting very particular sub-regions (mainly cross-border), some intermediary regions have been identified which illustrate innovative public and private cooperation.

In Europe, public authorities aim to target all the territories by addressing both developed and underdeveloped areas in accordance with the cohesion policy, and to simultaneously address both efficiency and equity. Structural funds are available even for highly developed regions but obviously to a lesser extent than for less developed regions. In other words, a combination of funds, crossing programs and measures to foster innovation goes hand in hand with a willingness to support lagging regions and marginalized social groups. For these reasons, the entire EU territory as such is included: Prosperous regions are not forgotten, and all lagging regions are kept within the scope of public intervention.[4] On the other hand,

---

[4] In EU, as Antola says, "If regionalization in the 1990s was seen as a part of reorganizing post-Cold War Europe, it is today and will be even more so in the future a version of integration differentiated on a territorial basis. Regionalization as a form

ASEAN targets its territorial intervention on some areas to the exclusion of others. Historically, maritime regions were first targeted because development was primarily concentrated throughout maritime channels. In a step-by-step process, development of Southeast Asian territories has shifted from coastal areas to territories in the interior.

As shown in Table 6.1, a comparison of the categorization of both regions from this territorial perspective allows us to better understand the regional integration process. Different steps are distinguished: From the more concentrated and local areas, to cross-border linkages and networks, to the largest and loosest entities associated with the more dispersed areas of Europe and Asia. Somewhere in the middle of the process different regional configurations take place, implying step-by-step formal cooperation agreements; they range from the sub-regional growth polygons including macro-regions, to the macro-regional frameworks in which several countries form a region, i.e., East Asia or the EU. Lastly, a few macro-regions can be isolated, such as the EU macro-regions involving EU members and non-EU members, or continental regions like Asia. We can use the Asian regionalization model set up by Christopher Dent in order to better understand EU regionalization, by starting from the most local — the Euro-region — continuing through to the more organized regions under INTERREG or ECGT rule, and up to the latest concept of macro-region, which emerged in the 2000s, involving several countries sharing a joint territory.[5]

The chapter is divided into two parts. The first part deals with EU cohesion policy, followed by ASEAN policies. The last part compares different aspects of the two regional development models, characterized by a mix of informal and formal rules.

---

of differentiation stems from the simple fact that Member States geographically close to each other share common histories, common values and common interests on a variety of issues".

[5] This is the case of the Baltic Sea and the Danube basin, the North Sea, and the Transalpine area, up to the Mediterranean Sea. See next chapter.

Table 6.1. From more concentrated to more dispersed areas in both regions?

	Southeast Asia	CEE
More concentrated geographic area	Selection of/Selected from East Asian-related regionalist forms	Selection of/Selected from East Asian-related regionalist forms
Micro-regionalism		
Region-wide networked associative, integrative and organizational linkages	IPNs	Euro-regions The Cohesion fund
Sector activities and infrastructures		
Sub-regionalism	RPN	
Growth polygons and other sub-regional or quasi-regional trans-border zones		INTERREG, C Macro-regions/EGTC (European Grouping Territorial Cooperation)
Macro-regionalism		
Organizations, frameworks and agreements involving most countries within a defined macro-region (= East Asia)	IMSGT TRADP BIMP EAGA GMS	INTERREG A
Trans-regionalism		
Organization, frameworks and agreements involving most countries across two or more macro-regions in a larger recognized trans-region (e.g., Asia Pacific) or continental region (Asia)	ASEAN/AFTA APT EAS ACD ADB APEC PECC ARF	European Neighborhood Policy (ENP)
Inter-regionalism	ASEM EALAF	ASEM
Organization, frameworks and agreements		
Two relatively distant macro-regions, e.g., East Asia and Europe		
More dispersed geographic areas		

Source: Adapted from Dent (2008, p. 14).

6.1. The EU Cohesion Policy

What radically differentiates EU regional development policy from ASEAN is the level of institutionalization. Institutionalization concerns not only legal and formal rules but also the cohesive unity that binds together a vision of European territorial development, using rules of coordination and important sectoral institutions, supported by various development tools. Together they represent one of the most sophisticated EU policies, with the second biggest EU budget after that of the common agricultural policy (CAP).[6] Moreover, by emphasizing the overarching role of the territorial dimension, EU cohesion policy is insisting on the general coherence of EU policy of development and highlights the fundamental role of governance. These very important formal indications contribute to defining what can be called a strong supranational ensemble. But formal aspects resulting from EU policy are not sufficient. Voluntary agreement is required from member states, meaning commitment to shared development. What are the tools the EU can use in order to force member states to comply with EU rules? Development is not a question of central policy. It is much more a result of coordination of different actors at different levels: The EU level, the state level, and, at the same time, the local level. For this reason, conditionality cannot be based only on constraining rules. It requires cooperation, and cooperation is based on trust. The main question therefore is how to create trust.

6.1.1. A vision of development: Efficiency and equity

The cohesion policy is a vision of balanced development which accompanies the building of the EU institutional architecture and each step of the process, and which makes increasingly apparent the desire to closely

---

[6]The Cohesion Policy budget during the period 2007–2013 is EUR347 billion of which 306 billion is for Objective 1 mainly intended for Eastern and Southern Europe. Of this EUR 347 billion, EUR 86 billion are to be dedicated to "innovation" (including regional programs, research, clusters, technological transfer, services); entrepreneurship; innovative ICT; human capital; and regional innovation systems (as well as special programs linked to the environment, education and research).

link economic, social and territorial policies.[7] Article 2 of the Maastricht Treaty clearly reflects this in its stated aim to "promote economic and social progress as well as a high level of employment, and to achieve balanced and sustainable development". Article 158 further states: "in particular, the Community aims to reduce the disparities between the levels of development of the different regions and the backwardness of the least favoured regions or islands, including rural areas". In order to define cohesion policy, Andreas Faludi distinguishes two story lines. The first and main line refers to the general objective of "convergence" for EU regions, which have to improve their competitive position by combining growth and employment through solidarity. The second strand, called the subsidiarity story line, emphasizes "software development" based on coordination, cooperation and capacity building (Faludi, 2010).

---

[7] If the *Treaty of Rome* mainly aimed at creating a "common market", that is, to eliminate the obstacles to free movement of goods between the founding states and to implement an integration strategy based on the economy. While taking into account the failure of the *European Defense Community* in 1954, it should be noted that the Social European Fund was established in 1958 "in order to improve employment opportunities for workers in the common market and to thereby contribute to raising the standard of living ... it shall have the task of rendering the employment of workers easier and of increasing their geographical and occupational mobility within the Community" (Title III, Chapter II, Article 123 TCEE). In 1965, the European Commission published a first Communication on the Regional policy and in 1968 DG REGIO was created. The European Regional Development Fund (ERDF), which aimed to redistribute a part of Member States' contributions to the least developed regions, dates from 1975. In 1986, the *European Single Act* introduced in the Part III of EEC Treaty on "Policy of the Community" a new Title V on "Economic and Social Cohesion" that provided the legal basis for consolidating and further developing the Community's action in this field. The *Treaty on European Union* 1992 listed the economic and social cohesion among the objectives of the European Union (Article B): development and pursuit of actions leading to the strengthening of its economic and social cohesion and aiming in particular at reducing disparities between the various regions and the backwardness of the less-favored regions (Article 130a, Title V Economic and Social Cohesion). In 1997, at the time of the revision of the EC Treaty by the *Treaty of Amsterdam*, the concept of "territorial cohesion" is set out in the Treaty in the new Article 16 EC consecrated to services of general economic interest. The *Constitutional Treaty* 2004, the *Green Paper on Territorial Cohesion* [SEC(2008) 2550] and then the *Treaty of Lisbon* 2009 went further by consecrating the threefold ambition of "economic, social and territorial cohesion".

The current program started in 2007 and will continue until 2013. It has innovated by emphasizing the importance of "territorialization", which points to three major dimensions that are too often disconnected from each other in the various phases of both developed or catching-up economies: Economic growth, boosted by improving competitiveness and connections between regions; social cohesion, improved by stressing cohesion between labor markets; and territorial balance, which aims to not only reduce regional disparities but also to make the two former pillars — growth and labor market — more efficient locally.[8] The first pillar concerns the production of quantitative wealth by focusing on innovation and R&D, the second pillar aims at creating and supporting employment. The last pillar looks for reduction of territorial disparities. As growth is often located in particular places where all the resources are concentrated, it tends to induce territorial imbalances. Highly developed places — usually big cities — are able to attract economic, natural and human resources and by doing so they divert resources from their surrounding environment and thus impoverish it. In order to counterbalance this common trend in territorial development, cohesion policy aims to develop connections between growth poles and lagging regions or between central places and peripheries. Developing infrastructures aims to facilitate communication between them by reducing the number of isolated people or regions. Accessibility is therefore a key component in ensuring that all citizens can benefit from public goods. In 2008, the Green Paper on Territorial Cohesion has summarized this ambition by proposing a more balanced and harmonious development of European territories, following three axes[9]: *Concentration by overcoming differences in density.* The objective is to avoid excessive

---

[8] The Lisbon Treaty has repeated what is a core European objective since the Rome Treaty: In Article 174 it underlines that "In order to promote its overall harmonious development, the Union shall develop and pursue its actions leading to the strengthening of its economic, social and territorial cohesion. In particular, the Union shall aim at reducing disparities between the levels of development of the various regions and the backwardness of the least favoured regions". In Article 175, it goes on to state: "Member States shall conduct their economic policies and shall coordinate them in such a way as, in addition, to attain the objectives set out in Article 174".

[9] [SEC(2008) 2550].

concentrations of growth and facilitate access to the increased returns of urban agglomerations in all territories. *Connecting territories overcoming distance*: The objective is to link territories to transport networks, energy networks, new technologies and services of general economic interest. *Cooperation by overcoming division*: The problems of connectivity and concentration can only be effectively addressed with strong cooperation at various levels (see Fig. 6.1).

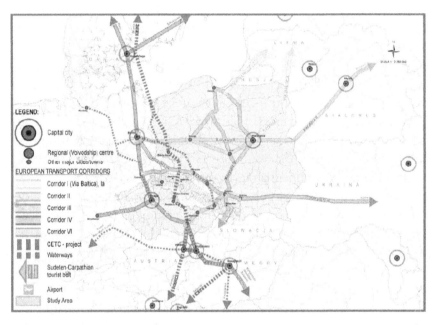

Fig. 6.1.   European transport corridors.

For these reasons cohesion policy is a "grande vision" of development that simultaneously embraces growth and social objectives by creating jobs and equal access to public goods for all. By insisting on these topics — growth, social and territorial development — EU authorities intend to emphasize two major dimensions. First, looking for efficiency cannot be achieved without also prioritizing equity. In other words, the market cannot manage all consequences that growth induces. Market failures cannot be ignored, and the unexpected effects of a totally free and deregulated market are exclusively at the expense of the poorest people and regions. Public interventions are required to guarantee equal access for all. Efficiency and equity are two faces of the same coin that only a territorial dimension of public action can achieve, because development is territorial. Indeed, unexpected effects of growth, both positive and negative, are territorial.

6.1.2. A hard public debate

This approach of efficiency and equity has been discussed in two major reports: the Sapir report published in 2005 (Sapir, 2003) and the 2009 Barca Report (Barca, 2009). Both seek to clarify the meaning of "subsidiarity". Subsidiarity defines which tasks are the responsibility of each EU actor, to the exclusion of the other partners. In other words "subsidiarity" defines the exact responsibility of the Commission, states, regions and local communities in matters of development.[10] For the Sapir Report, the EU level should exclusively concern itself with growth policies,[11] leaving responsibility for equity to nation states. To this extent, equity should not be a priority at the EU level. In accordance with this approach, fiscal policies implemented by each national state are much better placed than EU measures to achieve territorial balance (Begg, 2009).[12] The strict dichotomy

---

[10] Article 5 TEU clarifies the principle of subsidiarity: "Under the principle of subsidiarity, in areas which do not fall within its exclusive competence, the Union shall act only if and in so far as the objectives of the proposed action cannot be sufficiently achieved by the Member States, either at central level or at regional and local level, but can rather, by reason of the scale or effects of the proposed action, be better achieved at Union level. The institutions of the Union shall apply the principle of subsidiarity as laid down in the Protocol on the application of the principles of subsidiarity and proportionality. National Parliaments ensure compliance with the principle of subsidiarity in accordance with the procedure set out in that Protocol".

[11] The Sapir Report therefore recommended that 32.5% of the EU budget (not 5%) should be devoted to Research and Development, and that the agriculture budget, the CAP, be reduced from 40% to 15%.

[12] The rejection of the "planned EU territory" amounts to the rejection of the "French model" of "aménagement du territoire".

between growth and territorial policies means that regional development is said to exclusively depend on the state level. Any EU spatial planning proposal is considered to be an attempt to centrally organize a planned EU territory.[12] For the authors of the Sapir Report, the Lisbon treaty, which defined the EU's main economic and social objectives, was relevant as long as it did not concern itself with redistribution issues — be they social or territorial. Within such a vision of EU development the EU level is reduced to setting up the relevant institutions which can allow the free play of economic actors. EU prerogatives must not be widened[13] and EU conditionality strictly limited to market rules. Job creation and territorial balance are achieved by national fiscal policies.

The second approach — exemplified by the "Barca Report" — does not exclusively focus on closely linking together efficiency and equity. It also aims to combine them within the territorial dimension, arguing that growth development in a unified market impacts the EU territory as a whole. These observations lead Barca to propose major changes in EU policy. The first change would address policies that should be dealt with at the EU level, because they concern all European states, such as migration, climate change, child protection, and the environment. These issues are no longer a matter for isolated states but of the whole community. The second change would be at the local level. Considering failures in governance, the incapacity of political elites to think long term, as well as poor implementation of structural funds, it is suggested that local actors should be more closely involved in decision-making processes. They are in a much better position to identify local needs and allocate appropriate resources than the central authorities. These reflections have led to the so-called "place based approach", initially developed by some OECD studies,[14] as reformulated by Fabricio Barca. In his report, the

---

[13] This report was heavily criticized by both governments and EU DGs, not only because it conflicted with the interests of several European countries.

[14] "OECD territorial development policy" aims at "enhancing well-being and living standards" of regions and "generate and sustain regional competitive advantages" with a fuller and better use of regions' assets, by an approach "that is place-based,

former EU adviser of the DR Regio points out the need for public authorities to target excluded groups and poor people in order to integrate them into the public programs. Development of well-being at the level of the EU cannot emerge if populations are increasingly excluded from collective benefits linked to development. A place-based development policy, therefore, can be defined as "a long term development strategy aimed at increasing efficiency... designed and implemented by eliciting and aggregating local preferences and knowledge through participatory political institutions and by establishing linkages with other places, and promoted by a system of multilevel governance..." (Barca, 2009). Lastly, the "place based approach" is legitimized because it defines equity as being conducive to efficiency. Rather than opposing the two notions — efficiency and equity — Barca thinks they are intertwined, pointing out that poverty and exclusion can also be identified within the most developed regions. Moreover, only local people can develop what is rightly considered to be the basis of economic development: Trust, knowledge-based activities, linkages and networks. Exclusively focusing on growth and efficiency by leaving aside equity objectives brings several risks: The reinforcement of the power of ruling elites, the growth of "poverty traps", and a growing democratic deficit.

"Territorial capital" therefore becomes one of the major categories for thinking about development. By integrating different features of the "social capital" — like symbolic, cultural, individual or local community resources — "territorial capital" echoes the idea that "geography matters",[15] not only from a natural and physical perspective, but also in terms of the local milieu within which social networks are embedded. To this extent, EU cohesion policy provides a strong integrative vision for EU development, based not only on rules and institutions but also on a strong effort to integrate informal relations and loose networks for people located at very different and

---

multilevel, innovative and geared to different types of regions" (Bachtler and Méndez, 2007).

[15] The French geographer, Jacques Levy speaks of "spatial capital" in *L' espace légitime*, Presses de Sciences Po, 1994.

disconnected places. But how is social capital produced? Not from the center: Top–down policies have failed to guarantee long term development. Ruling elites are too often only preoccupied with their political survival and excluded people are not stable voters. Furthermore, more and more local people want to be involved in collective action. As globalization continues the more important the local level is, because only the local level embodies and qualifies global flows and goods by mirroring vivid identities. As Barca states, "there is no general recommendation for building trust or social capital. It needs to be designed place-by-place. But the information, which is necessary for this taylor-making, is certainly not held by those very public subjects that promote exogenous interventions. It is rather held by local agents. It should be up to their knowledge and preferences to decide what and how to intervene" (Barca, 2009, p. 23). But how can local actors be supported when they are not present? How can communities or associations be created when no local support exists? How can clusters be fostered when there is a lack of SMEs, and why build industrial parks and incubators from scratch when no knowledge capital is present?

Finally, this very important discussion about what kind of priorities the EU should set and with whom they can work reveals contrasting views among member states in their understanding of "solidarity" and consequently "spatial planning". This very French conceptualization of regional development is rejected by certain states, who suspect it to be no more than an attempt to rejuvenate the old idea of "planification", which they oppose. Such states favor a free market system in which states do not have to report to the EU level about regional development, and where the role of the supranational framework is confined to ensuring respect for rules about competitivity. In other words, a strong institutionalized "pro-market" EU is compatible with a very weak social and territorialized EU.

6.1.3. *Strategy, objectives and tools of development*

Linked to this global vision, in 2000 at the Lisbon summit, the EU developed a long-term strategy called the Lisbon Strategy. It aimed to make the EU the most developed region in the world by 2010, by emphasizing the development of a "knowledge society", based on the primacy of R&D transfer to SMEs and support of job creation thanks to life-long learning measures. In 2010, it was recognized that the main targets of the global strategy had not been achieved: Instead of 3% of GDP being spent on R&D as set out in the Lisbon Strategy, the final figure was 2.6%. In CEE, the situation was much worse: The equivalent figure was less than 1%.[16] Instead of the targeted employment rate of 70%,[17] 67% was finally achieved, and once again CEE trailed badly. Poland, for instance, only achieved 55% employment.[18] Following the Lisbon Strategy, a new strategy was set up in 2010: The Europe 2020 Strategy, which frames development strategies for the period 2014 to 2020. Some different targets were set to support the EU vision of sustainable development[19]: Investing 3% of GDP in R&D; 75% rate of employment for Europeans aged between 20 and 64[20]; reducing greenhouse gases by 20%, increasing the share of

---

[16] EU data. Poland, 0.58% in 2008. See the fifth report on economic, social and territorial cohesion. *Investing in Europe's Future: A Regional Development Strategy for 2020.*

[17] Based on population aged between 20 and 64.

[18] In spite of progress, Europe's employment rates — at 66% on average — are still significantly lower than in other parts of the world. Only 59% of women are in work compared to 73% of men. Only 46% of older workers (55–64) are employed compared to over 62% in the US and Japan. Moreover, on average Europeans work 10% fewer hours than their US or Japanese counterparts. Moreover demographic ageing is accelerating. As the baby-boom generation retires, the EU's active population will start to shrink as from 2013/2014. The number of people aged over 60 is now increasing twice as fast as it did before 2007 — by about two million every year compared to one million previously. The combination of smaller working populations, a higher proportion of retired people and higher levels of unemployment, places additional strains on European welfare systems.

The main innovations of Strategy 2020 are, firstly, "smart specialization", which stresses the performance of national and regional innovation systems, and, second, the energy objectives (3×20%).

[19] Communication from the Commission, Europe 2020, A strategy for smart, sustainable and inclusive growth, COM, 2020 final.

[20] But no explanation accompanies this upgrading level of 75% although the previous target of 70% has not been reached.

renewable energy to 20% and improve energy efficiency by 20%; increasing to 40% the percentage of individuals aged between 30 and 34 having completed tertiary education; and lifting at least 20 million Europeans out of poverty. These targets are, however, only indicative and a major concern is how the EU can use conditionality to achieve these goals.[21]

Based on these general guidelines, and in accordance with the territorialization of European interventions, some objectives have been set which take into consideration the level of development reached by European regions. Objective 1 is "convergence" and refers to the less developed regions, which are said to be "backward" because they are well below the EU average and therefore need collective assistance to ensure they catch up. The EU indicator of "backwardness" is, as mentioned above, linked to the level of the regional GDP per inhabitant. Regions that have a GDP of less than 75% the EU average benefit from the support of the structural funds. The other regions are involved in the objective of "competitiveness and employment". A last objective, "cooperation", concerns cross border cooperation.[22] The funds for these different objectives are allocated at

---

[21] The European Commission has delivered on 6 October its blueprint for the next generation of EU cohesion funds after 2013, indicating a start of €336 billion legislative package and connecting the use of funds with the EU's stability and Growth Pact. Few innovations have been introduced in this new package: Simpler rules, fewer investments priorities. In more developed regions, the bulk of investments will go to innovation, support of SMEs, energy efficiency and renewables, while in least developed regions these priorities are balanced 50/50 with development needs towards employment, education and poverty reduction. The only innovation of this package is the strong will to establish a tighter link between EU cohesion funding and the countries' economic and fiscal policies.

[22] The first objective, "convergence" has been granted the biggest budget, €199.3 billion, the second, "competitiveness", €4.5 billion, and the last one, *cooperation*, €7 billion. To these sums it is necessary to add those allocated to the so-called regions, for phasing in and phasing out, that define some transitory measures with budgets of €13.9 billion and €11.4 billion, respectively. Finally, the cohesion fund allocated to the countries having a GDP less than 90% of the EU average can target transport and environmental infrastructures. For the period 2007–2013, therefore, the total amount of structural funds available is €347.4 billion.

different levels: Funds for Objective 1 are managed by regions, whereas those for Objective 2 are managed by the state.

Lastly, three other funds should be mentioned. The first is the European Development Fund (ERDF) (€201 billion) which targets regional development, the reversal of economic decline in industrial or rural areas, as well as competitiveness and co-operation. The second fund is the ESF (€76 billion) which promotes employment, social inclusion and anti-discrimination measures. Lastly, the Cohesion Fund (€70 billion) finances initiatives concerned with the environment and transport. There is also a special tool forged to foster cross-border cooperation, which we will look at in the next chapter when considering different forms of cross border project.[23]

Finally, EU funds are seen as generators of development not only because of the significant amounts of money available, but also because funds are reshaping national budgetary strategies. An important aspect of EU conditionality is the obligation for national states to add to the EU allocation by making a contribution of their own. This size of these contributions depend on the nature of the individual project: Public projects may receive up to 75% of their funding from the EU, private projects up to 25% and public/private ones up to 50%. In each case, the EU funding has to be matched by a contribution from the recipient nation. This payment is said to be "additional". Furthermore, projects financially supported by EU funds have to fit in with national strategies. This principle is called "complementarity". It underlines the fact that the EU cohesion policy cannot replace national strategies. It follows from these two basic principles, additionality and complementarity, which are closely checked by EU services, that it is almost impossible to develop other public policies, as national budgets are low and EU funds of vital importance to these "catching up" countries. Once

---

[23] The initial "community initiative" INTERREG has been included in the programming period 2007–2013 within the third objective and address cooperation between borders (cross-border Interreg A), between regions (Interreg B) and between states (Interreg C). Moreover, a new legal tool has been created, the *European grouping for territorial cooperation* (EGTC).

Table 6.2. Programming periods (2000–2006 and 2007–2013) objectives and instruments.

2000–2006		2007–2013	
Objectives	Financial instruments	Objectives	Financial instruments
Cohesion fund	Cohesion fund	Convergence	ERDF/ESF/cohesion fund (81.5%)
Objective 1[24]	ERDF/ESF/EAGG Guarantee and Guidance FIFG		
Objective 2[25]	ERDF/ESF/	Regional competitiveness and employment	ERDF/ESF/(14.5%)
Objective 3[26]	ESF/		
Interreg[27]	ERDF		
URBAN[28]	ERDF		
EQUAL[29]	ESF	European Territorial cooperation	ERDF (4.5%)
Leader +[30]	EAGG Guidance		
Rural development and restructuring of the fisheries sector outside Objective EAGGF Gurantee	EAGG Guarantee FIFG		
9 Objectives	6 Instruments	3 Objectives[31]	3 Instruments

[24] Objective 1 targeted regions having a GDP less than 75% of the EU average.

[25] Objective 2 targeted parts of regions affected by industrial or rural crisis within regions having a GDP above 75% of the EU average.

[26] Objective 3 dealt with employment objectives and was considered unsuccessful.

[27] Interreg is the only Community initiative that remains in the current SF architecture. These community initiatives that represented 5% of the whole EU development budget were created in order to solve issues that emerged along the EU development.

[28] URBAN was an initiative targeting urban concerns.

[29] EQUAL targeted gender equality.

[30] Leader + was an initiative targeting particular poor rural areas with specific characteristics (mountainous areas, etc.).

[31] The current programming period has opened to simplification concerning objectives and instruments since Community Initiatives have disappeared leaving place to the only territorial cooperation; After 2008, in order to tackle the crisis more effectively, public projects could receive up to 80% finance.

the additional national contribution has been made the national state has very few resources left at its disposal. Lastly, it has to be mentioned that projects supported by the EU have to comply with some technical rules. One of the most important of them refers to the EU architecture of governance, which links the five EU levels (EU, state, regional, departmental, and local) vertically, and the public, private and non-public actors horizontally. This is so-called "multi-level governance", a system by which "the responsibility for policy design and implementation is distributed among different levels of government and special purpose local institutions (private associations, pacts among several local public authorities, districts and cooperation projects within national borders or across national borders, public–private partnership)" (Sabel and Zeitlin, 2008; Lolle, 2006; Gelauff *et al.*, 2008).

Let us quickly conclude about strong versus weak EU related strong states. Obviously, EU is strong because of "pooling sovereignty". EU rules can exert significant pressure on candidates because member states have transferred part of their national sovereignty to the EU Commission. Cohesion policy requires that the rules be strictly applied. Nevertheless, by having prioritized growth and left aside social measures, European rules have contributed to increasing territorial disparities and reinforced anti-European feelings among large sectors of Europeans. Second, conditionality is often missing and territorial homogeneity is not present. We will examine this more closely in the next chapter.

6.2. ASEAN: Cooperation, No Binding Rules and Step-by-Step Construction

Obviously, it would be a mistake to conclude that ASEAN lacks a regional policy just because the Southeast Asian organization has not developed something comparable to the highly regulated institutional architecture presented above. The context in which ASEAN emerged at the end of the 1960s reveals four major features of regional development in Southeast Asia. First, ASEAN was born from out of political considerations: The fear of communism, the desire for security, and the strong will of each of the five founding members to establish its own national development path. These three elements have limited any further attempts at more political integration. The enlargements of 1995 (Vietnam), 1997 (Laos and Myanmar) and 1999 (Cambodia) did not lead to "pooling sovereignty". In other words, coordination between member states has definitely been preferred to "pooling sovereignty". That is the major difference between the ASEAN and the EU. Second, far from blocking any evolution, such a point of departure led to a step-by-step construction of different arenas. Each arena has instituted rules for more deeply intertwined economic exchanges. Third, in a few places different models of regional cooperation have emerged which strongly structure Southeast Asian economic development. Finally, some informal cross-border exchanges were established which do not rely on fixed rules. What has been highlighted above, with the terms cooperation, connectivity and concentration, corresponds exactly to what the ASEAN targets with its "3 Cs": Connectivity, Competitiveness and Community.

6.2.1. *ASEAN: A loose regional ensemble*

The conditions of emergence of ASEAN and the profiles of its members explain why no strong institutional ensemble could emerge. As seen in Chapter 3, ASEAN was born out of the desire of some loosely connected countries to defend themselves against the threat of communism.[32] The search for security and affirmation of regional autonomy *vis-à-vis* the great powers were common goals among the founders of ASEAN. The objective of security has never been abandoned; if anything its importance has increased. The further evolution and instability of the region led member states to constantly reassert this basic objective despite strong internal division between them. Those of them who wanted to prioritize security — like Thailand, Philippines and Singapore — favored reinforcing links with the US,

---

[32] In a recent article, Lee Jones (2010) defends the thesis that during the cold war "the predominant cleavage in ASEAN societies was between forces committed to and opposing the prevailing capitalist order".

while other countries — like Malaysia and Indonesia — preferred to defend regional autonomy. During the 1990s and 2000s, the combined effects of the fall of communism, the withdrawal of FDI (reoriented to new EU member states and China), and the rise of China pushed ASEAN to welcome new member states, and cooperate with new northern partners (APT).

In the years preceding the creation of ASEAN, the five founding members — Malaysia, Singapore, the Philippines, Thailand and Indonesia — attempted to build a common arena.[33] However, they failed for different reasons related to clashes between some of them, notably disputes between Malaysia and the Philippines over Sabah, and between Indonesia and Thailand over Aceh. When ASEAN emerged a few years later very few people thought it would survive for very long. Rather than being based on a grand vision of development like the EU, from the very start ASEAN defined itself as a "non-communist arrangement to promote security of its members" (Pempel, 2005). Such a position represented no global idea of historical development, no sense of fulfilling a historical duty by deliberately overcoming the failures of history, and no shared identity. Here, obviously, lies the main difference between the two organizations; the EU was a "grand" political project with an economic basis: A community of steel and coal between France and Germany whose purpose was to prevent the organization of cartels and avoid the kind of economic imbalance that could lead to the nightmare scenario: Conflict between the two major European economies which could, in turn, once again plunge the whole continent into war. In contrast, ASEAN was a political project set up to protect the existence and autonomy of certain developing countries *vis-à-vis* the "Great Powers" of Russia, China and the US. ASEAN decided not to impose

---

[33] In 1962, The Association of Southeast Asia including Malaysia, the Philippines and Thailand was created, supported by the initiative of the Prime Minister of Malaysia Tunku Abdul Raman but failed because of the conflict opposing between Malaysia to and the Philippines concerning the region of Saba. A year later another forum, Maphilindo, was created under the initiative of the Philippines and attempted to join Malaysia, the Philippines and Indonesia, but failed once more for the same reasons.

any binding rules on its members.[34] There were no initial economic constraints, unlike the European Community which limited the use of certain resources. There was no common defense project. The Asian states decided to respect their mutual independence by immediately declaring two basic principles: The notion of non-interference in the affairs of other members — because of concerns about minorities or territories — and the commitment to operating by consensus. The former principle has allowed central states, notably communist states, to liquidate internal opposition. The latter principle has been constantly reasserted, and demonstrates members' desire to reach satisfying agreements. Under such conditions the least binding agreements tend to be adopted. Acharya (2009) rightly says, "They decided to form ASEAN as a mechanism for regional rapprochement, anticipating that participations in the Association would help moderate the currently unrestrained competitive dynamics between their countries". To this extent, regulations were seen as existing to facilitate each country taking care of its own problems. "the most appropriate standard of behaviour for a group of very diverse states having to work together on common problems" (*idem*, p. 35).

6.2.2. *Political changes and world-wide economic evolution*

Despite this firm position concerning consensus, two major sets of changes put pressure on ASEAN to evolve: First, the geopolitical situation, and, second, world-wide economic changes. But, under increasing pressure, rather than "pooling sovereignty", member states chose greater economic liberalization and decided against the

---

[34] "The ASEAN doctrine of non-interference was, in important part, an expression of a collective commitment to the survival of its non-communist regimes against the threat of communist subversion" (Acharya, 2009, p. 58); "the principle of non-interference in the internal affairs of member countries and the search for accommodation and consensus have traditionally guided decision-making and behavior in the association, collectively termed 'the Asean way' has remained a constant feature of ASEAN institutions" (p. 33, 34) Khong and Nesadurai (2007, pp. 32–82); "flexibility and search for consensus have remained key design features of all Asean institutions which continue to emphasize intergovernmental decision-making" (*idem*, p. 34).

creation of more common political rules. What makes ASEAN so unique is that it was able to target and achieve a more integrated approach within a politics of more open regionalism, based on strict adherence to its fundamental principles of non-binding rules, non-interference and primacy of national sovereignty.

In 1975, there was a major shift in the geopolitical situation when, following the US departure from the Indochina basin, Communism was left dominant in Vietnam, Laos and Cambodia. Moreover, because of the changing relationship between the US and China, some countries were afraid of being sacrificed as a result of "Great Power" maneuverings. Thailand, for instance, was particularly concerned, being heavily reliant on US aid. Furthermore, in the 1970s Great Britain decided, after 200 years, to withdraw from East of Suez, which provoked similar fears. Then, in the 1980s, the occupation of Cambodia by Vietnamese forces challenged ASEAN's position regarding territorial conflicts between Thailand and Cambodia. These events all contributed to reshaping the influence of the "Great Powers", in particular the US and China, and ASEAN was consequently forced to adopt a clearer position. Pressures further increased at the end of the Soviet era in 1990, and subsequently with rising tension caused by the dictatorship in Burma. As mentioned above, in Chapter 3, applications to join ASEAN from Cambodia and Burma presented the organization with a major challenge[35] and we have seen how the enlargements of 1997 (Myanmar and Laos) and 1999 (Cambodia) have changed the ASEAN.

6.2.3. *World-wide evolution and progressive construction: Economic exchanges and arenas*

New world-wide economic pressures in the 1990s, resulting from both the end of European communism and the dynamics of globalization, pushed ASEAN to adopt new economic directives. Rather than regarding regional development as a matter of "pooling sovereignties" and the promotion of new binding rules, ASEAN, in line with its fundamental principles, opted for a more step-by-step construction

---

[35] See Chapter 3 (p. 9).

of a new arena, which included both economic and security objectives. The first forms of cooperation that structure the common space are the Free Trade Agreements (FTA), which are bilateral trade agreements. These numerous FTA — often compared to "noodle bowls" — mainly address merchandise trade liberalization. In addition to FTAs, ASEAN has created more comprehensive agreements: the Regional Trade Agreements (RTAs). RTAs target goods but also other trade facilitation measures, such as investment protection and liberalization, harmonization, recognition of mutual certification, and the opening of government procurement markets.[36]

Obviously, the fall of Soviet type communism, the strengthening of the EU and NAFTA in Northern America, the rise of China, and the decrease of FDI from 35% in 1990 to 24.5% in 1992 in favor of China and other emerging markets have all exerted strong pressure on ASEAN. They forced ASEAN to address the following challenges: How could it overcome the development divide that clearly separates the ASEAN-6 from the CLMV group? How could it lift barriers concerning trade in goods and services, investment flows, labor migration, but also address issues of cross-border transport agreements and trade facilitation? How could it ensure inclusive growth? For these reasons, one of the most important trade bloc agreements was AFTA in 1992. The main objective of AFTA was to set up a new common effective preferential tariff scheme that would finally lead to a single regional market in 2020.[37] AFTA "may be

---

[36] As Kawai observes: "For East Asian economies, regional and bilateral liberalization is an attempt to achieve deeper integration with their trading partners on a formal basis, going beyond reductions in border restrictions — i.e., pursuing investment liberalization, promoting greater competition in the domestic markets, and harmonizing standards and procedures" Kawai (2003).

[37] Already in 1976 Singapore had proposed to immediately create AFTA, but the other neighbors were afraid of its power. At that time, they had high tariffs for protecting their infant industries. In 1986, the Philippines proposed the creation of a Custom Union (tariffs for non-members) but this was rejected by the other members. In 1990 at Bali, the idea emerged of a Common Effective Preferential Tariff on selected items like cement, pulp and fertilizer, which lead to the creation of some FTAs. In 1992, Singapore finally proposed more FTAs that were accepted.

perceived as a collective export-oriented industrialization strategy or simply a method for enhancing other more informal but perhaps more significant forms of regional integration taking place in Southeast Asia" (Kawai, 2003).

Then, in the aftermath of the major financial crisis of 1997, an important initiative was taken, the ASEAN Plus Three (APT), which brought Japan, China and North Korea into the collective talks. It was followed by the Chiang Mai initiative in 1998, which was adopted in response to the huge Asian crisis. It is a pool of currencies with bilateral swaps and includes an alarm system for capital flows and several forums for the exchange of views about the financial markets. Some scholars considered the meeting of the APT to be an important milestone in Asian cooperation. Finally, following the 1997 Asian crisis, at the November 2002 Summit, Singapore suggested that the ASEAN Economic Community (AEC) be established. This was achieved with the signing of the Ventiane Action Plan Program in 2004, which was seen as a response to shared concern about the loss of competitiveness of ASEAN to China. After the 1997 crisis it became obvious that the ASEAN states could not compete with China on labor costs. Moreover, FDI flows were now mainly directed to China.

ASEAN's final objective is to create an ASEAN economic community (ASEAN EC) open to the free flow of goods, services, investment and skilled labour, and promoting a freer flow of capital.[38] The main instrument of liberalization is the Common Effective Preferential Tariff Scheme, subdivided into four main product categories.[39] The basic idea is to maximize complementarities between ASEAN economies and create a single integrated production base from which to

---

[38] Declaration of the ASEAN Council in Bali, Indonesia, 7/10/2003.

[39] The first or "Inclusion" list addresses products with low tariffs of 5% to 20%, reduced to 0% to 5% (electronics). It was decided to postpone the deadline for the poorest CMLV to 2006. The second or "temporary exclusion" list concerns products which could be transferred to the first list (the Inclusion list) after a short period. The Sensitive list defines products for longer tariff liberalization (because of high tariffs). Finally, there is a General exception list that concerns products that involve national security or that are culturally sensitive. AFTA deadlines have been extended for Vietnam to 2013, for Myanmar and Laos to 2015, and for Cambodia to 2017.

upgrade production efficiency and labor productivity. Concretely, the AEC aims to organize a community with a free flow of goods, services, investment, skilled labor, and a freer flow of capital in 12 sectors.[40] Furthermore, in order to implement full trade liberalization a resolution mechanism was needed. Already conceived in 1996, it was finally created within the AEC in order to solve trade and investment issues, with a timeframe of 30 days for resolution. Although limited, such an innovation can be considered an important step towards institutionalization. Another step in the same direction was taken in 2000 when a notification protocol was added requiring members to inform the Secretariat before modifying any agreements. It was followed by the creation of the ASEAN Compliance Body (ACB), a group of experts which provides mediation services.[41]

The latest step taken in this long term construction of a common exchange space was the creation of the ASEAN Charter. Adopted at the end of the Ventiane Summit in 2008, it intends to build the community on three pillars: Economic (AEC); social (ASC) and cultural (ASCC). After indicating that the Charter would develop appropriate organs in accordance with the rights and duties of each member, he continued by further clarifying that "among these organs would be objective and credible dispute settlement mechanisms" (Yeo, 2009).

6.2.4. Step-by-step regional integration?

What lessons can be drawn from evolution of ASEAN compared to that of the EU? It is clear that, regarding regional development

---

[40]Electronics, e-ASEAN, healthcare, wood-based products, automotives, rubber-based products, textiles and apparels, agro-based products, fisheries, air travel, tourism, logistics.

[41]The ASEAN has also adopted two complementary programs: The ASEAN Investments Area (AIA) aims at opening all industries for investment by 2010 to ASEAN investors and by 2020 to all investors (coordination of investments and facilitations programs). The second program, AICO (ASEAN's Industrial Cooperation Program) promotes joint manufacturing industrial activities between ASEAN-based companies. (immediately preferential tariffs 0–5% for the enterprises). As of 2003, 126 AICOs had been accepted, see ADB.

policies, the Chiang Mai initiative cannot be compared with the EMU. APEC is of decreasing significance because of the fourth list (national security and cultural sensitivity), which is increasingly used by member states to avoid collective duties. In this way states remain the main actors, and no hegemonic state emerges. The project to create, in 1989, a massive economic community which would include non-ASEAN members — APEC — failed for a lot of reasons that have already been mentioned: Lack of regional identity, lack of regional unity, requirements to make too great compromises, and, finally, too great heterogeneity between APEC members. Moreover, the great economic disparities between members have hampered their ability to work together. This is even more the case for small states whose economies are not complementary (Beeson, 2009). Giving small states the capacity to resist stronger states is an important feature of the Southeast Asian organizations. Politically, some states have no interest at all in respecting the ASEAN charter commitment in favor of greater democracy. Economically, informal and less constraining rules prevail.

Despite the well-documented lack of homogeneity of the region, it must be acknowledged that all these agreements — even though they appear vague — contribute to the construction of a regional identity. Even though the Asian Regional Forum and Security (ARF) suffers from the same limitations as APEC,[42] it reflects the concern of strong Southeast Asian states to organize their own security, and to connect security objectives with economic ones. It should also not be forgotten that less than thirty years ago, the states which today make up APEC were strongly opposed to one another, ideologically and militarily. It is certainly easy to criticize the lack of concrete achievements. These failures are undeniable. Nevertheless, member states and their foreign ministers still manage to meet up with a view to setting up a common agenda for preventive diplomacy. Moreover, besides formal agreements and treaties, there are also very different and more informal intraregional agreements which are oriented to the market, in contrast to state ones, like FTAs. FTAs are state initiatives and seek to

---

[42] The ASEAN regional forum involves 29 members, including the Russian Federation, the US, the EU, China, India and Japan (p. 73).

create intra-regional blocks and regional investments by eliminating intra-regional tariff barriers. Growth triangles also originate from state initiatives. In contrast to these intergovernmental agreements, economic corridors — supported by ADB within the GMS — reflect the commitment to decentralization of some states or non-state actors. The basic idea is to facilitate communication by enhancing connectivity and supporting communities. We will come back to this in the next chapter.

6.3. Comparing Both Regional Areas

Let us now compare two types of regulation: Monetary union and the regional development policy. Other types of regulation, such as state aid, strategies and special economic zones will be compared at the end of the next chapter. Table 6.3 complements Higgott's table by adding the European dimension of regional integration.

There are huge differences between the first two items (economic and trade exchanges, and money). It would be interesting to isolate the conditions necessary for monetary union. Scholars who have analyzed the construction of the Euro currency first underline the crucial factor of political unity. No monetary union can emerge without "pooling sovereignty". The Chiang Mai initiative does not belong to this category of union.[43] The pooling of sovereignty in the EU requires rules, confidence, trust and commitment to be shared by the various partners. Obviously, states which accept this kind of monetary union derive great benefit from the elimination of transaction costs due to the liquidation of the exchange margin. In this respect monetary union is more beneficial for small states than large states, whose currencies are extensively used for international payments (Kang and Wang, 2002). Nevertheless, the costs are also very high. States, which agree to join the monetary union, may no longer manipulate their national currency

---

[43]Jabko (2005). Having said that the euro is "the world's only true regional currency", the author adds that, "the euro was created as a result of a political process and the Member States of the EU decided to create an EMU (Economic and Monetary Union) for political reasons" (p. 44).

Table 6.3. Some aspects of regional integration.

	ASEAN	EU
Economic and trade exchanges	Trade pattern CBTA, FTA, CEPT	Common market
Monetary agreement	Chiang Mai Initiative Asian Bonds	Monetary union
Production network	Business operations and investments, FDI, ethnic networks, and the different lines of production	FDI and relocated firms
Policies of regional development	Infrastructure IAI	The cohesion policy The cohesion and the structural funds
Political economy	Links between domestic milieu ("grandes familles" and state bureaucracy) and FDI	Rule of law
Policy community/ governance (multi-level, multi-channel, multi-actor mixture of formal and informal types of activity	The client/Boss employer/relationships Informal personal contacts Summits Policy communities (Elites from the same universities)	Policy networks, formal and informal ones
Regional cooperation	Sub-regional cooperation patterns GMS, Growth triangle	Euro-region, ECGT (interreg)

Source: Adapted from Higgott (2007).

in order to compensate for a lack of national efficiency. Nor can they print their own money or devaluate it. Raising revenues for public expenditures can be problematic because of EU policy on inflation. Furthermore, states have to accept to transfer a part of their national sovereignty to a supranational bank. The role of national banks is reduced to advising, and taking part in shared decisions. Lastly, members have to respect strict limitations on public expenditure. They also have to deliver accurate and reliable statistics to the EU commission, as the current crisis in Greece and Portugal clearly demonstrated. For all these reasons, it is clear the Chiang Mai initiative falls a long way short of EMU, which involves a single, well-executed monetary policy. Nevertheless, discussions concerning a possible Asian monetary union are still ongoing, and ASEAN conditions do not appear to be the same as those in the EU. What is much more important is whether Japan is able to take the lead (and whether the US and China will agree to this).

6.3.1. Regional policy and pro-poor program: The Initiative for Asian Integration (IAI)

At first glance, the two regional entities appear to have completely different regional development policies. As mentioned above, the EU Cohesion policy is a highly regulated framework supported by guidelines — the Lisbon Strategy and, later, Europe 2020 — which framed core development strategies (R&D, SMEs, export-oriented strategies, etc.), and used powerful regulatory and financial tools (Cohesion fund, EFRD, ESF). Thanks to these tools, the EU organizes economic, social and territorial development by targeting different regional levels of development guided by three objectives: "Convergence", "competitiveness and employment", and "territorial cooperation". This kind of EU "spatial planning" (let us accept this contested term, whatever some member states may think of it) has received funding of more than 340 billion euros. ASEAN did not develop such a policy and has no intention of doing so. A general regulated framework does not exist, and regional development policies are practically non-existent. Nevertheless, there are some similarities between the two regions. First of all, the founding document of ASEAN, the Bangkok Declaration of 1967, stated that "The countries of Southeast Asia share a primary responsibility for strengthening the economic and social stability of the region and ensuring their peaceful and progressive national development" (Acharya, 2009, p. 55). Secondly, as the IAI program is based on EU ones, it is interesting to compare the IAI, which is a "pro-poor policy", with EU social policies. Indeed, the IAI emerged after the last ASEAN enlargement, which dramatically increased levels of regional inequality due to the gap between the ASEAN 6 and the CLMV nations.

EU regional policy has influenced ASEAN and its "pro-poor policy". The Hanoi Declaration in July 2001 on "Narrowing Development Gap for Closer Integration" mentions an initiative that led to the working plan presented in Phnom Penh in November 2002. The plan was set up for a six-year program (2003–2008). Focused on the poorest countries and regions, it aimed at targeting intra-regional economic development through capacity building. The basic idea, largely inspired by the EU, was supported by the consideration that growth is not necessarily beneficial to all member states, and that some groups do not benefit from the general rise in the level of well-being. To this extent, the IAI program is a response to the increasing gap between the richest and poorest states,[44] launched at the very moment when the EU announced its commitment to supporting new members, thanks to a huge packet of structural funds. At that time Singapore had a GDP per capita of around USD25,000 and Brunei USD16,000; at the other extreme, the corresponding figures for Cambodia and Myanmar were USD338 and less than USD200, respectively. As mentioned in Chapter 2, the figures for the richest states were more than 100 times greater than those for the poorest, while in the EU, the highest per capita GDP — Luxembourg (45,000 euros) — was only seven times that of the lowest (Bulgaria (6,000 euros)).[45] So, in the view of ASEAN elites, the regional organization was under an obligation to better distribute the fruits of growth, by transferring resources from the richest to the poorest member states. The program is wide-ranging: It covers Infrastructure Development, Human Resource Development, Public Sector Capacity Building, Labor & Employment, Higher Education, Information and

---

[44] For Christopher Dent, IAI "was at least partly conceived as counteracting core-periphery divergence arising from AFTA commercial liberalization". He adds "the IAI's primary objective was to bridge the development gap among ASEAN members and is specifically focused on fostering intra-regional economic development and cooperation through capacity-building and other measures" (Dent, 2008).

[45] At a regional level this gap was much greater, as mentioned in Chapter 2.

Communication Technology; Regional Economic Integration and Production-based Development. Later some other fields were added, such as Energy, Investment, Climate, Tourism, Poverty Reduction and Improvement in Quality of Life.

Unfortunately the funds made available are not comparable. Whereas the EU devotes 340 billion euros for regional policies, 308 billion euros of which goes to the poorest regions, the second IAI program has a budget of only $45.1 million.[46] In September 2006, 132 projects were launched, of which 19 were for infrastructures, 11 for transport, 8 for energy, 48 for human resources, 22 for ICT and 32 for regional integration, mainly tourism. In 2008, the budget was $51 million; 203 projects were in the working plan. Funding was secured for 158 projects, of which 116 were completed. Compared to the huge sums allocated to EU projects, the IAI budget is tiny. The IAI program has been heavily criticized for inadequate inter-agency coordination, reporting mechanisms, implementation and follow-through actions. Controlled from the top of the ASEAN, it does not integrate the targeted countries, the CLMV, who are not involved in the project selection process. Some examples of specific criticisms are: The very poor level of English of the trainers, the lack of understanding of the rules by local actors, and the fact that training sessions are too short. Very low effectiveness is exacerbated by a lack of knowledge and poor skill dissemination. No impact assessment of projects is carried out. When we address local development in the next chapter we will see similar criticisms made of various levels of the EU and ASEAN.

6.4. Conclusion

We must acknowledge that the EU is strong because of its huge architecture of development rules, while the ASEAN is weak chiefly because

---

[46] The budget from the Asean 6 is around $28.2 million, (63% of the total), mainly from Singapore, 76.3%, ($21,544,456); Brunei, 5.3%, ($1,500,000) Indonesia, 2.1%, (599,000), Thailand, 1.7%, (480, 902), the Philippines, 0.1%, (30,932). The five foreign donors are the EU/Korea/Japan/Norway, contributing a total of $16.9 million.

of the unwillingness of its members to promote more binding rules. Nevertheless, the EU is not always able to enforce compliance with its rules. Faced with states that are very reluctant to pool more sovereignty, the EU is in a weak position to impose its views. The EU's fifth regional report[47] identifies conditionality as a major concern. We will see in the next chapter how the EU has failed to find new innovative tools or rules to impose conditionality more effectively. The Greek crisis has highlighted this major weakness caused by the absence of relevant tools to oblige a state that has bent the common rules to behave appropriately. ASEAN's lack of collective commitment has obviously impeded finding solutions for collective issues, be they political or economic. Examples of political problems whose poor handling seriously tarnished ASEAN's image are the SARS epidemic, the Indonesian haze at the end of the 1990s, and repression in Burma (Weatherbee, 2009). There are a number of longstanding problems which ASEAN has failed to properly address, such as the continuing conflict over the Vihear Temple in 2011 between Thailand and Cambodia (Askew, 2010). Nevertheless, anything that is said about the weakness of ASEAN must acknowledge the unwillingness of some regimes to change. Some domestic networks can maintain their authority because of certain alliances. Loose coupling and the ASEAN principle of non-interference are relevant for the MNEs, who are firmly resolved to continue to play the game free of further constraints.

From an economic perspective, AFTA fails to work efficiently because a lot of products are put in the most protective (fourth) category, which excludes products from liberalization. Vietnam, in particular, has been criticized for doing this. The reaction of ASEAN Plus Three to the 1997 Asian crisis was the limited "Chiang Mai Initiative", which is actually a swap agreement rather than a monetary union. The APT did not lead to a "grand" policy and disagreements between Japan and China hampered collective action. As Beeson (2009) says, "APEC looks somewhat redundant", given the fact that the WTO, which has the same trade liberalization agenda, plays a very similar role much more

---

[47] The fifth report on economic, social and territorial cohesion. *Investing in Europe's Future: A Regional Development Strategy for 2020.*

efficiently, because its rules are binding. Finally, the ASEAN charter has been criticized for not including NGOs and civil societies (Lebel *et al.*, 2007) in its preparations, and for strongly reasserting the basic principle of non-interference, which effectively blocks change by letting less committed members do what they want (Yeo, 2009).[48] In other words, ASEAN continues to reinforce its own incapacity to adopt any important regional policies. Rather than shaping paths towards change, new declarations and treaties seem to merely restate and reinforce the status quo. "To change so that nothing changes" appears to be the main shortfall of the Southeast Asian organization.

Despite all of these arguments criticizing ASEAN's inability to act collectively, it would be mistaken to simply conclude that it is a weak organization. Paradoxically, ASEAN is actually a strong union because its rules allow different elites to meet and elaborate shared visions. The constructivist approach is right in emphasizing the role of ideas in managing collective action and the capacity of shared norms to shape interests (Acharya, 1997). The initial "grand" objective of ASEAN was to exist in the eyes of the Great Powers — the US before the 1980s and then China — whose capacity to exert pressure on its member nations has been enormous. Indeed, ASEAN members succeeded to maintaining good relations with both the US and China. They also managed to assert their own security, and remain sovereign states capable of resisting external control. Furthermore, some local initiatives have demonstrated the effectiveness of local actors, as the next chapter will show in its examination of cross-border relations.

---

[48](64) The Asia Pacific Economic Cooperation: 21 members, not only from Asia (Japan, China, South Korea, Taiwan), but also from American (US and Canada) and Latin America (Chile and Mexico).

7

STATE, SUB-STATE DESIGNS AND CROSS-BORDER COOPERATION

Stretching back over decades and centuries, borders in Europe and Southeast Asia have been areas of disastrous conflict. They have frequently been displaced and re-drawn, and equipped with check-points and military quarters. Once conflicts end and peace treaties have been signed, the issue becomes how to get local people to cooperate through repairing historical injuries and consolidating stability. How do local populations recombine their legacies, and within what kind of institutions, and under what framework of rules?

Cross-border cooperation issues are of utmost importance for our understanding of development policies, because they demonstrate the importance of the State's capacity to secure its own territory, which it does by redistributing power among regional and local partners, and by creating new rules of cooperation with international partners. This is why, if cross-border co-operation is to be promoted, the creation of domestic and joint institutions is a primary concern. Appropriate infrastructures facilitate exchange and reduce transaction costs because they cut transit time. Efficient infrastructure networks allow developing countries to integrate into more complex supply chains, thus promoting trade. Joint rules organize shared markets and strengthen partnerships, which in turn guarantee security because of regular and stable exchange. In the end, cross-border exchanges promote trust and a reciprocal willingness to cooperate.

Nevertheless, this analytical framework — frequently used by OECD studies[1] — is only valid for borders which are already stable. This is not the case everywhere. A peaceful situation can sometimes be accompanied by very poor institutional support. Far from fostering clear rules and predictable legal behaviors, border situations can be very confused. Such confusion opens the door to a reestablishment of patronage relationships which strengthen certain pre-existing hierarchies between actors. This is often the case in the Mekong region where some peaceful local areas provide an opportunity for some actors to reassess links of dependence. A similar situation can be identified in some regions on the Eastern periphery of the EU in which outsider populations seek to evade EU rules which impose too high levels of cooperation. In both regions obstacles to fruitful border cooperation are numerous. Far from facilitating fluid governance, borders tend to offer the opportunity for different state authorities to reassess their power assets. In the Greater Mekong region, borders often provide an indication of profoundly deregulated territories in terms of economic development. This is what is incarnated by the special economic zones, whose remit is to attract FDI on the basis of extensive social deregulation. In the case of the EU, borders can indicate extensive peripheralization, especially on the Eastern perimeters. However, they can also signal the most developed places as is the case for the industrialized pentagon surrounded by the cities of Wroclaw and Katowice in Polish Silesia, by Prague (Czech Republic), by Bratislava (Slovakia) and by Györ in Hungary.

This chapter develops three theses. The first elaborates upon the thesis presented in Chapter 6 regarding state capacity within each region to organize various forms of exchange, thanks to a step-by-step construction of territories and public interventions. Different forms

---

[1] The OECD defines trans-border governance as "the establishment of and adherence to a set of incentives, norms and organizations that are set up to coordinate policy-making in a region where the functional area of economic activities does not coincide with the geographical patterns of political jurisdiction" (OECD, 2006, 2009).

of cooperation are analyzed: From trans-regional areas (Asian growth poles and EU macro-regions) through to the more local forms, such as special economic zones, as well as very local cross-border cooperation, seen in both Europe and Asia. By themselves supranational ensembles have no real power to impose spatial planning upon member states. Their main tactic is to provide attractive incentives to member states to comply. But what are the benefits of compliance? And who benefits? Both regions face similar issues regarding the facilitation of cross-border exchanges.

The second thesis, which we have already developed in previous chapters, is that states are still the main actors. While in both regions states often manage to agree on building shared infrastructure — to develop transport networks, for instance, at the local level, cross-border cooperation encounters many difficulties demonstrating the capacity of actors at all levels — state, regional, and communal — to resist external pressures. As Chapters 2 and 3 have shown, strong states are not only those which can hold out against more "pooling sovereignty" by arguing in terms of distinct historical legacies and local comparative advantages. There are also those who can put up obstacles in order to strengthen their particular forms of domination at all administrative levels. In short, strong states are those who can reinforce their internal coherence by using external partnerships and, in doing so, reinforce their particular forms of political economy.

The third thesis postulates that the different types of public intervention in economics were designed to attract vectors for development — in other words foreign investors. For this reason, new member states were considered to be excellent terrain for the establishment of globalization in its least regulated form.

This chapter is divided into three parts. The first part concerns the EU, while the second concerns ASEAN. Within each region, particular instances of cross-border cooperation are analyzed, such as EU Euro-regions and macro-regions, and ASEAN growth poles and special economic zones, in order to facilitate a final comparison of strategies, obstacles and keys to success.

7.1. EU Cross and Trans-Border Cooperation

A unique feature of EU policy is that it steadily maps its growing territory by classifying areas and social groups. This is done in order to reflect the increasing complexity, which results from successive enlargements. Each enlargement leads to new mapping. micro-regions like the Euro-regions, meso-regions like those defined by some INTERREG[2] programs, macro-regions — like the Baltic sea — and the European Neighborhood Policy reflect the ongoing EU development process. This process increasingly makes governance the crucial challenge, raising issues about conditionality and the EU's ability to make the whole dynamic coherent. In return, states are more able to oppose domestic arrangements in order to resist integration. The different forms of regional mapping analyzed below clearly demonstrate the EU's increasing difficulty in maintaining coherence among member states. Let us start with the *Grande Region* and then further consider different regional arenas resulting from increasing EU economic, social and territorial disparities.

7.1.1. *The initial model: La Grande region*

The features, which explain the success of the Grande Region,[3] show that an integrated region is an area where there is not only economic and trade exchange, but also a shared identity which supports common institutions and promotes strong political commitment.

This region shares the political and economic ambitions of the founders of Europe, mentioned in the last chapter. All founders had their roots within territories which had been the theater of many wars. The German Chancellor, Konrad Adenauer, and the French Minister of Foreign Affairs, Robert Schuman, came from this region and

---

[2] INTERREG involves different spatially limited programs: INTERREG A refers to trans-national cooperation; INTERRG B to the trans-regional; and INTERREG C to trans-border cooperation.

[3] La "Grande Region" currently covers 65,401 ha with 2.5 million inhabitants. It is located at the heart of one of the biggest transport and city networks in Europe, with 13% of the EU flows and manages 40% of EU imports/exports.

shared the same values and the same Catholic faith (Quevit, 2005). Economically, all the regions involved had long industrial traditions based on coal and textiles.

From the 1960s onward, the whole region experienced a large-scale industrial crisis which led to a painful restructuring of the coal mining and textile industries. Over the last 40 years, 400,000 jobs have been lost[4] and high unemployment has had an impact on urban areas. Initially the Community's main objective was to organize cooperation between the Northern European founding member states of Germany, Luxemburg, France and Belgium. There is a considerable amount of daily migration which is partially linked to this restructuring process, as well as to some of the comparative advantages of border regions and states. More than 170,000 inhabitants of these states commute to work in another country, representing 40% of European migration. Most of these migrants commute to Luxembourg, as 40% of Lorraine companies target this region, and 10% of Luxembourgian companies are located in Lorraine. Luxembourg is the part of the region most targeted by French and Walloon workers, mainly because of its fiscal advantages and efficient transport networks (see Fig. 7.1).

Because of these various transport networks one can speak of the Euro corridor. In Lorraine there are eight motorways, three harbors, four railway stations, and a river transport system between the cities of Metz (the largest port for agricultural produce) and Thionville (the number one port for steel). The German region of Sarre is located in the heart of the main North to South and East to West motorways, and along the Frankfurt/Main-Berlin TGV line. The Saarlouis Dilinger, Merzig and Völklingern harbors are linked to the North Sea. Finally, in the Belgian region of Wallonia many multi-modal sites are located in the cities of Liège, Charleroi, Mouscron, and Aubange. This has resulted in a new regional logistic network of infrastructures, highlighting the importance of metropolization,

---

[4] 160,000 jobs were lost in Lorraine. There was 240,000 miners in 1969 and 69,000 in 2007. In the region of Sarre, the number of people employed in the steel industry dropped from 95,000 workers in 1960 to 19,000 in 2005. In the shoe industry, in Wallonie, 24,000 jobs disappeared.

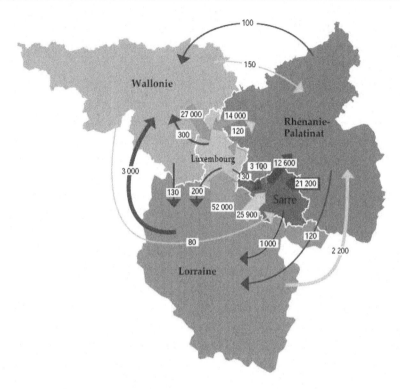

Fig. 7.1.   Worker migrations in the Grande region.

which increases the potential for sharing intertwined resources. New technology sectors are closely linked with a common labor market of highly skilled workers and backed by a dynamic network of transport connections. All these features contribute to achieving public authority ambitions to be a "model" of trans-border cooperation, not only because they give birth to other local initiatives called "Euro-regions", but also because such a "Grande Région" is a kind of blueprint for the new concept of 'Macro-region', elaborated in the 2000s.

Three macro institutions function at different administrative levels: Regions, municipalities and communes. The Sarre (German)/Mozelle (French) agreement joins four inter-communal organizations which bring the cities of Sarrebrück, Forbach, Sarreguemine and Freyming Merlebach together. Then, the "Quadropole" joins the four main cities — Trier, Metz, Luxemburg and Sarrebrücken — which are organized by a steering committee and an office that coordinates working groups in charge of transport, migration, labor markets, and tourism policies.[5] The third administrative level is represented by the Euro-region, which fosters cultural, tourist and youth projects. All these tightly interconnected institutions aim to strengthen city, university and business networks and thereby lay the groundwork for creating a strong regional cluster. This is done within a single INTERREG program, based on SMEs, networks, trans-border cooperation and social intervention in education, health, and social matters.

7.1.2. The Euro-region

Euro-regions are worth understanding in order to know what local identities mean within and outside EU territories. This more "local" program was initiated by the EU in order to foster local exchanges and to support local actors, NGOs, associations and communes. Cultural exchange is the core target of such micro-local initiatives. By encouraging these programs the EU wants to reinforce a common identity, based on trust and shared values, for people who have been divided by arbitrary historical decisions. The concept of "social capital" is very often mobilized when describing these policies (Grix and Wanda, 2002; Batt, 2001). Several Euro-regions appeared in the 1990s along the borders between former candidate countries and EU members, but also in the border regions of non-applicants like the Ukraine, Russia, and Belarus (Scott, 2002; Batt, 2001). Supported by small budgets, generally less than 50,000 euros, Euro-region projects aim to develop economic activities by supporting SMEs specialized in different sectors, such as cultural and youth program exchanges, cross-border trade, tourism, protection and joint management of the environment, information and communication networks, water, waste management, and energy management systems. Even judicial and administrative cooperation takes place, with the support of extended training courses.

---

[5] www.quattropole.org/; www.saarland.de.

Shared institutions established by border communities have to be registered by state authorities as well as by regional representatives. Many studies of Euro-regions stress that for them to function properly there is a need for political commitment at all levels, from the center out to the local authorities. If commitment from central elites is absent, trust between cross-border partners cannot develop. There are already a lot of challenges at the local level. Memories of atrocities or of unfair behaviors are too strongly anchored in local territories and in local populations to be overcome without outside support. If central state representatives do not make strong symbolic gestures, the risk of local development failing is high. It has been suggested that one of the main reasons for the success of the Nyssa region[6] and the partial success of the Viadrina region[7] was the strong commitment of the Presidents of Germany, Poland and the Czech Republic who, at the beginning of the 1990s, decided to act jointly to tackle shared problems which deeply affected all of these regions. For the "Nyssa region" the common enemy was acid rain. For the Viadrina Euro-region, it was the very large restructuring process during the 1990s along Polish and German borders (see Fig. 7.2).

Although commitment of the center is necessary, on its own it is not sufficient. It must be connected to a high local capacity to act if the regionalization process is to deliver. Lastly, success depends on the capacity of institutions from both local regions to work as partners. If the administrative asymmetry between partners is too great, cooperation initiatives will be undermined. The reasons for the success of partnerships in the West of Europe — or in Western regions of Eastern Europe — also serve to explain the lack of success of cooperation between cross-border partners in eastern regions of CEE. Presidents of Slovakian, Hungarian or Polish regions cannot manage shared projects with their Eastern partners from Belarus or from the Ukraine because they have no administrative partners at the same level. They have to negotiate directly with the central authorities in Minsk or at Kiev, who mistrust local cooperation, because there is no regionalization process in Belarus or in the Ukraine.

---

[6] Grouping German, Polish and Czech partners.
[7] Joining Germany from Frankfurt. Oder and Polish from Slubice.

EU map

Fig. 7.2. The euroregions in the EU 27.

Capacity to overcome historical legacies by taking innovative initiatives is thus a crucial ingredient for success. The great "Karpackie" region — involving parts of Poland, Slovakia, Hungary, Romania and the Ukraine — is a major example of how history can be an insurmountable obstacle to the development of trust between neighbors, even when both states are members of the EU. Identity is a very difficult challenge which sometimes, far from unifying people, divides them.[8] At the beginning of the 1990s, the official purpose of this Euro-region was to develop a Transcarpathian identity by transcending ethnic exclusivism, and by fostering broad reconciliation among local communities torn apart by history. In reality, the region has completely failed to support actual projects because of the persisting conflict between different players. The Carpathian region cannot bind its members legally. It depends on the free agreement of each partner and that limits the amount cooperation that can be achieved. Furthermore, Romania and Hungary are not official members of the region. Slovakia does not have its own managing authority, the Ministry of Regional Development takes responsibility for the Euro-region. Poland, on the other hand, has its own managing authority, is actually well organized legally, and has a strong association of 60 local authorities committed to common projects. The scope of action of these authorities is, however, limited by lack of cooperation from the other partners.

In order to explain this asymmetric organization, resulting from the lack of participation of certain members, it is necessary to recall some historical events. In the past Hungary was one of the major players in this region, perhaps the most important one. But, after its defeat and the Treaty of Trianon in 1920, Hungary lost two-thirds of its former territory and one third of its population, who since that time have been located in bordering regions: In Serbia (Vojvodina region), Romania (Transylvania) and Slovakia (the region of Kosice). This situation was never accepted by Hungarian authorities who after 1990 regularly promoted policies in favor of Hungarian minorities. This led to serious tension with neighboring states, who feared irredentism from their Hungarian minorities. That explains why Hungary wanted to

---

[8] To illustrate the complexity of the notion of "identity" in this region, prior to 1918, a person born in this region was a citizen of the Austro-Hungarian empire who then became Ukrainian in 1919, Romanian in the short period of occupation from 1919–1920, Czech from 1920–1938, German for the next three years and Hungarian until the end of World War II, then Soviet from 1945–1991 and since then, Ukrainian once again. In 1941, the population of this region of former Ruthenia was 27.41% Hungarian, 58.81%, Ruthenian, 1.55% German (more than 10% in 1910). In 1989, these figures were 12.50% Hungarians and Ruthenians were no longer recognized as such, but 78.41% were classified as Ukrainians and 3.97% as Russians (see Batt, 2001).

control what happened in the Carpathian Euro-region without actively being part of it. From the Hungarian perspective, full participation could be interpreted as an indication that Hungary accepts territorial partition. Hungarian authorities want to cooperate, but only within the territorial boundaries of the former Habsburg Empire, and only by supporting projects connected to Hungarian minorities. Therefore, Slovakians and Romanians suspect Hungarian partners of using the Euro-region to better disseminate the idea of a big supranational "Hungarian" region. In Chapter 3, we saw the same argument used for limiting regionalization. Moreover, Ukraine suspects Poland of using the Euro-region to increase its strength at the expense of its Eastern neighbors. Such a situation recalls the longstanding ill-feeling between the two states. Indeed, in the past the Polish landowners were the dominant players and Ukrainian peasants were very often exploited by Polish masters. Ukrainians, on the other hand, have been accused of committing atrocities against the Polish during WWII. Furthermore, while Poland is now a decentralized state, Ukraine remains what it has always been: A highly centralized one. All these reasons explain why cooperation within such a highly sensitive and symbolic region of the EU will probably continue to be problematic.[9]

---

[9] To better address cross-border cooperation, a new legal instrument was created in 2007: The *European Grouping Territorial Cooperation* has a legal personality and stipulates that member states are free to delegate management of an ETC program to an EGTC. With central state agreement, it became possible for local beneficiaries to have a legal personality, allowing them to manage funds, to hire people, and to sell goods. While the general principles remain the same — economic and social cohesion, sustainable development and territorial integration, with the new tool — the EGTC — peripheral regions can better "institutionalize" their cooperation with non-EU members. Therefore, besides having a legal personality, the second innovation is to name associations as potential beneficiaries of these tools by enabling them to reinforce their local and cross-border impact. Indeed, EGTC members can be member states, regional and local authorities, associations and other public bodies. In line with the new importance attached to territorial cooperation, financial support has significantly increased. The current EGTC budget is 13.2 billion euros, compared to 3.9 billion during the period from 1994 to 1999, and 4.9 billion during the last programming period for 2000 to 2006. Of the budget of 13.2 billion, 61% is dedicated to cross-border cooperation, 27% to transnational cooperation and 6% to interregional cooperation.

7.2. Beyond Enlargement Policy: Stabilizing Unsecured Borders with the ENP

The "big bang" enlargement in 2004 raised considerable issues concerning EU security. New members now border highly insecure countries, which are mostly undemocratic and connected to Russia. Located at the EU's external borders, these states are still characterized by high centralization, low economic development and considerable territorial imbalances.[10] If the 2004 Eastern enlargement can be rightly considered the biggest success ever experienced by the EU, this was only achieved by the quick and full adjustment to the *Acquis* by countries, which were under undemocratic rule less than 15 years before. It provided proof that EU strategy, tools and conditionality are applicable and that illiberal regimes can be defeated as long as a majority of their citizens declare themselves in favor of EU rules. The fact that such illiberal regimes (Vachudova, 2005) are numerous at the EU Eastern borders is sufficient reason to legitimize the EU will to export its values and standards, thanks to similar strategies and tools used during the Eastern enlargement. The EU's immediate task was to "make a particular contribution to stability and good governance in the immediate neighborhood [and] to promote a ring of well-governed countries to the East of the European Union" (European Commission, 2003b, 2004).

But far from reproducing the same logic of CEE adjustment, the number of countries that take the path of domestic transformation is very low. The EU therefore extends its norms and policies but does not guarantee integration. This is the radical difference from the eastern and Central experience, where conditionality was supported by reciprocal commitments. The EU conditioned the adjustment process upon a final integration and the candidates were forced to commit themselves by passing laws that complied with the chapters of the

---

[10] Already before the 2004 enlargement, security at the eastern border was the EU's utmost concern. "[...] threats to mutual security, whether from the trans-border dimension of [...] illegal immigration, trafficking, organized crime or terrorist networks, will require joint approaches in order to be addressed comprehensively" (European Commission, 2003a).

Acquis. In other words, the EU15 guarantees candidates the right to become EU members, including all political and economic rights, provided these candidates guarantee security for the whole community. In return, candidates commit themselves to guaranteeing collective security. Security and development are both poles that frame the collective game. Conditionality is embedded within a limited asymmetric game, forcing both players to respect their initial commitments. Path dependency is reinforced and leads to convergent actions. Candidates assume the costs of adjustments, persuaded that the benefit of integration will cover them.

7.2.1. *"No institutions"*

By saying that "everything should be shared with one exception: The institutions", Romano Prodi (2002), the previous President of the Commission, made it clear that EU members were afraid of the much greater asymmetric framework with new neighbors.[11] Indeed, the lack of firm democratic and market rules and security failures represented challenges never before met with former candidates. The difficulty of the challenges was compounded by the fact that these new neighbors had other options available to them. The crucial difference with eastern candidates is that they had had no real alternative to membership because they clearly rejected any return to the Soviet period. In contrast to new EU neighbors, who have the capacity to contest EU claims, the Ukraine is able to manipulate gas transport corridors. Russia exerts high pressure to maintain its domination over Caucasian states as well as over CEE states (see Table 7.1). Central Asian states use the weapon of oil to reorganize corridors. Some others can use the argument of terrorism to limit EU claims concerning human rights — even though the recent revolutions in Tunisia, Egypt and Libya clearly showed that the alleged Islamic threat had been manipulated by authoritarian leaders to enable them to reinforce domestic repression.

---

[11] The states involved in the ENP are: Ukraine, Belarus, Moldovia, Georgia, Marocca, Tunisia, Libya, Egypt, Israel, Palestine Jordania, Syria, Libanon, Algerie, Azerbaidjan, and Armenia.

Table 7.1.   Asymmetric resources at the disposal of EU neighbors.

	EU values	"Negative advantages"	Territorial alternatives
Southern Caucasus Georgia, Armenia, Azerbaïdjan	Respect of minorities	Oil and gas the EU supply	Russia
Moldavia	Human rights and drug trafficking	Romanian and EU security	Russia
The Ukraine	Respect of minorities, democracy	Polish and EU security	Russia
Maghreb Tunisia, Morocco	Democracy and Human Rights	Islamist threat	Great Maghreb
Palestinian authority	Recognizing Israel	Islamist war threat	

The ENP is a step-by-step approach of cooperation, transforming the initial concept of governance by making it looser and more flexible in conjunction with the four pillars that support this policy. The foreign policy of security is the first pillar, including border stability and security and the fight against crime, terrorism and illegal immigration. The Mediterranean policy is the second pillar, oriented by the EU's policy of promotion of democracy and growth, and reinforcement of civil societies and the rule of law. The third pillar comprises the enlargement policy with the *Acquis Communautaire*, the convergence process and the support of integration. The last pillar addresses economic and trade policy thanks to cooperation agreements and free zones. These different pillars are associated with different types of boundaries, which range from the loosest couplings to those with the most binding rules (Gänzle, 2009).

By intending to engage in a step-by-step transfer of norms and ways of acting, the EU uses the same procedures with non-EU members, in accordance with its traditions and habits.[12] By exerting its bargaining power it expects to have a normative resonance, capable of

---

[12] Such an approach legitimizes historical institutionalism (Tulmets, 2007) and Development Policy (Börzel and Risse, 2000, Kelly, 2006).

transcending narrow cost/benefit calculations (Kelly, 2006; Lavenex and Schimmelfennig, 2009; Barbé *et al.*, 2009). These calculations always disfavor a strong partnership because the crucial question always remains unanswered: If there is no carrot (the integration), but only a stick, why pay the cost of transformation? Why adjust? Why comply, particularly if the period of adjustment is very risky? Centrifugal forces are let loose because of administrative adaptation; civil society is required to go along with new forms of cooperation. Why adjust to EU rules and run the risk of provoking the emergence of alternative powers which put the ruling elites in danger? EU normative resonance is, on the contrary, supposed to promote "appropriateness" in neighboring liberal forces by reinforcing strategic alliances with coalitions in favor of a stable partnership. This logic of partnership is based on common action plans that support candidate strategy and which are monitored and assessed by EU civil servants. Different programs exist, such as Tempus, and trans-border cooperation (ENPCBC), programs for transport and energy, and programs for immigration and human rights.

Does it mean that there has been no progress at all on the Eastern border and that the "step-by-step" EU approach is a failure? Measured by the scale of its initial objectives — the transfer of EU norms and standards — the results have been disappointing. Illiberal domestic coalitions still seem to be the norm. For the past few years, Ukraine has not shown any willingness to adjust to EU standards, in fact quite the contrary. Russia stands in the way of Georgia's ambitions to join NATO and the EU. The ceasefire set up in 2008 clearly indicated the limits of both partners, Russia and the EU. Moldova cannot rid itself of Russian influence, which is supported by highly corrupt domestic networks which have close connections with Russian criminal networks. Belarus continues to stay out of the EU game, more or less protected by its Russian neighbor. Certain instances of trans-border cooperation, however, give some grounds for optimism. Agreements have been signed with Ukraine and Moldova concerning illegal immigration. The principle of return to the last transit country is generally accepted, even though a very negative consequence of this has been the spread of large refugee camps at the Ukrainian–EU border, where refugees can wait months, even years, for papers which are not forthcoming. Furthermore, human trafficking at Moldavian, Romanian and Bulgarian or Turkish borders has not been brought under control. In January 2011, finding that Bulgarian and Romanian borders were not sufficiently equipped with the relevant security and information systems, France and Germany refused these countries Schengen member status. The Schengen zone aims to strengthen border controls (internal borders, external borders) through police cooperation,[13] using the Schengen Information System that makes visa cooperation (Common Consular Instructions) and data protection[14] feasible.

7.3. The Macro-Regions

The latest type of regional entity to be created by the EU commission is the "macro-region". The first is the Baltic Sea macro-region, the second is the Danube basin macro-region (EU, 2011). Although further areas are in the works — like the Black Sea, the North Sea and the Mediterranean Sea — the EU is waiting for results from the first two macro-regions before extending this experiment to other regional entities. The EU's is taking a cautious approach because of the importance of this regional initiative: It is important not only because it embraces a very large number of EU citizens — 80 million in the case of Baltic Sea region and 52 million within the Danube basin — but also because it is expected to perform better than previous regional development policies.[15] Furthermore, and perhaps of greatest significance, it intends to achieve regional integration based

---

[13] Articles 39, 40, 41 Schengen Convention: Are Also Connected to Schengen Legislation the Law on the Border Guard, Law on the Participation of the Different States in SIS and VIS, Act on Aliens, and Bilateral Agreements.

[14] Strategic Documents are needed (like Schengen Action Plan, Master Plan, Integrated Border Management Strategy), Adjustment of Legislation, Infrastructure and Procedures and finally, Financial Measures.

[15] "Opportunities that EU membership provides have not yet been taken and the challenges facing the region have not yet been adequately addressed" (EU, 2010).

on common resources, shared identities and reoriented strategies. In a word, what is expected from "macro-regions" is for them to be laboratories for future EU regional policies, by bringing innovative solutions to the complexity resulting from previous enlargements, new border uncertainties and key global issues like environment and security. Therefore, the Baltic strategy has identified four pillars that cover the main EU development objectives: Prosperity (innovation), sustainability (environment), security (energy), and accessibility (transport). These four pillars cover 15 priority areas which encompass over 80 flagships programs.[16] As an EU document observes, "Full advantage of the … opportunities that EU membership provides has not yet been taken and the challenges facing the region have not yet been adequately addressed" (EU, 2010). Some issues, such as the environment and sea pollution or security and energy transportation have still not found acceptable solutions (*ibid.*) Also, heterogeneity and interdependence of the region make cooperation and coordination essential (*ibid.*). Finally, important non-EU state actors must be involved in decisions concerning all riparian states.

Before explaining the originality of the macro-region it has to be mentioned that the Baltic Sea macro-region was not the first regional framework to be established in this region. Many previous commissions and transnational organizations were already established in the 1990s. All of them targeted common challenges concerning the environment (the Baltic Sea is one of the most polluted seas in the world), security and social development. The first such organization was the Helsinki Commission (HELCOM)[17] dealing with pollution prevention measures; the Council of Baltic Sea States (CBSS), established in 1992 in response to the end of the Cold War, aims at creating a political forum for regional inter-governmental cooperation.[18] Since 1992, "The Vision and Strategies

---

[16] Flagship projects are either strategic — addressing specific and important issues, or cooperative initiatives aimed at improving partnerships between members.

[17] HELCOM website http://www.helcom.fi/helcom/en_GB/aboutus/.

[18] The Members of the Council are the eleven states of the Baltic Sea Region as well as the European Commission. The states are Denmark, Estonia, Finland, Germany,

around the Baltic" (VASAB) outlines a spatial development perspective for the region in order to unify the different spatial planning policies. Since 1999, the Northern Dimension (ND)[19] intends "to provide a common framework for the promotion of dialogue and concrete cooperation, to strengthen stability and well-being, intensify economic cooperation, and promote economic integration, competitiveness and sustainable development in Northern Europe".[20] Lastly, the Euro-region Baltic (ERB), established in 1998, targets cooperation in the South-East of the Baltic Sea region, involving eight regions of Denmark, Lithuania, Poland, Russia and Sweden. It is the first euro-region to have formally included a partner from the Russian Federation. Two city-networks, set up in 1991 and in 2002, were created to mobilize cities and metropolises, and later, in 1998, an information network to create a platform for exchanging information (see Fig. 7.3).

7.3.1. *"3 nos": No new institutions, no new rules, no new funds*

There are, however, no new funds from the EU side to achieve the tasks linked with the new Baltic strategy. This is one of its principal failures because a new way of acting collectively is expected and must be developed using no new rules, no new funds, and no new institutions (Bafoil and Michal, 2011). These three "nos" are supposed to incentivize stakeholders who are invited to re-orientate their own strategies and budget. By doing so, the responsibilities of each participant — the EU commission, states, and regions — are expected to be reasserted within a renewed multi-level system of governance.

Iceland, Latvia, Lithuania, Norway, Poland, Russia, Sweden and a representative from the European Commission Council of Baltic Sea States. (Website http://www.cbss.org/CBSS-The-Council/the-council).

[19] By four equal partners: the European Union, Norway, Iceland and the Russian Federation.

[20] European Union External Action (Website http://eeas.europa.eu/north_dim/index_en.htm).

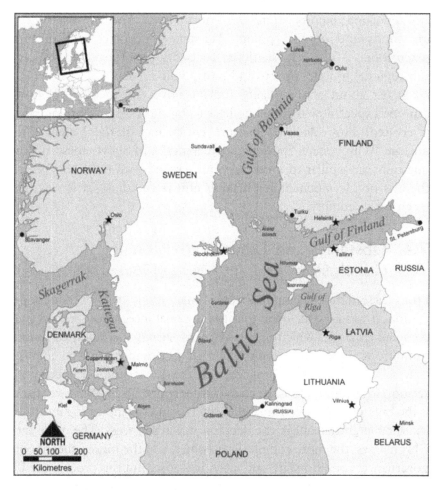

Fig. 7.3.   The Baltic macro region.

As a EU document states, the Commission is expected to exert "soft power" in the role of "overall coordinator", "external facilitator", and "impartial honest broker" (European Commission, 2009, pp. 4, 6), while the strategy is drafted and implemented "from within" (European Commission, 2009, p. 5), meaning by the national and sub-national governments and different stakeholders. The European Commission fulfils the tasks of coordinating, monitoring, facilitating and reporting; member states are Priority Area coordinators, directing funds and contact points. Partners — project owners and practitioners — are transnational (network), national, regional or sub-regional, public, private and non-public actors.

Issues about conditionality and incentives are crucial. But how can one expect new regional policies to be successful if nothing new is created? How does one ensure compliance if the benefits are unclear? Why restate "pooling sovereignty"? In short, these major questions are similar to those previously raised with the ENP: When there is no clear benefit for making efforts to adjust, where is the incentive to comply?

7.4. Obstacles and Limits Provisional Conclusion

From these different empirical case studies about cross-border cooperation, it can be concluded that the regional integration process is a complex dynamic, which is created from shared identities, common institutions and political commitment. This dynamic must be empirically differentiated in accordance with the size of the community in relation to the importance of cross-border cooperation. What we stress is the causal link between enlarging the EU and the increasing incapacity to coherently manage the decision-making process. The more the EU enlarges, the more complex it becomes, and the more issues about governance, conditionality, and incentives arise. But this process of EU weakening is counterbalanced by a process of reinforcement of member states. Institutional complexity can be useful for states, as it can enable them to manipulate increasing uncertainties in order to avoid mounting collective obligations. The more EU enlargement there is, the more the member states are able to resist collective pressures.

7.5. Southeast Asia, from Coastal Regions to the Interior

The Southeastern Asian model of cross-border cooperation displays a large variety of representations, from growth poles to "economic corridors", along which special economic zones are located, irrigating a mushrooming border activity and low level exchanges. The basic forms of these cross-border exchanges are rather simple: Asymmetric exchanges of cheap labor for high financial investments. But such an exchange is not enough to support development. Political commitment is of definite importance in understanding the dynamic of institutionalization or a lack of development. Fiscal exemption, land-leasing and infrastructures facilities can lead to development but can also appear to be a waste of resources if they do not take place within institutions. It is worth mapping the Southeast Asian territory in a step-by-step way by considering different forms of cooperation between states and also between regional and local partners. Regional integration is first of all supported by "hard" and "soft" infrastructures.

Some factors can be highlighted to explain successful local development based on combined asymmetric exchanges — low wages versus financial flows — anchored in particular territorial areas and framed largely by institutions. The Asian Development Bank considers the Chinese case — particularly the Shenzhen Special Economic Zones (SEZ) — as a model not only because it succeeded in promoting growth but also because it has provided a long-term growth model. In a very systematic way it succeeded in linking urbanization and industrialization; universities, skills and production, R&D, and infrastructures and tax incentives and OSS (ADB, 2007). Analyzing Southeastern Asian SEZs, Ishida (2005) emphasizes the importance of harbors and a large labor market for export-oriented economies, which explains the location of SEZ close to seas and ports. Aveline-Dubach (2010) completes the picture by emphasizing four features: "A large-scale area where land is developed in accordance with a comprehensive plan ... An area served by roads, infrastructures, utilities and services ... Sale and lease of factory buildings for manufacturing purposes ... Controlled development with restrictive covenants for the benefit of both the occupants and the community at large". Recent studies have shown how and under what conditions transport infrastructure can lead to very limited regional development and how some SEZ open the door to enclaved growth without any surrounding spillover (Bafoil and Lin, 2010).

Because of the remarkable and rapid progress of China, its Southeast Asian neighbors could not afford to ignore this model.[21] They saw in such development the opportunity to secure peace and development and a way to make ASEAN stronger. Different pictures of territorial mapping emerged: Growth zones, growth poles, then SEZs. All of them take place within an ASEAN strategy that intends to be competitive and urgently needs to attract FDI in order to guarantee growth. For Krongkaev, the Growth Triangles concept "refers to the exploitation and complementarities among geographical contiguous countries to help them gain greater competitive advantage in export promotion" (Krongkaew, 2004). Obviously, China provides the model of the SEZ. But it also represents the most serious competition for ASEAN, because China has attracted and continues to attract the largest share of FDI, particularly since 2000.

7.5.1. *Growth poles and special economic zones*

By supporting the most successful growth zone in the 1990s — the SIJORI growth triangle — the ASEAN vision was to guarantee both regional security and the reinforcement of the core actor of the region — Singapore — as a hub of activities (Parsonage, 2003). From this perspective, regionalization is understood as simultaneously

---

[21] Taken together, some components of the Chinese experience of local development can provide an attractive "model" for southern Asian territories, although there are clearly large differences in levels of political commitment between China and Southeast Asia. Political commitment — in other words governance — was of definite importance in opening the Chinese economy to worldwide exchanges, thanks to the setting up of SEZs. Within these equipped zones, a low-paid Chinese workforce could find employment from investors from the north who wanted to develop products for exports. Central and regional Chinese authorities used this opportunity to step-by-step develop their own territories by equipping them, thanks to educational institutions and economic firms, which both organized the supply chain of foreign investors (Naughton, 2009). Linguistic and territorial proximity to rich Hong Kong and Taiwan represented the optimal option for the establishment of SEZs in coastal areas, such as Shenzhen, Zhuhai and Shantou in Guangdong Province and Xiamen in Fujian Province.

based on intergovernmental agreements and cross-border cooperation, because only this type of cooperation can be conducive to peace,
security and development. In such a process, the special zone wit-
nesses a double level of intervention: From states and from MNEs.
The state regulates economic activities and provides a legal framework. For Parsonage "The extensive nature of state intervention in
Southeast Asia SGZ illustrates the necessity for the continuation of
functions traditionally provided by the state, such as provision of
infrastructure and maintenance of a legal and social environment conducive for accumulation, to be maintained as capital transcends formal national borders" (Parsonage, 2003, p. 271). Jenkins defends the
same idea by arguing that the real superiority of new industrializing
states is not that they have succeeded in shifting from an import substitution strategy to an export oriented one, but that they exemplify
"the ability of the state to direct the accumulation process in the
direction which is required by capitalism development at particular
points in time which is crucial" (Jenkins, 1991, p. 224, quoted in
Rigg, 2003). This is the definition of the developmental state. It is
based on the capacity of central states to promote rules capable of
both securing control at the borders, fostering flows of capital, and
elaborating international rules of cooperation with international partners.[22] By doing so the state reinforces links with regional and local
authorities and attracts foreign investors linked to domestic
interests.[23]

---

[22] "What distinguishes this strategy from wholly domestic policies designed to further
the same interest is the requirement of formal or informal intergovernmental agreements to foster enterprise through the liberalization of legal and political restrictions
inhibiting 'natural' economic integration in contiguous state territories in order to
share the factors of production" (Weatherbee, 1995).

[23] "... states are important actors in resolving the contradiction inherent in the transnationalisation process. ... For though national boundaries are becoming increasingly
irrelevant for flows of capital, states also have an interest in preserving national borders as a means of constraining highly values services and industrial niches in order
to enhance national economic competitiveness. ... Capital is also dependent on the
state to maintain the conditions for economic regionalism and manage potentially
fractious political and social consequences" (Parsonage, 2003).

Many sub-regional cooperation zones have been created: The Indonesia–Malaysia–Thailand Growth Triangle (IMT-GT in 1989), the Brunei–Indonesia–Malaysia–Philippines–East Asia Growth Area (BIMP-EAGA in 1994), the ASEAN-Mekong Basin Development Cooperation (AMBDC in 1994, the AEM-METI Economic and Industrial Cooperation Committee (AMEICC), and the Mekong River Commission (MRC in 1995). The GMS was created in 1992. Their main objective is to facilitate the connection between different countries and regions, thanks to infrastructures, railways in the case of IMT GT, and roadways within the GMS.[24] In contrast to the previous Chinese model, Southeast Asian regional development schemes are not so much based on tariff reductions as on structural impediments of infrastructures like roads and checkpoints which permit easier customs procedures (see Fig. 7.4).

Other than the GMS "economic corridors", only SIJORI can be considered a relative success. The other Southeast Asian growth poles have been much less successful. The reason for this failure is the fact that the comparative advantages of each side are too similar: They are based on the same low-paid workforce, while financial and powerful investors are absent, which in turn leads to inappropriate transport investments. Concerning the first areas mentioned (IMT-GT and BIMPT), the most important criticisms address the unclear potential economic complementarities and a lack of regional importance of national infrastructures (Verbiest, 2012b). Finally, joint agreements are criticized for being too formal. For these reasons, the key to success seems to be strong asymmetries between partners, a presence of financial investors and a strong commitment from the central authorities. SIJORI clearly shows this as do the "economic corridors", and to a much greater extent, because of their more effective governance.

---

[24] "in summary, growth areas contribute to closer governmental communication, greater people mobility, joint-venture business investments, expanding tourism earnings and an economic up lift for specific areas that had been neglected in the past. Trade and people mobility have always been the backbone of growth areas" (Thambipillai, 1998, p. 263).

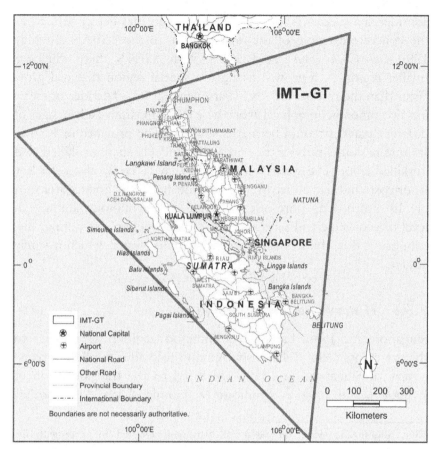

(ADB Map)

Fig. 7.4.   The IMT — GT.

7.5.2. *The case of SIJORI: Reinforcement of the central states*

In December 1989, Singapore launched the proposal of a "growth triangle" made up of Indonesia, Malaysia and Singapore". Step-by-step, the project took shape, expanded, and very soon it was considered a success.[25] Indeed, ASEAN authorities depict SIJORI as the concrete example of the entire future of the ASEAN. In May 1990 *Goh Chok Tong* stated that "within ASEAN there will be a smaller region — a growth triangle, a special region that will grow faster than the rest of ASEAN" (Parsonage, 2003). The idea of creating a common geographical area where the comparative advantages of different partners could be met is simple.[26] The province of Riau in Indonesia could provide raw material, and cheap semi-skilled and unskilled labor. The state of Johor, in Malaysia, could also offer low labor costs and had a thriving tourist industry, and a good water supply. In return, Singapore offered capital and technology, and a high level of economic and service activities (e.g., design, marketing, distribution). But, the city-state urgently needed water, which it sorely lacked.

7.5.3. *History and geography matter*

Singapore and Johor have a long common tradition dating back to the pre-colonial era. Relations were reinforced after the British rediscovery of Singapore in 1819, which led to the transformation of a poor island into a significant economic Asian "entrepôt".[27]

---

[25] On August 28, 1990, Indonesia and Singapore adopted an agreement, the Singaporean Riau Economic Cooperation Agreement that extended the economic zone to the Island of Batam and to the whole surrounding region of Riau. In February 1992, the three heads of government adopted an agreement to increase their cooperation, and in December 1994 they concluded a memorandum of understanding (MOU) foreseeing a series of regular meetings. During the first semester of 1996, the Malaysian provinces of Pahang and Negri are similarly integrated into the project, and in 1997 so were five other Indonesian provinces: W Sumatra, S Sumatra, Lampung, Benkulu, Jambi.

[26] Speaking of SIJORI, which we will analyze below, Patronage (2003) states "the basic concept of growth triangle is deceptively simple, in that a vertical division of labor in industry is proposed to exploit differentials in industrial development and production cost, in effect creating a sub-regional 'theater of accumulation' based upon external manufacturing capital stradling state borders".

[27] Turnbee, Singapore Present and Past NUS, especially the 1st chapter, "The New Settlement," pp. 21–50.

Furthermore, the three partners are geographically connected: Johor is only 2 kilometers from the Singaporean straits, and Batam only 20 kilometers away. 50,000 Johoreans commute daily to Singapore while Johor attracts Singaporean tourists, who possess the highest purchasing power of the region. The cooperation between Singapore and Riau — only 35 kilometers away — is more recent. An international airport is located at Batam, which is experiencing increased international exchanges (Thambipillai, 1998). But Singapore urgently needs to diversify its partnerships.

7.5.4. *Asymmetric exchanges and reciprocal dependency*

Thanks to this economic zone, a new division of labor in Southeast Asia emerged. It is based on an asymmetric exchange of capital and cheap labor (see Table 7.2): Malaysia and Indonesia supply cheap workforces to the firms that will be financially supported by Singapore. Johor receives massive funding for its textile, chemical, electronic and agro-industrial sectors, while Riau attracts investments in electronics, textiles and tourism. In the space of a few years, cooperation in the tourism sector reached USD10 billion, 60% of the investments being Indonesian and 40% Singaporean. The Singaporean development benefited from EU, US and even Asian joint ventures which invested in Johor, while the Singaporean state supports domestic firms and sets up strategic alliances with foreign investors in the island. At the

Table 7.2. Comparative cost of land and labor in the IMS-GT 1989 (in USD).

	BATAM	JOHOR	SINGAPORE
Land (per square meter)	2.30	4.08	4.25
Unskilled labor (per month)	90	150	350
Semiskilled labor (per month)	140	220	420
Skilled labor (per month)	200	400	600

Sources: From Harvest International (1990) in the Hong Kong and Shanghai Banking Corporation Ltd's Guide to the Growth triangle Batam–Johor (Singapore, 1992, quoted Smith, 1997).

beginning, FDI mainly targeted textile, rubber, light industry, food processing and low value electricity sectors. Then, step-by-step, as skills were upgraded and Singapore became highly institutionalized, and FDI became more technologically oriented. Malaysian development was based on FDI, tourist facilities and a reliable supply of a female working force — mainly unskilled rural women.

But beyond the official declarations praising cooperation and partnership, there are much more straightforward reasons for the huge reciprocal dependency between the three states. Each of them is highly dependent on the others. 40% of Malaysian trade goes through Singapore and Singaporean tourism reached USD400M per year. 50,000 visitors and 18,000 cars go across the bridge daily (Thambipillai, 1991). On the other hand, at the beginning of the 1990s Singapore faced a serious crisis because of the dramatic decrease in FDI. Furthermore, the City Island urgently needed basic resources, like water of which it has suffered serious shortages since the separation from Malaysia in 1965. Lastly, huge daily migrations of people from Malaysia must be controlled and fixed. For some observers these steady migrations should be a wake-up call to Singapore, which seems unable to control them. To this extent, SIJORI is an attempt to control this important security issue. As Parsonage (2003, p. 269) says, "the regularization of labor migration also enables participating states to preempt intra-regional friction over illegal immigration and guest labor from undermining sub-regional linkages". Strict legislation was adopted which controls daily commuting by imposing a work contract limited to two years, and provides dormitories in Batam where workers are forced to live.

Indeed, Singapore and Johor cooperate, as do Singapore and Riau, but there is no tripartite cooperation. An agency was created, but nothing more came of it. There is no common industrial policy, because of the perceived danger that it would result in strengthening of Singaporean leadership. Such reinforced cooperation is avoided for fear of intensifying the rivalry between Johor and Riau. They share the same industrial advantage: A cheap, low-skilled workforce. While there is a formal agreement between Singapore and Riau, no such thing exists to regulate relations between Singapore and Johor. Finally, reciprocal dependency has been increasing and solutions to date have been inadequate. In order to combat the Singaporean idea of developing partnerships with other regions, Indonesia seeks to transform Batam into the most important deep water harbor in the region.

In the end, the SEZ of SIJORI strengthens the cleavage between the core (Singapore) and the periphery (Malaysia), hence the widespread feeling of resentment among Malay citizens. Huge social animosity is fueled by the increasing cost of land and the resulting inflation. But worse, it appears that SIJORI is not the success story that it is claimed to be by the ruling elites, who benefited most from this new cooperation. The most frequently cited firm is the Singaporean Technologies Industrial Corporation, the first firm specialized in electronics and defense material, and in Indonesia, the Batam Indonesian Park, whose factories cover 500 has and employ 8,000 people (under Indonesian contract), and the Holding Salm Group. Suharto's sons and Prime Minister Habibie are closely involved with these firms. On the Singaporean side, the situation is very similar.

7.5.5. *The case of GMS: States and a non-state actor*

The GMS "economic corridors" correspond to the highest developed form of regional development schemes in Southeast Asia. Compared to the previous regional initiatives, they encompass a wide vision of economic development which addresses the CLMV divide and embodies the ASEAN strategy.[28] This vision is based on the articulation of transport infrastructures[29] with cross-border trade agree-

---

[28] "ASEAN has in fact used the GMS framework as it determinedly pushes to integrate the four less developed members more deeply and more quickly with the rest of ASEAN ... 9 of the 16 projects have become integral parts of ASEAN highways". Available at http:/www.aseansc.org/3256.htm.

[29] The objectives of economic corridors is to "(1) provide a spatial focus to GMS activities, with the backbone, growth centers, and nodal points catalyzing the development of surrounding localities; (2) open up many opportunities for various types of investments from within and outside the sub-region; (3) promote synergy and enhance the impact of sub-regional activities through the clustering of projects;

ments and other development policies regarding, for example, the environment and tourism. But the originality of the GMS economic corridors lies not only in this conjunction of "hard" strategies — road infrastructures — and "soft" strategies, represented by the Cross Border Trade Agreements (CBTA). It is also found in the involvement of states, businesses and NGO players (see Fig. 7.5).

From a geographical perspective, the main difference between growth poles and economic corridors is the fact that the corridors cover much more spatial territory, as growth poles were limited to borders. From 1992 to 2010 the whole Great Mekong sub-region territory was covered by these economic corridors. They connect metros from Kunming to Bangkok, from Bangkok to Saigon through Phnom Penh and, to a lesser extent, from Kunming to Hanoi and from Yangoon to Danang. They enable the opening of trade facilities and the development of very remote regions. Whereas once, during wartime, the GMS regions were in a very disadvantageous position, they have now become the main link between China, Singapore and Indonesia. From a broader perspective, its geographical location makes it a land-bridge between the Southeast (islands), the East (India) and China. Indeed, these "economic corridors" not only map the ASEAN mainland, they also connect it to two sub-continents: northwards to Chinese territory through Thailand, Myanmar, Laos PDR and Vietnam, and eastwards to India through Cambodia, Thailand and Burma.[30] These corridors can therefore be considered the first attempt to achieve a Southeastern spatial planning comparable to what the EU intends to do with the Trans European Network

---

(4) provide a mechanism for prioritizing and coordinating investments among neighboring countries; and (5) generate tangible demonstration effects."(ADB, 2009, p. 3).

[30] One of the most important Cambodian strategies is to integrate The Mekong-India Economic Corridor (MIEC) joining Cambodia, Myanmar, Thailand and Vietnam with India through its east coast. This corridor links the most important Cambodian cities: Sihanoukville is the deep Cambodian sea port (83 meters), linked with the Phnom Penh railway, and where a large number of SEZs and industrial investments are planned. Moreover, it is an emerging tourist destination close to Oil & Gas production areas.

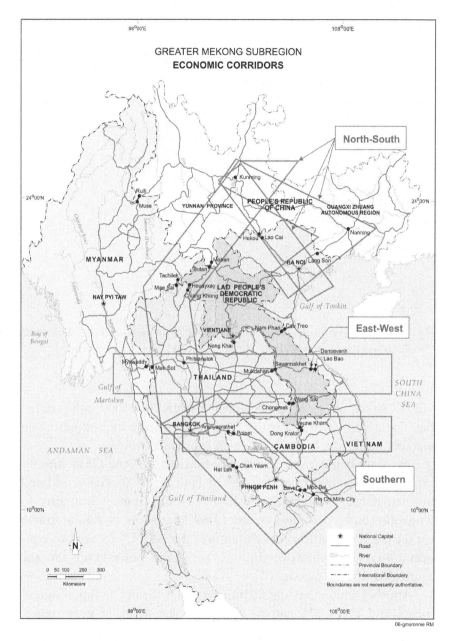

Fig. 7.5.　The Greater Mekong Sub-region corridors.

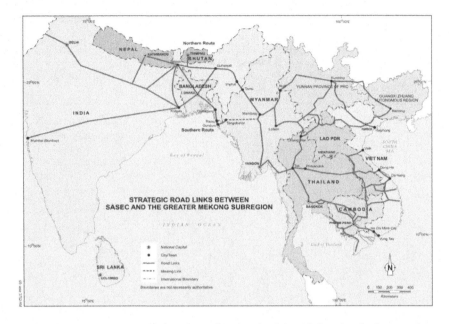

Fig. 7.6. Strategic roads between the South Asian Subregional Cooperation (SASSEC) and the Greater Mekong Sub-region (GMS).

(TEN), which will be supported financially by cohesion funds (see the Fig. 7.6). The GMS is a major connection to the biggest emerging markets and a new frontier for Asian economic growth.

Far from being limited to road infrastructures, the GMS strategy now encompasses railway strategy. In January 2010, Hanoi adopted the first railway strategy that would not only connect Kunming to Singapore but would also create 4,069 kilometers of railway tracks within CLMV countries. In the future, the ASEAN intends to connect other GMS infrastructures to the Asian power grid and the Trans-ASEAN gas pipeline.[31]

Another important distinction between former regional agreements and the GMS can be found in the form of governance.

---

[31] Avaiable at http://www.vmekongmedia.com/content/view.php?code=tot290910-20320128.

"Economic corridors" are mainly supported by a non-state actor, the Asian Development Bank (ADB), even though cross-border agreements remain under state responsibility. ADB financially supports the construction of motorways but the project of "economic corridors" is much more than that. Its objective is to connect different regional areas by facilitating trade and, therefore, by lifting up barriers at the different borders (Banomyong, 2005). ADB has developed a multilateral instrument covering all aspects of cross-border transport facilitation that needs to be ratified by all GMS members. These cross border trade agreements (CBTA) were made in 2007 at seven key border crossing points and the plan was properly launched in 2008 when all the annexes and protocols to the CBTA were ratified. In 2009, CBTA have been fully implemented and by 2010 sub-regional institutional coordination arrangements have been formulated in order to monitor the full implementation of the CBTA. Accompanying CBTA the strategic framework for action on trade facilitation and investments (SFA-TFI) has been set up to facilitate the movement of goods, people and vehicles.[32] Obviously that is the main challenge that ADB can manage by training qualified people, financing local technical equipment and facilitating dialogue between partners. But the final decision — the border agreement — depends on member states. For these reasons, the type of governance that supports this intervention is less multilateral than bilateral because the core issue is about cross border agreements.

CBTA unify and simplify procedures of control by organizing both a single-window inspection — customs, quarantine, immigration — and a single stop inspection of entry and exit ways. They are of the utmost importance because everything depends on the final stage of cooperation and communication at the local level. If there is no trust between partners, nothing can happen. A single window inspection can only succeed if it is based on a strong partnership

---

[32] GMS (2010, p. 4). The SFA-TFI led by the Trade Facilitation Working Group placed under ministerial responsibility. This group develops a regional work program by mapping national and regional mechanisms to support trade facilitation.

between representatives of different ministries who are not used to working together. For example, people from the Agriculture Ministry, in charge of animal control, must work in a single room with people from the Trade ministry and with the Ministry of Home Affairs in charge of immigration.

7.5.6. The 3 "Cs"

As of 2011, because these economic corridors as "hard infrastructures" are almost complete, the most important challenge for member states is to organize their local and regional development. Economic corridors, therefore, provide not only the best ways of reducing transport logistics costs (Rolant-Holst et al., 2008), they also support emerging local sub-regional economic zones which can specialize in various sectors such as tourism, water management, environment, biodiversity reserves, etc. These developments can make zones safer by controlling illegal immigration, trafficking of women and children, and the spread of communicable disease. Different programs targeting the development of tourism[33] or environmental protection[34] are supported by ADB in cooperation with national, regional and local populations. For these reasons, "economic corridors" contain the most general representations of ASEAN regional development embodied by the 3 "Cs", mentioned above: *Connectivity* because the CBTA intends to maximize the benefits of sub-regional transport infrastructure; *Competitiveness* because that will result in improved efficiency arising from smoother flow of goods and people across borders; and *Community* because the CBTA fosters a greater sense of community and promotes harmonization of rules and procedures.

---

[33] 2005, *GMS Tourism Sector Strategy* (2006–2015) — seven strategic programs and 29 priority projects, including development of 16 thematic strategic projects and 13 priority tourism zones.
[34] with selection of core areas of biodiversity and implementation of performance measurement.

However, as said above, aside from formal agreements and legal procedures, success is based on the establishment of trust at a local level between population and officers. If civil servants at the local borders do not play the game by respecting common rules, there is no chance of projects being successful. As Verbiest (2012b) says, "the software part of cross-border transactions is very much dependent on people and institutions". Several studies are critical of obstacles that impede CBTAs. They point to a serious lack of communication within the administrative hierarchies because some documents are written in English and not available in the domestic language. They also criticize the fact that local people are not involved in the decision-making process. Legal regulations within CLMV are absent. Lastly, many local civil servants are frequently moved from one place to another, making training sessions useless. Institutional capacity is weak and poor governance remains the main obstacle to improved institutional performance.[35]

7.5.7. *The special economic zones*

One of the positive effects of these economic corridors upon their immediate environment is the mushrooming of SEZs which emerge along borders, in metropolitan areas, and by rivers and seas (Ishida, 2005).Thant insists on the importance of political commitment at the regional level: All infrastructure (water, power supply, roads, navigation lines and telecommunications) needs to be part of international production networks (Thant *et al.*, 1998). Last, the ADB (2009) defines a SEZ as "a specific geographic region with economic laws that are more liberal than a country's typical economic laws".

---

[35] as Bafoil and Lin (2010) note "there are still several resource constraints, problems of streamlining and harmonizing border control documents due to conflicting issues and differences between the legal and regulatory frameworks of the respective member countries, the lack of understanding of the agreement by local officials and also the lack of available information for the private sector" (p. 111).

7.6. Developing Dependencies

The development of SEZs mirrors the strong divide between the founders of ASEAN, where SEZs are flourishing, and the CLMV countries, where there is less support for SEZs (see Table 7.3). Compared to other maritime Southeast Asian countries, the CLMV countries' comparative advantages are linked to their plentiful supply of cheap labor, due to the continued presence of a large agricultural sector, in which worker remuneration is low. These conditions are, however, shared by all riparian Mekong states, which results in fierce competition within the CLMV group (see Table 7.4). In this context, being competitive means offering the best conditions regarding fiscal incentives and land use; in other words, the winner is whoever can increase its dependency by offering the most advantageous benefits for the external partner. The poorest countries — Lao PDR and Cambodia — are offering land use for up to 99 years and exemption from corporate tax for 10 years. Within CLMV, all these SEZs base their strategy almost exclusively on fiscal incentives, low costs, and trade facilities.[36] They aim to attract foreign investors by offering them optimum conditions for free trade, and by organizing within the SEZ a "one-single-shop", within which all customs documents are delivered. A place is provided for investors to negotiate with representatives

---

[36] For instance in Cambodia, corporate tax is 20%, tax holidays are up to 9 years. Full Import Duty Exemption, repatriation of profit (withholding tax and reinvestment of earnings (special depreciation) are allowed. In Laos, there is a corporate profit tax of 8–10%; tax holidays go from 2–10 years starting from the first profit making year; personal income tax: 5% for both local and foreigners with SEZ. Losses carry forward 5 years. Investors enjoy 12 years lease exemption, subleasable within lease period. All exports and imports of manufactured products receive exemptions from tax and customs duties. There are corporate income tax holidays of up to 8 years. Reductions last 5 years. Import duty reductions or exemptions exist on machinery and raw materials. There is a double deduction for public utility costs, deductions for construction/installation costs infrastructure, and 100% land rights ownership for foreign investors. Foreign investors can repatriate profits and enjoy full property rights over land (100% freehold ownership) (in other Southeast Asian countries it is said that joint venture with 51% ownership is more often the rule).

Table 7.3. Number and trends of SEZ in GMS (2011–2015).

Country	Total (2011)	On-going (operational)	On-going (implementing)	Proposed	Total (2015)
Burma	6	0	0	6	6
Cambodia	24	6 (2009)	1	N/a	24
China	1	1	n.a	na	1
Laos	8	5	—	3	32
Thailand	6	0	1	5	6
Vietnam	4	4	n.a	n.a	4

Sources: ADB (NSEC, EWEC, and SEC Action Plan).

Table 7.4. Labor costs in the greater Mekong sub-region.

COUNTRY	Minimum wage (US$/ month)	Standard workday	Maximum working days per week	Minimum daily rest required by law (hours)
Cambodia	43	8	6	14
China	182.5	8	6	13
Laos	63.7	8	6	no express minimum number (12)
Thailand	279.5	8	6	1
Vietnam	49.9	8	6	no explicit provision, but a limit of 12.

from the central ministries of labor, health, customs and home affairs, without having to wait for long hours at the central ministries to obtain the relevant documents.

Deep social divides and developing dependency result from this policy based on a new public/private partnership. The top elites in the central ministries are able to negotiate with private organizations in charge of developing these zones, and allow them carte blanche there, as long as they pay up. All the SEZs are sold to foreigners — mainly Taiwanese, Malaysian and Japanese organizations — by central authorities who are handsomely paid for their cooperation. At the local level, firms are managed by foreigners while workers are nationals. In Cambodia the latter are paid $61 per month (for working 10 hours days), while the former earn over $1,000 a month. Organizers intend to attract foreign investors whose only contact is with representatives of central ministries, who are in charge of preparing the legal documents. Representatives of the Labor or Health ministries are not responsible for worker safety. Therefore, working conditions are very hard, trade unions not allowed, and strikes forbidden. Furthermore, "anything goes" when it comes to guaranteeing that poor territories "catch up". Countries like Laos and Cambodia have developed a kind of "casino economy" close to Laotian and Cambodian SEZs. So-called "casinos", located along borders, are centers for gambling and prostitution, and attract Thai and Vietnamese customers who have a much higher purchasing power than local people. A strong dependency on foreign investors and considerable degree of corruption result from these various public initiatives. Based on such observations, some studies have determined that a developing dependency exists (Bafoil *et al.*, 2011). Critics address the lack of functioning governance by stressing how the one-shop-service falls short: Business people are forced to sign documents at both cross borders and not at just one place. Incentives are criticized, particularly those related to land leasing, for creating a heavy dependence on foreigners. Low wages lead to high turnover, and in the end there is no spillover.

7.7. Comparison between European and Southeastern Asian Schemes

Finally, what kind of lessons can be drawn from cross-border cooperation? Strategies, state aid and obstacles can be compared in order to better highlight some of the keys to success.

7.7.1. Strategies

As seen in the previous chapter, ASEAN has not developed a "grand" strategy of regional development comparable with the EU Cohesion policy. The EU "grand policy" targets, in a coherent manner, growth, employment and balanced territorial development objectives, thanks to funds and a set of rules. Whatever their institutional differences, both regions consider development of transport infrastructures as their main public policy. Infrastructures support growth by reducing transaction costs and increasing agglomeration externalities and knowledge accumulation. They favor development by facilitating access to public goods (Bafoil and Lin, 2010). By connecting main cities and regions, transport infrastructures are expected to open up landlocked regions and increase local markets, tourism and local assets. Connectivity promotes development by enhancing competitiveness. Therefore, transport infrastructures are key, both for the GMS strategy with its "economic corridors" and for the EU, where transport infrastructures represent about 28% of all structural fund expenditures.

In both regions the flagship terms refer to the same objectives: "Connectivity" is used in the EU and in Southeast Asia; Southeast Asian "Competitiveness" targets exactly what European "Concentration" aims at developing: Growth. Both "Community" and "Cooperation" are considered the best ways to foster people-to-people contacts in order to re-build shared identities rooted in local territories. Moreover, the first objective, "connectivity", is supposed to be the causal link supporting the two other main objectives. Improvement of infrastructures is the basic policy expected to be conducive to development.

7.7.2. State aids and regional policies

National states are the major players not only because they use fiscal policy to support SEZs, but also because they orchestrate connections with main investors. All of them base public aid on the same formula: A combination of tax exemptions, excise taxes and diverse facilities (see Table 7.5). In Eastern Europe, state aid has relied on tax relief, soft loans, guarantees for banks loans, credit incentives, depreciation allowances and subsidies. In some regions, these kinds of aid may be coupled with some conditionality related to job creation, as in

Table 7.5.   Policy incentives in GMS Special Economic Zones (SEZ).

Country	Tax holiday	Corporate income tax	Import Duty and other taxes	Others
Cambodia	Up to 9 years	Standard: 20%	Tax exemption: Import of equipments, construction materials and production inputs	Custom duty exemption on the import of machinery, equipment for construction of public services infrastructure.
China	Exemption for 2 years and reduction for 3 years (local portion).	Standard: 25% 15% preferential tax rate.	Exemption from import duty and customs-levied import tax; export overseas exemption;	Financial support; The traffic fee incentives: The traffic regulation fee will be levied at a 20% to 35% discount
Laos	Z1 Up to 10 years Z2 Up to 8 years Z3 Up to 4 years	Standard: 20% (outside the zone) 8%–10%		Custom duty for plant, equipments and raw materials; tax exemption in Business turnover tax and excise
Myanmar	Manufacturing: 5 High-tech: 8 years	Standard: 15%. 50% for the second 5 years;	Free trade on export; Custom duty free on import commodities.	

(Continued)

Table 7.5. (*Continued*)

Country		Tax holiday	Corporate income tax	Import Duty and other taxes	Others
Thailand	Z1	3 years	Standard: 30%.	50% reduction on machinery; 1 year exemption on raw material.	
	Z2	7 years		Exemption on machinery; 1 year exemption on raw material.	
	Z3	8 years;	50% reduction in income tax rate for an additional 5 years	Exemption on machinery; 5 year exemption on raw material.	Double deduction on public utility cost;
Vietnam		Up to 4 years	Standard: 25 % Reduce rate: 10% in 15 years: EZ, HTZ; 10%: E&T, Health, environment;	Raw materials, machinery and equipment in preferential sectors and locations.	

Bulgaria,[37] with the amount and duration of investments, as in Poland,[38] or with fiscal facilities and regional programs, as in Hungary.[39] In Hungary a few crisis-hit regions have been targeted, such as the Northern and Northern Southern Great Plains, and the Central and Southern transdanubian regions. In Germany, the so-called "New Länder" are supported through regional programs that particularly target both very fragile sub-regions, and mono-industrial sectors that have almost exclusively shaped the regional profile. This is the case of the Eastern part of Brandenbourg and the city of Eisenhüttensdat, which before 1989 had 50,000 inhabitants, 12,000 of whom worked in the local steel mills.

Some Southeast Asian national measures for economic development are not very different from European ones.[40] New Vietnamese policy incentives applicable to cross-border economic zones allow provinces to retain more than 50% of total tax revenue collected in the border economic areas, providing that the total revenue is less than VND 100 billion per year, and up to 50% if total revenue is more than VND 100 billion per year. Also in Vietnam, regions face high unemployment benefit from public aid and fiscal incentives. Use of the state budget and preferential credit is allowed in order to develop infrastructure within the locality. Concerning trade, tourism, and banking systems, duty-free areas and exchange counters may be set up. In all GMS countries, land rental, land and water use are offered at low prices for both domestic and foreign investors in

---

[37] In Bulgaria, investors are exempted from corporate tax in several regions (mainly where unemployment is high), there are some additional grants for salaries and social insurance, training and retraining of staff.

[38] In Poland, financial support for new investments may be granted if the following conditions are met: Investment of a minimum of €10 million; Investment of a minimum of €500,000 and creation of a minimum of 100 jobs for five years, and creation of at least 20 jobs/year, and lastly, introduction of technological innovations or environmental improvements.

[39] In Hungary there are two forms of incentives: Aid granted under the decree relative to the incentives/ Investment and tax incentives. Income tax can be reduced up to 80% for investments in some preferred regions.

[40] See footnote 3 in Chapter 2.

border economic areas. Everywhere, immigration formalities are simplified to become "one door" procedures at border checkpoints using a "single-window". Support is given to import and export activities, such as temporary import for re-export, transit of goods, duty-free shops, trade fairs, exhibition showrooms, export-processing industries, and domestic and foreign branches and representative offices.

7.7.3. Obstacles

For all these reasons, cross-border cooperation obviously has the positive effect of opening up marketplaces; people can thereby supplement the meager revenues they earn from unprofitable small-scale agriculture. This is the case in both regions, particularly EU eastern peripheries and Mekong riparian locations. Poverty alleviation is certainly achieved, because most of the poor populations live at the cross-borders. Nevertheless, while poverty has undoubtedly declined near the Thai and Vietnamese borders,[41] this is less clear in the cases of Myanmar, Lao Pdr and Cambodia. There, people living close to Thai borders are very dependent on exchanges — garments, trade, transport, services — and seasonal movement of agricultural labor to Thailand. Furthermore, there is no general agreement concerning the development of transport infrastructure capacity to efficiently combat the landlockedness of certain regions, like Laos. Some people are afraid that economic corridors will reinforce this isolation by only addressing the needs of the extremities of corridors — Bangkok and Kunming — and not the regions in between. In Laos NGOs point to the environmental destruction caused by the numerous transport projects undertaken in that country. Within the EU, infrastructure

---

[41] In Thailand, a positive impact is noted within 5 km of the checkpoint (higher incomes and consumption, direct benefits with labor markets, hostelry, restaurants, guest houses etc. The authors conclude that "poverty reduction impacts from these activities are likely to be considerable" (p. 13). In Vietnam, it is the same because people can acquire cheap products and for this reason, "it has been a way for people to escape from poverty" (Myers and Wharton, 2007, p. 239).

policies have met with the same kind of criticisms. In 2008 a serious conflict occurred between Polish central authorities, who had decided to build a motorway from the capital to the Baltic area, and NGOs who were determined that the very well-known ecological region, through which this hard infrastructure would need to pass, would not be sacrificed. The arguments of the NGOs finally prevailed, thanks to support from the EU Program Natura 2000, and the project was abandoned. In both regions, connecting two regions or the capital to a peripheral region seems to be unproductive and even counterproductive if the connection reinforces a sole migration path, at the expense of the periphery. Development does not result from growth if it not also accompanied by crossed policies — education and services — which must be anchored locally.

The positive argument about transport infrastructure must also be mitigated by the fact that people living in Southeast Asian border regions are rather poorly educated. Furthermore, illegal immigration and trafficking of human beings are widespread, and women and children are often forced into prostitution and other work. In Southeast Asia, competition is very intense, demand is limited, and local situations are dominated by powerful cartels that are able to limit regulation. This deregulated situation allows organized corruption, fraudsters, prostitution and trafficking to flourish. Some similarities can be found at the eastern periphery of the EU, concerning seasonal work in very small and labor-intensive farms in Eastern Hungarian, Slovak and Polish regions. Throughout these Eastern borders regions, Moldavian and Ukrainian (and Caucasian) trafficking is commonplace. Trafficking involves not only cars and drugs, but also women. Many studies stress the same failures of the market and the public sector: Lack of management at the local level, incomplete decentralization, and no delegation of power at the local level.[42] There is also a

---

[42] see *Economic Cooperation Strategy* 2003 Office of Area development NSDB which "points out the rapid growth of the cross-border economy of Thailand, that need immediate attention, such as the unpreparedness of the province to accommodate development and the resulting social and security problems, drugs trafficking and degradation of the environment" (p. 148).

lack of adequately functioning agencies and banking systems. Insufficient rules for industries increases disorder.[43] Finally, in both regions, various critics point to a number of ways in which governance is inadequate. A too vertical bureaucracy and uncoordinated decentralization are criticized for hampering local initiatives. On the other hand, the lack of regulation induces growing corruption which only works in favor of groups that are already organized and have connections with local authorities. Also, in both regions, the lack of well-defined local priorities by regional authorities is frequently criticized (Bafoil and Lin, 2010; Barca, 2009).

7.7.4. Core and periphery: the "grey zones" at the local borders

Finally, relations between core and peripheries show some similarities. The stronger the core, the more regulation there is, which in turn leaves peripheries unprotected and insecure. Indeed, the stronger the periphery, the more deregulation there is, leaving local political economies unchanged. Although the highly regulated Schengen system provides a lot of protection for EU members, it makes the local and informal cooperation that was previously developed along eastern borders that much more difficult. During the 1990s, these eastern borders were the scene of immense disintegration, resulting from the breakdown of the Soviet-type economy, and an absence of FDI or appropriate measures from local actors to adapt to the new rules. Suddenly, a lack of state subsidies left populations, who had previously been accustomed to a high level of support from the central authorities, in a desperate situation, which was made worse by the fact that no FDI went to the most backward regions (OECD, 2008). As a result, during the 1990s, various informal markets emerged along eastern borders, where a lot of immigrants from former Soviet Republics came to sell small things and to look for employment. They

---

[43] "While trade, tourism transactions and other economic activities have been spurred, the absence of specific regulations on these operations has often led to chaos and market disorder" (Myers and Wharton, 2007, p. 220).

found work in very small privately owned Polish, Czech and Slovak farms, which were now able to survive because their wage bills were much lower than their counterparts in the west of these countries.[44] The second shock affecting these eastern regions came with the *Acquis* adjustment. Chapter 21 of the *Acquis*, dealing with regionalization, imposed a reduction in the number of former administrative city regions in favor of a few bigger regional cities, mostly located far from the borders. The third shock came with the adjustment to the Schengen law, strictly regulating the granting of expensive short term visas to non-EU citizens, which lead to the destruction of this informal economy.

The "grey zones" on the Eastern borders of the EU have Southeast Asian counterparts. In a detailed empirical-based study, researchers from the Cambodian CDRI analyze the very particular local political economies backed by the same trade chain (Myers and Wharton, 2007): Principals and suppliers, suppliers and producers, traders and cartels, cartels and public authorities. All of them are strongly intertwined through close links which frame a stable political economy often interpreted in terms of "patrimonialism".[45] Loans are granted by the "patron" (or by the local trader to the petty local traders) who in return commit themselves by selling their whole stock to the patron. In some Thai cases, patrons send their orders from Bangkok to the cross-border intermediaries or send raw materials to local clients, who proceed with the transformation and then sell it at the border or re-export it to Bangkok. In contrast to this Thai method, petty trade predominates at Vietnamese and Cambodian

---

[44] Such a difference about hourly wage rates helps to explain why eastern territories managed to survive during this period.

[45] "Usually small payments have to be made at the border. Key elements frequently associated with these informal flows include dependence on personalized relationships that have evolved over time and are sustained by repeat transactions between traders or between traders and customers. The rapid growth of the Thai–Cambodian garments processing and trading system is an excellent example of how informal arrangements based on simple incentive mechanisms (for example repeat transitions that enable credit relations to develop and promote trust) can generate large, complex exchange systems cutting across international frontiers" (*idem*, p. 12).

borders.[46] Cambodian petty traders come by bicycle or motorbike, bringing small volumes — of a value of less than US$5 — made up of all kinds of products that they then sell to intermediaries. These intermediaries work at the border and represent four or five Cambodian traders who visit Vietnam once a week. These intermediaries have their own shops located a matter of kilometers from the border, while big intermediaries, based in the capital city of Ho Chi Minh City, collect all the goods traded within the city, following the Cambodian orders.

7.8. Conclusion

From a more general perspective, the main key to success for regional development policies, and particularly cross-border cooperation, can be found in a combination of different factors. They are related to the history and politics of each state, as well as consistency in governance, connecting different actors from the top to the bottom, including public, private and non-public actors.

The histories of both regions have been full of conflict. Trade and cross-border cooperation aim at supporting big or small development projects connecting people and traditions. Historical legacies can be a positive asset as long as central actors are willing to use them as resources by implementing good policies. In Southeast Asia, as Thambipillai (1991) writes, "only the full support of political forces can help sub-regions within a federal system and promote cooperation without risking political reprisals". But central policies must be launched with the cooperation of decentralized authorities. A major condition for success lies in the complex combination of central and regional commitments to local projects. Decentralization has a positive effect as long as it is backed by strong institutions.

At the local level, confidence and trust are vital. For Thambipillai (1991) "confidence in the benefits of participation through the triangular relationship would be the only guarantee of success of the new ventures in sub-regionalism". But how is trust created? How can one

---

[46] "very small traders who deal fully on their own" (p. 232).

have confidence in a partner when in the past that partner had offended you? This is an issue of major concern for the EU. Euroregions are created in order to respond concretely and very locally to such a challenge by developing local networks. Trust is expected to emerge thanks to the networks of proximity and close cooperation.

This implies for the social agenda the need to contextualize public policies by targeting the less privileged groups and by harmonizing the different institutions and policies. Regarding territorial agenda, it must be understood that development occurs thanks to different groups and communities, that public policies must target the least privileged groups in order to foster social inclusion, and that coherent, efficient, and different institutions and policies must deliver public goods in order to foster business activity.[47] Therefore, "the social agenda must be territorialized and the territorial agenda must be socialized. The place-based approach to social inclusion should be the result of these two shifts" (*idem*, p. 33). Therefore, in both our cases, at the regional and cross-border levels, formal and informal links are of crucial importance.

---

[47] "We define social inclusion as the extent to which in a set of multidimensional outcomes that define people's substantive opportunity to live according to their values and choices and to overcome their circumstances, all persons (and groups) can enjoy, through a participatory and fair process, essential standards and the extent to which in the same set of multidimensional outcomes and through the same process, the degree of disparities among persons (and groups) is close to what is socially acceptable" (Barca, p. 27).

8 EU AND ASEAN ENLARGEMENT: ENLARGED GLOBALIZATION DYNAMICS

There are four reasons to conclude this work with a look at the latest enlargements in both the EU and ASEAN. The first reason is the generally accepted assumption that enlargement in both regions has mainly been brought about by political motives and not directly by economic ones. Challenges to security have prevailed over any other considerations. The second reason is that even if political motives underpinned enlargement strategy, the major drivers of the globalization dynamics that began in the 1980s, have been the new members in each region who had hyper-liberal visions of both enterprise and decentralization. In this context, industrial relations have become significantly less important, as seen in Chapter 5, and the state has greatly reinforced its capacity to redistribute power as it sees fit. Third, because enlargement in both regions has been an important driver of globalization, helping to "depoliticize" the decision-making process, the perception of the national state as the most neutral and expert actor has been reinforced. For these different reasons, enlargement closed one dynamic and gave birth to another characterized by lesser regulation. Lastly, a final reason — and perhaps the most important — must be mentioned. It is connected to internal opposition to these two regions created by the latest enlargements and which have sometimes led to blockages in collectivity. These difficulties linked to the integration of new members have led to the suspicion that once they were integrated the new members would not obey the interests of collectivity if these interests clashed with their own.

The realist perspective postulates that a given state only joins a supranational ensemble because it has to and on condition that the final benefit will be worth the cost of adjustment. The benefit drawn from membership must be superior to the cost of entry into the group. When political conditionality is strong and though it may sometimes be difficult for new member states to accept additional pooling of sovereignty the possible benefit to be drawn from membership must be seen to represent a greater interest. However, once integration is achieved, the reasons for making an effort must be made explicit. It would otherwise be difficult to understand why the very difficult process of adjustment should be undergone if the effort were not compensated for by the promise of finally becoming a member of the group. Rational action postulates that self-interest must be satisfied to support collective action. Political conditionality stops once membership is accomplished or when potential benefit is seen to be lacking. From the moment when a new sate joins the group, either the benefits of belonging or other appealing alternatives must become clear.

The most obvious benefit of becoming a member is the political legitimacy associated with belonging to an international ensemble. However, for older members the negative aspect of the arrival of these new members into the EU is that it slows down the process of integration. This is because further political integration would impose a greater pooling of national sovereignty on the new members. To put it bluntly, it is in the interest of ASEAN and EU candidates to comply with regional rules during the process of integration but once they become members, reinforcing the political mechanisms of collective action is less of an issue for them. That is exactly what happened with Slovakia when as a very new member of the euro-zone it was one of the most ardent adversaries of financial support for Greece in 2010 and 2011. Earlier, Ireland and Poland hesitated considerably before signing the Lisbon Treaty which was designed to increase the EU's institutional capacity but which limited Irish and Polish representation. When the CLMV joined ASEAN, the challenge was to turn the principle of non-interference to their advantage in legitimizing their own non-democratic regimes. Having succeeded in their mission, they demanded that the shared principle be strictly respected so that they might continue on the same domestic path.[1] In conclusion, it is evident that small states have no immediate interest in reinforcing regional EU or ASEAN institutionalization because increasing regulation implies increasing control of the group over its members, in effect forcing them to be more accountable. Increasing control entails too much reassessment of the political weight of larger members. On the other hand, limiting control is equivalent to reinforcing non-binding rules, informal exchanges, and fewer multilateral agreements.

The first part of this chapter looks at the political reasons for enlargement in both regions. Enlargement has resulted in remarkable political and economic gains for all new member states in both regions. The second part considers the conflicts between "old" and "new" member States within each region. In the third part, the losses resulting from these enlargements are analyzed by showing how the types of dynamics characterizing the earlier decade were later blocked. The last part compares both regions from the historical perspective.

8.1. Political Reasons for Enlargement

Recent enlargement in each region is much better explained by political motives than by economic ones. Even if administrative requirements prevailed in the EU during the last phase of preparation, in the end only political considerations counted in achieving enlargement. However, before examining these considerations let us look at three main reasons not to make a comparison between the enlargement that ASEAN underwent in the 1990s and the EU a decade later.

First, the economic levels were too different for a valid comparison to be made. In 2000, the average purchasing power in the EU of 15 was about US$26,500 yearly per citizen while it was US$11,500

---

[1] "Decision are hard to reach when any participant can wield veto power. According to the view, the institution's evolutionary pace is deliberately held back by the lowest common demonstrator" (Solingen, 2005).

for the 10 EU candidate countries, a difference of 43%. In Southeast Asia, the situation varied depending on the country. In Singapore and Brunei, purchasing power was at $20,500 per citizen as opposed to $5,200 in Thailand, Malaysia, and the Philippines — a difference of 25.3%. This was much higher than in Cambodia, Laos, Vietnam and Myanmar, where it stagnated at $1,650 (8%) (Yap, 2007). Second, the two most important economic leaders in each region, cannot be compared if the correlation between demography and political weight is considered: With 4.5 million inhabitants and less than one million respectively, Singapore and Brunei are not at all in the same playing field as Germany with a population of 82 million and France of 65 million. Finally, there is three times as little intra-regional trade in Southeast Asia as there is in the EU. This reflects Southeast Asia's rather weak regional integration as opposed to very strong integration in the EU (Bafoil and Lin, 2010).

It is nonetheless difficult to refrain from comparing when the nature of the "political shock" in each region and its impacts are considered. In the EU, the term "political shock" as used here refers to the integration of ten former Soviet-type satellites into the EU. In Southeast Asia, it refers to the merging of two former and still communist countries (Vietnam and Laos), as well as two very authoritarian ones — Cambodia and Myanmar. The economic shock was equally significant as evidenced by the increase in internal differences already discussed in the previous chapter. Two pieces of data should be underlined: In the EU, before 2004 the gap between the top 10% of the richest regions versus the bottom 10% of the poorest was less than 1:3. This ratio more than doubled after 2007. Similarly, in Southeast Asia, the level of GDP per inhabitant in Singapore was around US$28,000 in 1990, more than 80 times more than in Laos or Cambodia. Moreover, in both regions, new members were not only much poorer than older ones, they were also much more diverse in their composition. Ethnic and border conflicts refueled tensions that were not as acute among former members, at least in the EU. Hence, the basic principle of national sovereignty was reinforced at the expense of other more federalist dynamics. Lastly, beyond political and economic challenges, enlargement united people who had followed completely different historical paths, paved with entirely different representations and sometimes values. For these reasons, scholars of both areas consider that enlargement has weakened the former regional ensembles. For Dent (2008), "one problem that both ASEAN and APEC have experienced over recent years is that organizational coherence can be significantly weakened by enlarged membership. Encompassing too much economic, political and socio-cultural diversity can hinder the progress of regionalist projects". However, both regional ensembles decided to enlarge in spite of these huge "political and socio-cultural" differences, and the reasons for this merit attention.

This is mainly because of the huge economic gap between both parts of each region. It was obvious from the outset and indeed before it even took place that, at the very least, enlargement would result in economic fragility. In the EU, it was widely acknowledged that economic and social recovery would take a long time and be expensive. It was plainly obvious that German unification had overstretched the German public budget by more than 100 billion euros in just one decade. German unification affected 17 million inhabitants while in Eastern and Central Europe continental reunification directly concerned over 100 million. In 2000, the EU commission published a report asserting that Central European states would need at least 30 years to reach the EU average growth rate (GDP) while this period would be over 60 years for Baltic and Balkan States. This issue was all the more relevant as at that time there was already tough and divisive debate among EU members not only about the size of the EU budget for structural funds but also about the effectiveness of structural funds. In Southeast Asia where compensatory financial mechanisms do not exist, the debate was of a much more political nature. It focused on how to ensure that shared visions for common regional development would be forged among enemies so often divided by war and destruction. In both regions however, political reasons have been the main force behind unified regions.

8.2. Beyond Economic Challenges

For EU members, enlargement was driven mainly by political motives, namely by the idea that the division of the continent imposed at Yalta in 1945 was an arbitrary consequence of the war. The law of victory was not acceptable in an EU based on rule of law. Moreover, it was only a matter of luck that Western population was on the "right" side in 1945, as opposed to the "wrong side" in Central and Eastern Europe. To this extent, enlargement was a mix of moral duty and a desire to repair historical unfairness. Barbara Lippert rightly speaks of an EU feeling of moral responsibility *vis-à-vis* its eastern "cousins" whose strong desire to join the EU was legitimized by East European intellectual and political authorities advocating a "return to Europe" (Lippert, 2006). Europe was considered to be a family deprived of unity by mere historical accident. Sedelmeier has rightly stressed this shared representation of a common cultural EU between West and East to explain the fundamental basis of the unification process, despite the economic difficulties that have constantly accompanied the process of adjustment for the East to meet Western prerequisites (Schimmelfennig and Sedelmeier, 2005). To this extent, German unification in 1990 represents a kind of model on how to proceed between two different economic units, even if disparities there have been claimed by some observers to refute the idea of any unification between both parts of Europe. Although German unification encountered such enormous difficulty, even bigger economic gaps elsewhere would be impossible to overcome. On the contrary, it is because neighboring countries do not share the same sense of identity and values, and because domestically illiberal majorities prevail that they cannot — and do not — want enlargement (Vachudova, 2005). Such remarks call for a consideration of the various reasons that legitimize enlargement.

In a very similar manner, enlarging ASEAN to include Cambodia, Laos, Vietnam, and Myanmar has responded to the same objectives from a historical perspective. Acceptance of these four very poor "small countries", was part of the "old dream" of a united region

(Boisseau du Rocher, 2010). However, no actor in the past, either foreign or regional, had been able to create something resembling a Southeastern identity. The Great Powers — British, Dutch, American, French, Chinese and Russian all failed (Pholsena and Banomyong, 2004). As mentioned in the first chapter, the colonial empires failed to create a Southeastern identity; nor did the Dutch "ethical mission", the French "mission civilisatrice" or the Japanese "Co-prosperity area" succeed. Communism also failed to create a Southeastern identity (Pholsena, 2006b), even though anti-Communist feeling was the main reason for creating ASEAN. As Lee Kuan Yew writes, "Anti-Communism provided a sense of identity to states that were otherwise so diverse that they were referred to collectively as the "Balkans" of Asia. They joined forces primarily for "political objectives, stability and security" (Webber, 2001). Subsequently, post-colonials and post-Communists failed to build a Southeast Asian community capable of competing as a block against either the former Great Powers — the US, Russia and China, or the economic giants — Japan and China. Uniting the main Southeastern Mainland with the founding ASEAN members would diminish the risk represented by the ever-changing politics of the "Great Powers". Reinforcing ASEAN would mean quelling their desire to consider Southeast Asia as their own playground or as a shared battlefield. Moreover, in 1967, ASEAN appeared to be an "improbable" entity that nobody could imagine would last more than a few years. To this extent, reinforcing the links was a clear signal of the project's sustainability. Enlargement meant the end of the Cold War and an opportunity for ASEAN to proclaim itself as a peace-keeping organization capable of competing with Western states on human rights issues. Lastly, enlargement was a shared preoccupation for "middle" states such as Thailand and Vietnam who had become more insecure as a result of the new rules of the international order. For Thailand, the main reason for accepting enlargement was the changing geopolitical order: Continually changing US policy, the new alliance with China and constant conflicts with its Cambodian and Laotian neighbors also forced it to secure its position. For Vietnam, there was an urgent need to find an alternative to three acute challenges: The disappearance of its Soviet ally, the very difficult position resulting from the Cambodian occupation from 1979 till 1991, and the economic policy pursued during the last decade through the *Doi Moi* reform. Belonging to ASEAN allowed the *Doi Moi* policy to be continued and provided the best option to secure political resources. Thanks to the principle of non-interference, Vietnam could continue to proclaim its Communist orientation and the situation was similar for the Cambodian Hun Sen. ASEAN was therefore perceived to be the best ally in the legitimization of authoritarian regimes.

Finally, the enlargement which took place in 1997 and 1999 corresponded both to preoccupations linked to security in the member states and to shared values which facilitated the creation of a regional identity. From this point of view, ASEAN closely resembles the EU whose goal was as much to secure borders to the east of the union as it was to reformulate European identity. According to the constructivist approach, shared values support collective action not only because they create satisfaction, but also because they shape preferences and decision-making processes. For both these reasons, shared norms shape collective identities. In many of his works, Acharya emphasizes the long-term perspective of norms in Southeast Asia that are peace-oriented.[2] Material interests and making a profit do not suffice to explain the importance of rules and the survival of institutions if they are not backed up by a strong consensus of norm-sharing. This is the basis of the "Asian way", which according to Acharya, "… consists in a code of conduct for inter-state behavior as well as a decision-making process based on consultations and consensus.… "in this respect, the 'ASEAN way' is not so much about the substance or structure of multilateral interactions but a claim

---

[2] "Ideas and cultural norms provide a crucial inter-subjective framework for interactions and socialization leading to the creation and maintenance of multilateral institutions even in areas which previously had no experience of such institution-building. But the impact of ideas and norms especially if they originate from outside a given regional socio-political context, depends to a great extent on self-defined identity of the local actors" Acharya (1997).

about the process through which such interactions are carried out" (Acharya, 1997).[3]

8.3. Political Challenges: Large versus Small States

In ASEAN as in the EU, small states have the same *de jure* capacities as larger states. *De facto*, they have even better ones. Those candidate countries who defended the principle of national sovereignty in order to adhere to EU rules later recognized that membership of such a worldwide community was actually the best way to protect themselves against any external threat. Moreover, as EU members they became more visible and recognizable on the world scene. Few people were familiar with Latvia before it assumed the EU presidency. Small members could never have dreamt of having such a worldwide audience outside the EU. The Baltic States for instance receive EU support when they are in conflict with their powerful Russian neighbor as was the case in 2009 when a crisis occurred subsequent to the removal of a statue representing a Soviet soldier from Estonia. Romania can advocate Moldavian interests and denounce the arbitrary and artificial existence of the Transnitrie State without the risk of being sanctioned as in the past, when Soviet rule prevailed. In 2009, Poland could postpone the ratification of the Lisbon Treaty as long as it wanted to, without being sanctioned by other members who were forced to respect its choice. Likewise, by joining ASEAN, Cambodia and Laos found an excellent arena to prepare to join the WTO. Cambodia has been a member since 2004 but Laos has not yet joined. Hun Sen, the Cambodian Prime Minister, could use the

---

[3] Alan Dupont adds an interesting perspective by stressing the fact that Southeast Asian identity relies on the conviction of that self determination is possible. "Finally, Asians are determined to deal with their own problems in their own way. The fact that their own 'way' may not be as uniquely Asian or culturally driven as some contend, is not as important, ultimately, as the widespread Asian conviction that the region's destiny is in the hands of the Asian for the first time in nearly 500 years" Dupont (1996).

principle of non-interference to reject any criticism of his politics by blaming ASEAN for not having respected its own principles.[4] The Junta in Myanmar used the same arguments to continue its arbitrary and inhuman politics, despite Aung Sung Suu's liberation in November 2010.

However, serious the problems which the Myanmar Junta created for the image of ASEAN by constantly violating human rights, its military chiefs were guaranteed the silent support of member states defending the principle of non-interference. Malaysia criticized the ASEAN position concerning Hun Sen's coup, and proposed a "constructive intervention" consisting of direct assistance with elections, administrative and legal reforms, the development of human capital, and receptiveness to civil society and the rule of law. Thailand was more in favor of greater intervention, wanting to shift from the "diplomacy of accommodation" to a more politically and economically oriented "flexible engagement" or "enhanced interaction".[5] However, other countries feared the growing power of Thailand. Although they were ready for a more "constructive intervention", they were nonetheless reluctant to delegate more domestic powers to ASEAN and to Thailand. Human rights were not values shared by other members who were afraid of the emerging NGOs that were better connected to international networks. Non-interference remained the core principle. Therefore, the alternative principle of "constructive engagement" failed and the "participative regionalism" as suggested by Acharya did not occur (Acharya, 2003). After the events of September 11, 2001, campaigns against terrorism provided a useful tool to preclude any delegation of power and reinforcement of democracy.

Finally, some observers accuse new member states of being "free riders" because they use collective resources, whether principles or institutions, only in order to better defend their own national

---

[4] Hun Sen: "I am afraid of joining ASEAN because of ASEAN interference in internal affairs" quoted in Acharya (2009, Chapter 2, p. 117).

[5] "Constructive engagement" in the words of an official source in ASEAN "means that each ASEAN country can do what it wants, say what it wants but not take a collective six-countries position" Acharya (2009).

interests. This was the major reproach made to Myanmar which was considered to be unwilling to satisfy expectations concerning human rights by continuing to plead the non-interference cause. This same reproach was made to new European members when in 2003 they decided to support the Bush initiative to invade Iraq.[6] They sent the famous "letter of the eight" to Bush without informing the other member states who were deeply opposed to such an "alignment" with the US position. Poland, particularly, was sharply criticized for having supported pro-Atlantist choices while at the same time demanding more financial support for its own economic development. Another great disappointment was the very low turnout in the June 2004 European elections, in spite of the fact that the new member states had joined the EU only two months before.[7] Overall, it was clear that new member states had taken advantage of political and economic benefits but had not reciprocated with any sense of duty. More generally, the capacity to challenge the hegemonic power of "big" states can be counted as one of the "major strengths" of "weak" states.

8.4. Lack of Hegemony

Both the EU and ASEAN were born out of a fear of Communism and fears of hegemony (Webber, 2001). In parallel with the emergence of regional ensembles as a result of the threat of Communism, medium-sized and small states were given the opportunity to secure their own interests by reducing the influence of the bigger states. It was imperative to reinforce the European community in order to confine German power just as it was imperative to reinforce ASEAN in order to limit Indonesian influence. Both Germany and Indonesia were potential hegemonies and were clearly recognized as the most powerful actors within their own areas. For many observers, the European community

---

[6] It is interesting to note that among these eight signatures, only three were "Eastern States": Denmark, Spain, Italy, Great Britain, Portugal, Hungary, Poland and Czech Republic.

[7] Although a wide majority had welcomed membership in May 2004, in June of the same year, only 20% of Poles and less than 16% of Slovaks went to the polls.

provided an important arena to ensure that Germany subscribed to collective goals. In Southeast Asia, Thailand, Singapore and Malaysia joined forces to restrain Indonesia. By leading the political coalition, France obtained the status of main EU political driver as long as Germany was split into two states and was thus reduced to the status of political "dwarf" — even if it was actually an economic giant.

In Southeast Asia, the situation was different. Considering that "what is still missing in the Asian community is a common set of political values", Frost (2008) asks who and where are the equivalents of Monnet, Schuman, Adenauer and Gasperi in Asia. In other words, where are the leaders capable of supporting a cultural project such as the supranational ensemble, sharing the same vision of worldwide development, based on common religious — (Catholic) — and political convictions — (the fight against Nazism). Moreover, an equivalent of the French–German duo or in other words, the vital hegemonic driver likely to propose a common model of economic and political development has yet to be identified. Could the USA play a leadership role in Asia or perhaps China or Japan? The US is unable to assume this role because of the Asian population's widespread resentment of it.[8] Japan cannot play this role due to its historical role in Southeast Asia and because it is forbidden from doing so by the US. Singapore is the most powerful economic member of ASEAN and the biggest beneficiary, but it is also the smallest country (apart from Brunei) and the member most often blocked from becoming the political leader due to the economically liberal and Chinese origin of its President Mentor Lee Kuan Yew. Indonesia lost its status of hegemony after the 1997 crisis and even before that when the smaller ASEAN countries questioned Suharto's leadership. All states fear that China could play this role in the near future because of its power and capacity to present an alternative to Japan and the US. Higgott echoes this view when he considers that leadership is a key factor in the building of an

---

[8] "…what they saw was when Russia and Brazil had their crises, they (the Americans) rushed in, and they didn't do that for Asia, and even though these countries had been considered very loyal friends by the Asians" in *Financial Times 2000* quoted in Webber (2001).

integrated union, and for ASEAN, this leadership depends on the position of both economic giants — China and Japan.[9] Reinforcement of institutionalized exchanges does not create more institutionalized cooperation and indeed, one feature which is particular to Southeast Asian states is that there seems to be no policy coordination. As Mark Beeson (2006) stresses "… most of the ASEAN economies are competitive rather than complementary and they are consequently often locked in struggles to attract the same sorts of investments and penetrate the same sorts of markets". This is very similar to the situation in CEE where the cohesion policy has not managed to impose close coordination.

Self-interest and political conditionality legitimize the process of integration. The idea of "shared identity" itself could play a major role for both the EU (Sedelmeier, 2010) and Southeast Asia, (Acharya, 2009) even though at times it may seem to be just an illusion as the reactions of new EU members to the Iraq war, or those of ASEAN members to Myanmar reveal. As shall be examined further below, new members from both ensembles have made decisions that have deeply angered older member states, who considered these new members to be displaying a lack of gratitude for the privilege of membership. Therefore, ideas about "social construction" can sometimes resemble empty shells, covering only the illusions of their authors (Jones and Smith, 2007). Current initiatives can seem to legitimize national interests at the expense of collective ones; the dynamics of consolidating integration are no longer part of the game.

8.5. The End of a Dynamic?

Beyond short-term political considerations the key issue is indeed the fact that enlargement has put an end to a dynamic which

---

[9] "The presence of, or the absence of, the emergence of some kind of collective leadership, or at least consensual cooperation, is the major instrument for, or obstacle to, any advancement of regionalism in Asia. Without a 'historic compromise' between China and Japan economic integration will remain a distant prospect" Higgott in Delo (p. 77).

strengthened collective action in both regions. New members are criticized for having hampered the impetus by securing their own national interests. In this respect, rather than having empowered each region, enlargement has in effect weakened them.

8.5.1. *The limits of western deepening*

In the 1980s and at the beginning of the 1990s a strong dynamic which extended the vision of a more federalist community pervaded EU member states. The Single Act in 1986, the Maastricht Treaty in 1992 and the introduction of the euro in 1999 were the result of more sovereignty pooling and brought with them the promise of more political integration. At that time, public debate focused on the question of whether the member states were ready to move on to the next step, which would be a sort of "European economic government" implying more collective regulation. Clearly, several member states were opposed to more federalism. Backed by Great Britain, they advocated more market liberalization through the alleviation of EU rules. The notion of "flexibility" gained momentum in industrial organizations. In Germany, the growing burden of unification clashed strongly with the German model of industrial relations based on intricate regulation between social actors. For this reason, East Germany was the "ideal" location to test new models of management and organization that were less constraining for employers and much more flexible with regard to the amount of time spent at work. At that time, East German trade unions were demanding more centralized decision-making in order to defend employment at any price while West German unions simultaneously advocated more qualitative results such as better training and improved working time (Bafoil, 2009a). In this sense, traditions and realities were polar opposites from one part of Germany to the other. CEE unions followed the same path by committing themselves to one single issue: The preservation of employment at the expense of any other social issue. Wages were forgotten about. Western investors used this unique historical moment to impose updated methods of management on both West and East, to reduce the power of collective agreements and to force workers to accept uncertain working conditions. "Decentralization" in this sense meant putting traditional regional and sector based collective bargaining aside and bringing it to the level of workshop negotiations.

In the 1980s–1990s, public debate was largely concerned with social proposals, which were strongly supported at that time by the EU Commission. By the next decade, this was over. In retrospect enlargement to the East and Center appears to have hampered social and political progress, at the very least in EU public debate (Landvai, 2004). Having frozen federalist trends, it reinforced the national rationale for less collective commitments and sovereignty pooling. Such a position was obviously understandable coming from countries that had to make long, difficult and considerable efforts to adopt the entire *Acquis Communautaire*. Indeed, after 1998, day after day, month after month, under tough and cautious scrutiny from EU experts most of whom were unfamiliar with Central and Eastern Europe, all CEE public administrations had to adjust their norms, rules and procedures in accordance with the EU package of rules. One negative consequence of this extraordinary push towards adjustment on the part of CEE candidates was the emergence of firm opposition to any further collective effort. This period of adjustment to Western rules broke the historical dynamic for more collective bargaining in the workplace. Moreover, from a social perspective, this opposition echoed strong liberal options in favor of reducing or even eliminating social constraints for employers at the expense of employees.[10] In this respect, the EU commission's lack of interest in collective social ambition was very much in step with enlargement to the East. Indeed, many economists and EU commission representatives were strongly in favor of adopting a very low priority position on social affairs arguing that in such a historical situation it was necessary first to produce in order to then better redistribute. Social guidelines were therefore reduced to being a mere accompaniment to the

---

[10] As the Hungarian sociologist, Zusza Ferge (2001) said: "There is no recommendation to attempt full employment, while direct pressure for the privatization of pension and healthcare are apparent in all accession reports."

implementation of EU market rules, as recommended by Chapter 13 of the *Acquis communautaire*, but without considering the exceptional character of the historical situation. For example, proposals dealing with "life-long learning" and "qualification measures" in the workplace were considered to be a mere formality, and all the more so as there were no institutions to implement such proposals. As the Czech sociologist Vladimir Rys said: "To the extent that social criteria are not taken into account alongside political and economic criteria, social protection questions are reduced to their economic aspects only" (Rys, 2001). Because the EU was unable to make its social program clear, EU rules made weak states even weaker.

From a political perspective, voting behavior in the June 2004 European elections did not reflect the strong popular support for entry into the EU expressed in 2003. Meanwhile, the dynamics of enlargement were following the US trend of the 1980s that aimed at encouraging more flexibility and fewer social norms in order to facilitate the quickest possible movement of goods and finance. In following these trends, CEE states adapted to globalization and liberal ideas much better than their Western partners did. The new ideas of "management by flexibility" and "new public management" were strongly advocated by new members hoping in this way to escape from the "old" administrative and social constraints of Western Europe. Such divergences can help to explain the huge misunderstandings between the two parts of the EU during the whole process of adjustment and the deep resentment felt on the Western side after 2007. When the American Secretary of State Rumsfeld pegged EU15 as the "old Europe" everybody clearly understood which European states were "modern" and "adaptive" and which were "old".

8.5.2. *Agricultural policy*

The same remarks can be made about the common agricultural policy (CAP). From the 1950s up to the end of the 1980s, European agriculture experienced a fundamental revolution as a result of the CAP, shifting from a cyclical series of shortages and crises to becoming a net exporter of agricultural products. In less than 40 years, the EU became the biggest world-wide exporter (Hervieu *et al.*, 2010). Public policy measures supporting products and prices led to the end of previous crises and the production of adequate supplies for the feeding of growing populations. However, this remarkable success also paved the way for some unexpected side-effects. The traditional small family farming model gave way to a much more industrial one. Success was also brought about by increasingly bigger farms and more intensive use of fertilizer. Land surface diminished. Certain crops and animals were mass produced at the expense of more ecological farming. The "productivism model" prevailed, destroying traditional land use and forcing traditional agriculture to disappear. By the end of the 1980s, this model was close to the limits of its success under pressure from both profound internal ("mad cow" disease being the most notorious) and external crises. The Doha Development Agenda, which commenced in 2001, aimed at reducing tariff barriers and subsidies and denounced the EU for its strong protective laws which discriminated against developing countries. Simultaneously, "Green" actors fueled political debate, criticizing an overly results-oriented agricultural policy and defending local and environmental ways of life and work. The quality and origin of products became the focus of public debate. The time had come to change and a recognizable shift occurred away from a method of agriculture based on quantitative results which were not respectful of the environment to a much more qualitative view of agriculture. European subsidies were now linked to environmental incentives. Within the CAP, besides the first pillar devoted to agricultural products, a second pillar emerged targeting environmental criteria. Rural aspects were finally considered, implying a much more "territorial" approach to agriculture and greater attention to rural actors. Governance was reinforced and 10% of the CAP budget was reserved for this new pillar, the intention being to balance both pillars as quickly as possible. Apart from efficiency indicators, environmental conditionality became more and more apparent.

The fundamental shift towards a more "rural" mode of agriculture was connected to both a decreasing agricultural population and share of GDP and increasing environmental awareness. The process of CEE enlargement would bring a halt to this environmental shift for four fundamental reasons deriving from the strong differences between Eastern and Western agriculture.

First, the percentage of farmers counted in the CEE working population was not comparable to the equivalent percentage of Western farmers. In 1990, Poland's farmers represented over 25% of the working population whereas in Romania and Bulgaria they represented more than 30% compared to an EU15 average of 4%. By way of comparison, France, which is considered to be one of the most agriculturally productive countries had less than 3%. Second, the average farm size was radically different: In 1989, the average size was around 60 hectares in the Western part, as opposed to 6.8 has in Poland and 3.5 has in Romania (Von Hirschhausen, 1997). Third, this resulted in a very low level of productivity due to an over-employed population in CEE (population referring to plot size). Agricultural methods differed because there was such a large technical gap. Fourth, agriculture in CEE was characterized by a lack of specialization and was focused on mixed farming, in contrast to very highly specialized agriculture in Western Europe (Bafoil, 2009). Even if the second rural pillar became an important criterion for the delivery of subsidies, and even if the CAP budget increased between 2007 and 2013, this pillar experienced a large overall decrease because of the huge needs of agriculture in CEE. Moreover, the importance of qualitative conditionality was reduced as CEE farmers used less fertilizer, and in the meantime, large amounts of EU money were reserved for poorer Eastern agricultural sectors (Seliec and Trouvé, 2010). In the end, in order to avoid massive lay-offs of farmers unable to compete with market rules, EU funds functioned as a "model" saving small farmers that the Western part of Europe had been unable to save in previous decades when productivity was all that counted. The paradox of the CAP as applied to CEE was that it shifted from focusing on a competitive objective to a social one by supporting millions of poor farmers enabling them to survive. It was indeed an ironic paradox to see non-competitive farms being saved after 2004 by an agricultural policy that supported very productive and highly competitive farms in the Western part of the EU. The cultural gap between the two parts of the EU increased: Western farmers blamed the CAP for being too generous with lazy Eastern competitors, while Eastern farmers blamed the EU for not supporting them as much as their Western competitors.

8.6. Comparing CEE and Southeast Asia

What makes sense in comparing former Soviet-type economies with Southeast Asian ones when technical aspects of the transforming process are considered, is that neither had much interest in democracy. Furthermore, the immense advantage for politicians of this representation of the way public affairs were decided on in such a context was its supposed "de-politization". Experts were considered to be better placed to solve economic issues than others, who were suspected of being corrupt. Technical measures prevailed over political policies because they were deemed to be much more neutral. In East Germany, the privatization office (the *Treuhandanstalt*) benefited from extraordinary public privileges in comparison with other German public institutions (Seibel, 1994). The public office was immediately placed under the responsibility of the Ministry of Finance but it was considered to be an extra-federal level as former Chancellor Schmidt suggested. No one had control over this public office and no independent body could verify the decision-making process. At the end of the process when the *Treuhandanstalt* finally closed its doors, that is, four years after German reunification, nobody was allowed to assess criteria, costs and benefits. Very often in CEE, privatization policies followed the same pattern, being placed under the responsibility of public offices, like the Ministry of Finance or an Agency of Privatization, and not under parliamentary control (Bornstein, 1999). Due to a lack of relevant control over institutions and also because of a political unwillingness to publicly control decisions through public channels, privatization very often escaped public debate. In Southeast Asia, the same model with a domination of experts and tacit consensus often prevailed. Here, the "Washington Consensus" joined camps with the "Asian Consensus" by favoring the role of experts who framed policies aimed at bringing macro-economic policies that would foster foreign investments to the fore-front. This "Asian Consensus" rested on two pillars — a strong network

Table 8.1. The main macro-economic recommendations from the EU and ASEAN.

EU Washington Consensus	ASIAN Miracle
• Fiscal discipline and austerity	• Fundamentally sound macro-economic policy
• Public expenditure priority	• High level of domestic saving and investment
• Tax reform	• Tax policies favoring investment
• Financial liberalization	• Secure, bank-based financial system with
• —	strong regulation and supervision
• —	• Competitive exchange rates
• Exchange rate reform	• Pro-export trade incentive structure
• Trade liberalization	• Openness to foreign technology and
• Foreign direct investment	investment
• Privatization	• —
• Deregulation	• —
• Property rights	• Legal and regulatory environment hospitable to private investment and security of property rights

Source: EU, see Lavigne (1999, p. 34); Asean, see Rigg (2003, p. 10).

of trade policies and a strong banking system. As has often been observed, these policies were implemented in Asia in order to secure growth, and were seen as the only way to legitimize political power due to its redistributive effects. To this extent, there is a strong parallel between the two sets of measures, as explained in Table 8.1.

8.6.1. *Beyond enlargement*

In conclusion, enlargement in both regions has resulted from internal regional challenges. More precisely, the end of the Cold War brought regional security issues and the ensuing uncertainties with it. What is remarkable, as Douglas Webber (2001) underlines, is the fact that the end of the Cold War eradicated the very reasons that had legitimized the birth of ASEAN and the EU: ASEAN because it was born out of a desire to protect itself from Communism; the EU because it arose from a strong desire to limit the risks of creating an economic monopoly associated with the concentration of economic resources in one place — Germany — by sharing its economic assets with other countries. The most recent process of EU enlargement has greatly modified the notion of Germany and France as the driving force in the EU not only by highlighting the central place of Germany (and not France) in Europe, but also by removing Germany's "moral duty", a legacy of its responsibility for the Nazi era. Despite its declaration of loyalty, Germany now feels much less constrained by collective commitments. This was inevitable since German reunification marked the end of inequalities and the arbitrary order imposed brought about by the Yalta agreement.[11] Helmut Kohl was the last "European" German Chancellor, and it is clear that his successors, Schroeder and Merkel, are less committed to the war generation. The ultimate consequence of enlargement in both regions might well be the end of hegemony. This is the case in ASEAN firstly, where the retreat of Indonesia following the Asian crisis in 1998 coincided with the entry of small new nationalistic states. Secondly in the EU, where Germany no longer needs French political support, as it has now become the most powerful — and unrestrained — state, having access not just to the whole European market, but also, and primarily, to the worldwide market. This interpretation defended by Moravick in 1998 can be confirmed in light of the recent Greek crisis, where Germany once again imposed its own vision of budgetary discipline and European regulation on its partners, and this at a very high financial cost for itself indeed.

ASEAN is now complete — at the very least from a territorial perspective. No state remains on the outside and all Southeast Asian states are involved. This is not the case in the EU. A majority of states having emerged from the former Yugoslavia remain detached from the EU and a question mark remains over membership for Turkey.

---

[11] The Yalta agreement was drawn up in 1945 by the allies who had defeated Nazism and partitioned Germany and Europe according to their own vision.

8.7. Conclusion

The latest enlargement to take place in both regions has greatly modified the internal capacities of each regional ensemble, ASEAN and the EU. These new states are not only the poorest in each ensemble, they also share former political, economic and institutional features inherited from the former Soviet-type system. For historical reasons, they also appear to be the most nationalist states. The end of Communism, macro-regional economic changes and the stabilization of international relations have more or less forced each of these new states to join their surrounding regional institutionalized ensembles.

Rather than following pre-existing dynamics, new member states have modified them. More precisely, they have blocked the former dynamics which consolidated the institutions by radically stopping any attempts in favor of more "sovereignty pooling". In both areas, the EU and SEA, enlargement has resulted in a reduction rather than an increase in regional capacities. Because of this, in certain circumstances smaller states have more power than bigger ones as they can block the emergence of strong leadership. Fewer political rules and less interference in state affairs are more beneficial to the small states than to larger ones.

Because of recent enlargement, national sovereignty has become the strongest measure by which political negotiation makes sense. Because they disappeared gradually over time under foreign, colonial or imperialist rule, these states are relatively "new" from a historical perspective and at the same time are new member states from a regional perspective. However, the dimension of national sovereignty prevails over all other perspectives. States alone can provide an understanding of the way in which supranational rules are formed. They impose limits and rules. Supranational rules can be understood only in relation to states that produce and implement shared collective rules. If regional supranational ensembles are understood to be the intermediary units buffering the impact of the dynamics of globalization, states are the main players to organize collective rules.

PART III
CONCLUSION

Let us now review the conclusions reached in the previous chapters, in which Southeast Asia and Central Europe were compared. Both entail state capacities I questioned by using the terms "strong" or "weak" to describe states and the political economies supporting them.

Concerning Southeast Asian and CEE states, it is difficult to draw conclusions solely on the basis of which states are weak and which are strong. Why? Because both regions and states can be simultaneously regarded as weak and strong. From an empirical perspective, EU states can be seen as strong in that they produce strong collective rules. This is a matter of fact. And, in the same way, EU architecture reflects great institutional strength. The *champ reservé* of EU binding rules (*règlements*) is impressive. Agricultural policy is not decided by states but by the EU Commission. Competitiveness is framed by "state aid" rules that strongly limit individual nations' margins of maneuver. Within the Eurozone, no single state can make decisions regarding its own currency. But, despite these examples of the pooling of sovereignty, the EU's current major concern is the weakness of conditionality. In 2011, Greece and Portugal clearly showed that states can get around shared rules, deliver misleading information and endanger the whole EU community. In 2007, it was reported that Romania and Bulgaria were in compliance with EU rules. Less than three years later, both these states were denounced for breaking rules of good management. Conditionality can be lacking and indicators can be inadequate. But without the right indicators how can the right policies be launched? Hence, the hard reality of the limits of the last EU regional innovation: The macro-region. Lastly, the EU as a whole is clearly defined and EU growth is increasing. Nevertheless, at the same time regional inequalities are increasing within certain member states and unemployment is rising. Poverty and exclusion affect many people, despite EU social cohesion rules. EU structural policies have been praised for fostering growth, but at the same time they have also been criticized for having financed too many motorways or too many housing programs. These investments not only fail in terms of development but also damage the environment and end up wasting a lot of resources. So there are clearly great discrepancies between EU principles and European national realities.

Similarly, there is profound "dissonance" between what ASEAN proclaims and the reality on the ground in its member states. ASEAN has a common declaration but no binding rules. It has been criticized for producing norms and speeches but nothing more: For a lot of people, ASEAN remains an empty shell. Numerous declarations against terrorism have been made, but no concrete measures have been taken, except for the creation of a center for counterterrorism and a few think tanks. No concrete institutions have been set up in response to either the Southeast Asian haze or the SARS crisis. Myanmar continues to violate human rights. The Chang Mai initiative should not be mistaken for anything like monetary union. ASEAN member states cannot compete with the US, who never wanted such a union in the first place. The final stage of a common market is always postponed, and the number of products protected by APEC's fourth list has not decreased. Finally, ASEAN has been heavily criticized for failing to reduce the gap between core and periphery. It is neither a binding organization nor is it in favor of multilateralism. Both conclusions are paradoxical since both strong and weak states are capable of limiting any further pooling of sovereignty; strong ensembles are able to exert little or no pressure on member states, while weak states are actually able to be stronger and exert more pressure on members precisely because of their weak rules.

Let us conclude by saying that the facts regarding both regions do not point to any definite conclusions. Indeed, whether a state is regarded as strong or weak depends on what theoretical stance is taken. As Eaton and Stubb state, realists favor the international relations approach, while the constructivists are more inclined to use a sociological perspective (Eaton and Stubbs, 2006). The two approaches may be differentiated in a number of ways: First by self-interest versus norms and values, then by their contrasting visions of what power and legitimacy refer to, and, lastly, with respect to time span. From a classical realist perspective, which stresses the fundamental principle of self-interest, power is not negotiable. It sits with a single camp and does not circulate between players. States do not move unless they are obliged to comply with a foreign force. Hierarchy is always perceived through a top down perspective. Legitimacy depends where one is placed within the system of exchanges, which clearly differentiates strong and weak states. A weak regional ensemble depends on a collection of weak states, which are characterized by their dependency on "great powers". Weak states can only produce weak rules. Therefore, neo-realists restrict their analysis to the short term while, in contrast, constructivists take into account the long-term perspective, within which step-by-step and inchoate processes are embedded. In fact, the constructivist perspective emphasizes shared representations which create strong links, leading to formal and informal agreements which are conducive, under certain condition, to more engagement. Whereas neo-realists focus on elites, constructivists look to local exchanges between different social groups. The latter highlight the ability of local actors to use resources in order to increase their margin of maneuver, either by respecting rules or by getting around them. States are strong if they can reinforce their own positions, irrespective of the nature — strong or weak — of the supranational ensemble they belong to.

In other words, binding or non-binding rules can both reinforce a state's position. A collection of strong states can use strong supranational rules to reinforce themselves but a collection of weak states can get the same benefit in an opposite way. Weak from the perspective of the top-down pressure it can exert, a regional ensemble can be very strong if it produces weak supranational rules, which contribute to the strengthening of domestic arrangements. For this reason, a state's political nature does not necessarily give any indication of its strength or weakness. Both democratic and authoritarian regimes can be characterized as strong or weak. Authoritarian and communist regimes are strong in the sense that their highly centralized polities limit centrifugal forces and reinforce internal coherence. On the other hand, both these kinds of regime tend to be controlled by central elites, "grandes familles" or the nomenklatura. Democracies are strong as well because frequent democratic elections limit the power of interest groups and help to insulate elected officials from private interest groups. Nevertheless democracies can be ineffectual in preventing the rise of extremist forces, and the balance of power is often very fragile. There is also the danger that they can degenerate into totalitarian regimes. Lastly, European states — particularly the smaller ones — can be regarded as strong because they obtained legitimacy by virtue of being represented within a worldwide forum. Similarly, we have seen that the authoritarian leaders of ASEAN states benefit from not pooling sovereignty because foreign states are thus prevented from intervening in their internal affairs, and because ASEAN states can extend their economic trade and in return increase domestic redistribution (and consequently generate resources which can be redistributed domestically). By doing so, they increase their legitimacy and are able to reinforce their authoritarian dimension.

GENERAL CONCLUSIONS
TYPES OF CAPITALISM IN CENTRAL EUROPE AND IN SOUTHEAST ASIA

The analysis undertaken here leads to a conclusion on the nature of capitalism in Central and Eastern Europe and in Southeast Asia. The categories defined by Hall and Soskice do not seem to apply here as the categories of "coordinated market economy" or "liberal market economy"[1] do not seem to adequately define them. These economies can perhaps be better described as "hybrids". In both regions, this term reflects a particular combination of liberal and protectionist dimensions which are oriented differently depending on the founding principles of each region. In this sense, the different types of capitalism are at least partially defined by the relationship between national configurations and their corresponding regional environments.

1. The Geopolitics of Capitalism

This book has highlighted two main aspects of capitalism in these regions. The first of these is internal and concerns work organization; the second is geopolitical and concerns regional belonging.

In CEE countries, in spite of the numerous types of dependence listed above (in terms of R&D and domestic bank capital) assembly units were not the only type of entities to be set up. Growth peaks, in

---

[1] Hall and Soskice (2001). In both regions, this reflection has exerted a strong influence. On Central Europe see: Bohle and Greskovits (2006), Bohle and Greskovits (2007), Nölke and Vliegenthart (2009). Concerning Southeast Asia, see Tipton (2009), Ritchie (2009b), Carney *et al.* (2009), Nölke and Vliegenthart (2009).

turn giving rise to clusters, also occurred (OECD, 2005). Although a great many of them were set up in the first post-communist decade they are still there today as wages continue to be more competitive in the region than elsewhere in Europe. Added to this, production processes and work organization have been considerably improved by many factors: The presence of an industrial culture, which was one of the reasons for the development of several SEZs as already mentioned; availability of the relevant qualifications for private companies and particularly the banks and automobile and electronics sector; finally, the availability of a considerably increased number of third level graduates.

The situation is altogether different in the Mekong countries where, apart from Thailand, there is little potential for qualifications. There are few qualifications among the existing workforce and not much research activity. On the other hand, a considerable amount of labor is available and wages are extremely competitive which has caught these countries in a trap. As they are at the heart of their partners' geo-economic strategies, they serve as intermediaries within the inter-regional value chains rather than as independent partners likely to develop their own *savoir faire*. This was incontestably the original scenario for other founding ASEAN countries in the area as well. They however did catch up whereas external geopolitical and economic conditions and the globalization of trade have made it all the more difficult for new arrivals to do the same and even to take off. One of the issues at stake for future development is to see whether CLMV countries will follow the same path as their predecessors and leave the under regulated form of capitalism they have so far adopted behind them.

The second aspect is relative to the geopolitical direction taken by the two regions. This means that when deciding what kind of capitalism to implement, the territories themselves and the way in which they have been built by public and private policies are vital decisive factors in each of the regional ensembles. Interaction between public and private partners is a powerfully determining factor for the organization of private companies. In the CEE countries, policies designed to assist the development of private companies — special zones or other types of territorial support — are massively directed at supporting the European market. This aid is distributed according to territorial particularities. It is limited by very restrictive legislation — state support and structural funds — and determines the contracts between public and private partners. For this reason, capitalism is territorialized. This territorial dimension is essential in understanding the implantation and organization of private companies and merits further exploration taking the great variety of existing territories into account. Finally, border regions promote a particular type of development which differs from the way development takes place in cities.

In Southeast Asia, sub-regional infrastructural policies — similar to those promoted by the ADB in the Greater Mekong Sub-region — or indeed Japanese, Chinese, and nowadays Malaysian and Singaporean business networks — are not so much seeking to develop their territories but rather to connect them. This is the result of a geo-strategic vision where oceans, ports and border regions are seen as the places where economic activity is concentrated. The way in which they are linked through value chains provides a framework for the conception of development even if these chains are slow to appear in this region where Thailand is practically the only country which can claim to have identified them today. Nonetheless, the territorial effect particularly when linked to the crossing of borders is essential and the question of trans-border agreements is of primary importance in understanding the concentrations of capital in these areas together with the limits to its circulation.

2. Hybrid Types of Capitalism

In Europe, the absence of a system of firmly established industrial relations together with policies supporting foreign investment are combined with protectionist property policies which reflect the strong presence of national sovereignty issues within otherwise liberal economic tendencies. The regional dimension of the

EU provides a framework for this liberal tendency while linking it to policies aimed at lessening the negative effects of growth. Strategies for economic, social and territorial development are used (Cohesion policy) together with development tools and funds to do this. However, in this area the EU principles are mandatory but impossible to combine. The deregulation of labor law, the multiplication of tax shelter zones and the weakness of industrial regulations suggest the predominance of an extremely liberal type of capitalism which is all the stronger as certain historical traditions (as described in Chapter 5) are lacking in some countries. And yet this liberal European configuration also combines a large number of policies in support of employment and training through structural aid and growing welfare systems. In other words, in CEE countries as a whole, liberal labor and capital policies at a national level, which contribute to the deregulation of labor relations, are attenuated by European development policies. In the same way, the rules surrounding the European market favoring private property that have transformed access to public goods have encountered policies for the defense of national sovereignty and the constitution of a "hard core" in non-privatized companies at a national level. The conclusion can thus be drawn that a general type of hybrid capitalism which mixes liberal and protectionist aspects largely supported by EU objectives exists throughout CEE countries.

A similar dialectic between the desire to maintain sovereignty and economic liberalism in the national economies and in ASEAN can also be found in Southeast Asia. This has given rise to the co-existence of a very large amount of private property alongside a large number of foreign companies. This is as far as the comparison with CEE countries goes because of the prevailing principles in each regional organization. ASEAN is driven by the same principle that drives each of its individual members for whom the principle of non-interference in the affairs of a member country takes precedence over all others. This principle echoes the principle of national sovereignty, signifying that ASEAN has no right to an opinion on how capitalism is carried out in any individual country. Because of its liberal tendencies, regional organization offers the best protection to authoritarian regimes and is even used to justify dictatorships. For this reason, the category of political capitalism is also pertinent.

3. Political Capitalism: Clans, Families, Networks

The basic "political" figure of capitalism is defined by a combination of the absence of rule of law, the absence of industrial relations and more broadly speaking of civil society, dependence on foreign capital and the creation of pre-bends controlled by a monopoly.[2] We have seen above how this figure has provided an ideal screen for the authoritarian domination it supports in ASEAN. Many variations of this figure, depending on the status of the law which is not always easy to predict, can be found in Southeast Asia. At one extreme, Cambodia and its pre-bend system can be found. At the other, Singapore, which has little in common with Cambodia apart from the presence of a dominant party and therefore the authoritarianism of the government. However, what essentially distinguishes these countries is the domination of *rule by law*. Between these two extremes, familial capitalism which is very widespread in Southeast Asia is developing. The big families who function like cartels can be found in all Southeast Asian countries as mentioned in Chapter 2. This type of familial capitalism can give rise to more regulated figures as in Thailand or to less regulated ones as in the Philippines where crony capitalism seems to flourish.

These figures are part of an open regional economy whose extension they encourage by means of partnership agreements, whether these be border agreements in the shape of Growth Poles or trade agreements with FTAs. For this reason, familial capitalism is also

---

[2] In Economy and Society (Weber, 1978), the category of "political capitalism" is subdivided into predatory capitalism, (which illustrates a state of war), colonial capitalism and capitalism exercised by political authorities. Moreover, commercial capitalism which is the second most important type of capitalism includes several activities linked to the management of money. Finally, market capitalism expresses the highest level of technical rationality because of the superior calculation techniques it activates.

rooted in networks,[3] rather than in countries,[4] as shown by the dissemination of Chinese business groups. While states cannot push for supranational rules which would be difficult for them to implement, the networks can encourage national institutional frameworks and adjust them as needed. In this attempt at classification, Singapore presents a particular case as seen in Chapter 3.

4. Liberal Capitalism: Protectionism, Controlled Openness and Social Consensus

Three main characteristics define the types of capitalism present in CEE countries. The first of these results from the industrial legacies which have enabled the territories which collapsed after 1989 to redevelop. This redevelopment was accompanied by a whole series of educational and training policies notably inspired by the EU. Liberal capitalism in the region is not the result of a mere external transfer of capitalist norms and practices. It is also marked by older legacies such as the presence of skilled working classes and a strong industrial culture.

The second characteristic is the result of infrastructural policies made possible by European funds. Apart from transport, these policies have been extended to include all measures designed to enhance the environment of private firms. The same is true for urban and educational policies, and those surrounding housing and culture which have been widely used by foreign investors as a way to gain a

---

[3] "This Asian form of capitalism which is increasingly found in the APT countries is rooted in business networks — both Japanese and ethnic Chinese networks — and is characterized by strong business — links. It emphasizes production rather than consumption, and results rather than ideology, and tends to place a premium on market share as opposed to short term profits. East Asian capitalism is also based much more on social obligation and social trust than on the rule of law" (Stubbs, 2002).

[4] "What is distinctive about Southeast Asian nations...is that they have very little capacity to influence the transnational environment in which such activities occur. In short they are rule takers, not rule makers, and this has major implications for the way they are incorporated into the wider global political economy" (Beeson, 2003).

footing and to promote their human resources recruiting policies. Rather than restricting the analysis of capitalism to internal industrial regulations which are not very developed anywhere, the interaction between private and public policies provides a more useful focus. This approach allows the massive arrival of investors in the region over the last ten years to be understood.

The third characteristic is related to the various types of majoritarian social consensus, which have defined the approaches adopted by each of the countries since the beginning of the transition. They partly explain why there has been so little conflict in these countries and why there has been such a strong desire to attain the expected outcomes. The EU played a huge part in the reshaping of mindsets and the institutional frameworks in which both public and private actors have evolved. The variables needed to understand the emerging forms of capitalism and the broadening of regional integration include: The geopolitics of cross-border flows of all kinds, the overhauling of qualifications, EU structural support, massive social consensus, systems of representation, and standards of practice.

BIBLIOGRAPHY

Acharya, A (1997). Ideas, identity and institution-building: From the ASEAN way to the Asia-Pacific way. *The Pacific Review*, 10(3), 319–346.

Acharya, A (2003). Democratization and the prospects for participatory regionalism in Southeast Asia. *Third World Quarterly*, 24(2), 375–390.

Acharya, A (2004). How ideas spread: Whose norms matter? Norms localization and institution of change in Asian Regionalism. *International Organization*, 58(2), 239–275.

Acharya, A (2006). Europe and Asia: Reflections on a tale of 2 regionalisms. In *Regional Integration in East Asia and Europe, Convergence or Divergence?* B Fort and D Webber (eds.). London: Routledge.

Acharya, A (2009). *Constructing a Security Community in Southeast Asia: ASEAN and the Problem of Regional Order*, 2nd edn. London: Routledge.

Acharya, A (2010). Asia is not one. *The Journal of Asian Studies*, 69(4), 1001–1013.

Adamski, W, J Buncak, P Machonin and D Martin (1999). *System Change and Modernization*. Warsaw: IFIS Publishers.

ADB (2007). Special economic zones and competitiveness. PRM Policy Note Series Review Committee, ADB, Manila

ADB (2009). Designing and implementing trade facilitation report. ADB, Manila.

Aghion, P and O Blanchard (1998). On privatization methods in eastern Europe and their implications. *Economics of Transition*, 6(1), 87–100.

Alice, D (2006). Who's socializing whom? Complex Engagement in Sino–ASEAN relations. *The Pacific Review*, 19(2), 157–179.

Amess, K and BM Roberts (2007). The productivity effects of privatization: The case of polish cooperatives. *Internal Review of Financial Analysis*, 354–366.

Anderson, BRO (1983). *Imagined Communities: Reflections on the Origins and Spread of Nationalism*. London: Verso. Avila, JL.

Arghiros, D (2000). *Democracy, Development, Decentralization in Provincial Thailand*. Richmond, Surrey, UK: Curzon.

269

Arvanitis, R and Z Wei (2008). Les politiques parallèles du développement industriel en Chine, Chapter 8. In *Entreprises et Territoires. Une comparaison Europe/Asie*, F Bafoil (ed.). Available at http://etats-entreprises-et-territoires.contenu-numerique.com/

Asean Competitiveness Report (2010). NUS Singapore.

Askew, M (ed.) (1985). *Legitimacy Crisis in Thailand*. Thailand: Silkworm Books.

Askew, M (2010). Four Thai pathologies, late 2009. In *Legitimacy Crisis in Thailand*, M Asew (ed.). Thailand: Silkworm Books.

Aveline-Dubach, N (2010). The role of industrial estates in Thailand's industrialization: New challenges for the future. In *Sustainability of Thailand's Competitiveness. The Policy Challenges*, P Interakumnerd and Y Lecler (eds.), pp. 175–206. Singapore: ISEAS Publication.

Avila, JL (2003). EU enlargement and the rise of Asia. FTA implication for EU Asia relationship. *Asia Europe Journal*, 1, 213–222.

Bachtler, JF and C Méndez (2007). Who governs EU cohesion policy? Deconstructing the reforms of the structural funds? *Journal of Common Markets Studies*, 45(3), 535–564.

Bafoil, F (1998). Post communist borders and territories: Conflicts, learning and rule building in Poland. *International Journal of Urban and Regional Research*, 23(3), 567–582.

Bafoil, F (1999). From corruption to regulation. Post-communist enterprises in Poland. In *Privatizing the State*, B Hibou (ed.), pp. 48–76, London: Hurst.

Bafoil, F (2007). *La Pologne*. Paris: Fayard.

Bafoil, F (2009a). *Europeanization and Globalization in Central and Eastern Europe*. New York: Palgrave Macmillan.

Bafoil, F (2009b). Regionalisation and decentralization in Poland: A Europeanization process in a comparative perspective. In *Regional Development and the European Union. A comparative Analysis of Karabück, Valenciennes and Katowicz*, F Bafoil and A Kaya (eds.), pp. 61–85. Istanbul: Istanbul Bilgi University Press.

Bafoil, F (2010a). Marché, pouvoir et bureaucratie. Une économie politique wéberienne, *Question de Recherche, CERI*, 35 pages. Available at http://www.ceri-sciencespo.com/cerifr/publica/question/qdr.php#1.

Bafoil, F (2010b). East European civil societies in the 90's. A legacy of solidarnosc or different historical paths? Governance and Globalization — Sciences Po in China. Working Papers Series 18, Beijing.

Bafoil, F (2011). Dependent Growth, SEZ in the Greater Mekong Sub-region, Report. Nicolas Diaz, Sophie Guerin, Allison Morris, Sophia Sen, MPA sciences Po, 120 pages. Available at www.coesionet.com.

Bafoil, F and T Beichelt (eds.) (2008). *L'européanisation d'Ouest en Est*. Paris: l'Harmattan.

Bafoil, F and R Lin (2010). Relooking at the role of transport infrastructure in trade, regional growth and governance: Comparing Greater Mekong Subregion (GMS) and Central Eastern Europe (CEE). *Journal of Current Southeast Asian Affairs*

2010/2. Available at http://hup.sub.uni-hamburg.de/giga/jsaa/article/view/ 262/262.

Bafoil, F and D Michal (2011). Territorial Cooperation in the EU: EU Strategy for the Baltic Sea Region, Report. M Armali, N Ramos, P Villasenor and D Wang, MPA Sciences Po. Available at www.coesionet.com.

Baisnée, O and R Pasquier (2007). *L'Europe Telle Qu'elle se Fait. Européanisation et Sociétés Politiques Nationales.* Paris: CNRS Éditions.

Baker, C and P Phongpaichit (2006). *A History of Thailand.* Cambridge: Cambridge University Press.

Balcerowicz, L (1995). *Socialism, Capitalism, Transformation.* Budapest: Central European University Press.

Balisican, A, H Hill and SF Poza (2006). *The Philippines and Regional Development. An Overview.* Japan: ADBI.

Balme, R and C Didier (2008). *European Governance and Democracy. Power and Protest in the EU.* Lanham: Rowman & Littlefield Publishers.

Balme, S and M Sidel (2007). Introduction. In *Vietnam's New Order. International Perspectives on the State and Reform in Vietnam,* B Stéphanie and M Sidel (eds.). Canada: Palgrave.

Baltowki, M and T Mickiewicz (2000). Privatization in Poland: Ten years after. *Post Communist Economies,* 12(4), 425–443.

Banomyong, R (2005). The pilot demonstration project for construction of an advanced trade and investment environment. Report, Japan External Trade Organization.

Banomyong R and V Pholsena (2004). *Le Laos au 21ème siècle, les défis de l'intégration régionale.* Bangkok: IRASEC.

Barbé, E, O Costa, A Herranz and M Natorski (2009). Which rules shape EU external governance? Patterns of rule selection in foreign and security policies. *Journal of European Public Policy,* 16(6), 834–852.

Barca, F (2009). An agenda for a reformed cohesion policy, a place-based approach to meeting European union challenges and expectations. Report, EU, DG Regio, p. 218.

Barr, MD (2000). Trade unions in an elitist society: the Singapore story. *Australian Journal of Politics and History,* 46(4), 480–496.

Barret, R and S Chin (1987). Export-oriented industrializing states in the world systems capitalism. Similarities and differences. In *The Political Economy of the New Asian Industrialization,* FC Deyo (ed.), pp. 23–43. New York: Cornell University Press.

Batt, J (2001). Transcarpathia: Peripheral region at the Centre of Europe. Working Paper, (ESRC) One Europe or Several, p. 28.

Bauvois, D *et al.* (2004). *Histoire de l'Europe Centrale.* Paris: PUF.

Beeson, M (2003). Sovereignty under siege : Globalization and the state in southeast Asia. *Third World Quarterly,* 24(2), 357–374.

Beeson, M (2007). *Regionalism and Globalization in East Asia. Politics, Security and Economic Development.* Canada: Palgrave.

Beeson, M (2009). *Institutions of the Asia–Pacific, ASEAN, APEC and Beyond.* London: Routledge.

Begg, I (2009). The Future of Cohesion Policy in Ruicher regions. Working Paper, EU Regional Policy, p. 14.

Benz, A (2007). Comments on Bafoil's contribution. In *La citoyenneté démocratique dans l'Europe des vingt-sept,* C Lequesne and M MacDonagh-Pajerova (eds.). Paris: L'Harmattan.

Benz, A, D Fürst, H Kilpert and D Rehfeld (2005). *Regionalisation. Theory, Practice and Prospects in Germany.* Östersund: SIR.

Berend, IT (1996). *Decades of Crisis. Central and Eastern Europe before World War II,* Berkeley/London/Los Angeles: University of California, 1996et en Asie du Sud – Est,Tripton, art.cité

Berendt, I (1984). Agriculture. In *The Economic History of Eastern Europe, 1919–1975* (2 Vols.), MC Kasers and EA Radice (eds.). Oxford: Clarendon Press.

Berendt, I and G Ranki (1974). *Economic Development in East and Central Europe in the Nineteenth and Twentieth Century.* New York: Columbia University Press.

Beresford, M (2001). Vietnam: The transition from central planning. In *The Political Economy of South–East Asia, Conflicts, Crisis and Change,* 2nd edn., G Rodan, K Hewison and R Robison (eds.), p. 220. Oxford: Oxford University Press.

Berkowski, A (2006). Comparing EU and Asia integration processes. EU a role model for Asia? European Policy Centre, Issue Paper, 22, Brussels.

Bernard, F and W Douglas (eds.) (2008). *Regional Integration in East Asia and Europe, Convergence or Divergence?* London: Routledge.

Bertrand, R (1999). Asal Bapak Senang: Tant qu'il Plaît à Monsieur. Le gouvernement pastoral comme matrice et comme alibi de la privatisation de l'Etat en Indonésie. In *La privatisation des Etats,* B Hibou (ed.). Khartala.

Bibo, I (1984). *Misère des Petits Etats d'Europe de l'Est,* Paris: Albin Michel (trad. française).

Bohle, D and B Greskovits (2006). Capitalism without compromise: Strong business and weak labor in eastern Europe's new transnational industries. *Studies in Comparative International Development,* 4(1), 3–25.

Bohle, D and B Greskovits (2007). Neo liberalism, embedded, neo-liberalism and neo-corporatism: Towards transnational capitalism in central-eastern Europe. *West European Politics,* 30(3), 443–466.

Bornstein, M (1999). Framework issues in the privatization strategies of the Czech Republic, Hungary and Poland. *Post-Communist Economies,* 11(1), 47–77.

Borrus, M, D Ernst and S Haggard (2000) *International Production Networks in Asia, Rivalry or Riches.* London: Routledge.

Bozoki, A and JT Ishiyama (2002). *The Communist Successor Parties of Central and Eastern Europe.* Armonk, NY: M.E. Sharpe.

Börzel, T (2001). Pace–Setting, Foot–Dragging and Fence–Sitting. Member State Responses to Europeanization, Queen's Papers on Europeanization, No. 4. Available at http://www.qub.ac.uk/ies/onlinepapers/poe4-01.pdf.

Börzel, T (2003). Shaping and Taking EU Policies: Member State Responses to Europeanization. Queen's Papers on Europeanization, No. 2/2003. Available at http://ideas.repec.org/p/erp/queens/p0035.html.

Börzel, T and A Buzogany (2010). Governing EU accession in transition Countries : The role of non stateactors. *Acta Politica*, 45 ½, 158–182.

Börzel, T and T Risse (2000). When Europe Hits Home: Europeanization and Domestic Change. EioP. Available at http://eiop.or.at/eiop/text/2000-015a.htm.

Börzel, T and T Risse (2003). Conceptualizing the domestic impact of Europe. In *The Politics of Europeanization*, K Featherstone and CM Radaelli (eds.), pp. 57–80. Oxford: Oxford University Press.

Brooks, D and H David (2009). *Infrastructure's Role in Lowering Asia's Trade Costs*. Tokyo and Cheltenham, UK: Edward Elgar Publishing.

Brus, W (1985). *The Economic History of Eastern Europe 1919–1975*. Oxford: Clarendon Press.

Buhman, K (2007). Building blocks for the rule of law? Legal reforms and public administration in Vietnam. In *Vietnam's New Order. International Perspectives on the State and Reform in Vietnam*, Chapter 13, S Balme and M Sidel (eds.). Canada: Palgrave.

Bunce, V (1999). *Subversive Institutions: The Design and the Destruction of Socialism and the State*. Cambridge: Cambridge University Press.

Cachavalpongpun, P (2010). Temple of doom: Hysteria about the Preah Vihear temple in the nationalist discourse. In *Legitimacy Crisis in Thailand*, M Askew (ed.), p. 84. Thailand: Silkworm Books.

Caporaso, J and M-H Kim (2009). The dual nature of European identity: Subjective awareness and coherence. *Journal of European Public Policy*, 16(1), 19–42.

Caraway, TL (2004). Protective repression, international pressure, and institutional design: Explaining labor reform in Indonesia. *Studies on Comparative International Development*, 39(3), 28–49.

Caraway, TL (2008). Explaining the dominance of legacy unions in new democracies: Comparative insights from Indonesia. *Comparative Political Studies*, 41(10), 1371–1397.

Caraway, TL (2009). Labor rights in East Asia: Progress or regress. *Journal of East Asian Studies*, 9, 153–186.

Carney, M, E Gedajlovic and X Yang (2009). Varieties of Asian capitalism: Toward an institutional theory of Asian enterprise. *Asia Pacific Journal of Management*, 26(3), 361–380.

Caroline, H (2003). *The Political Economy of Cambodia's Transition*. London: Londres, Routledge.

Caspersz, D (2006). The talk versus the walk: High performance work system, labour market flexibility and lessons from Asian workers. *Asia Pacific Business Review*, 12(2), 149–161.

Chaloemtiaran, T (2007). *Thailand, The Politics of Despotic Paternalism*. Thailand: SilkwormBooks,

Chandler, D (1983). *The History of Cambodia*. Boulder, Colorado: Westview Press.

Charbenloet, V (2000). Industrialization and labour fragmentation in Thailand. In *Social development in Asia*, K-L Lang (ed.), pp. 99–125. Netherlands: Kluwer Academic publishers.

Clarke, S (2006). The changing character of strikes in vietnam. *Post-Communist Economies*, 18(3), pp. 345–361.

Connors, MK (2003). *Democracy and National Identity in Thailand*, Chapter 3, pp. 34–59. NIAS Press.

Cooney, S (2006). Labour market regulation in comparative perspective. In *Labour Market Regulation and Deregulation in Asia*, C Brassard and A Acharya (eds.), pp. 233–254. Singapore: Academic Foundation, Lee Kuan Yee Schoool of Policy.

Cowles, MG, JA Caporaso and T Risse (eds.) (2001). *Transforming Europe: Europeanization and Domestic Change*. Ithaca, NY: Cornell University Press.

Cumings, B (2005). *Korea's Place in the Sun: A Modern History*. New York: WW. Norton & Company.

Dauvergne, P (ed.) (1998). *Weak and Strong States in Asia-Pacific Societies*. Sydney: Allen and Unwin Australia.

Davies, N (1981). *Gods Play Ground: A History of Poland in Two Volumes, B and 2*. Oxford: Oxford University Press.

de Tocqueville, A (1856). *L'ancien régime et la révolution*. Paris: Gallimard.

Dent, C (2008). *East Asian Regionalism*. London: Routledge.

Dexia (2008). Sub-national Governments in the European Union: Responsibilities, Organisation and Finances. Dexia Editions.

Deyo, FC (ed.) (1987). *The Political Economy of the New Asian Industrialization*. New York: Cornell University Press.

Deyo, FC (1989). *Beneath the Miracle, Labor Subordination in the New Asian Industrialism*. California: University of California.

Deyo, FC (2001). The social construction of develoment labor system South East Asia Industrial restructuring. In *The Political Economy of South East Asia. Conflicts Crises and Change*, 2nd edn., G Rodan, K Hewison and R Obison (eds.), pp. 252–282. Oxford: Oxford University Press.

Djankov, S (1998). *Ownership Structure and Enterprise Restructuring in Six Newly Independent States*. Washington, DC: World Bank.

Doner, RF (1991). Approaches to the politics of economic growth in southeast Asia. *The Journal of Asian Studies*, 50(4), 818–849.

Doner, RF (1992). Limits of state strength: Toward and institutionalist view of economic development. *World Politics*, 44(3), 398–431.

Doner, RF, BK Ritchie and D Slater (2005). Systemic vulnerability and the origins of developmental states: Northeast and Southeast Asia in comparative perspective. *International Organization*, 59, 327–361.

Dore, J (2003). The governance of increasing Mekong regionalism. In *Social Challenges for the Mekong Region*, M Kaosa-ard and J Dore (eds.), pp. 405–440. Thailand: Chiang Mai University.

Dosch, J (2007). Decentralizing Cambodia: The international hijacking of national politics? In *The Changing Dynamics of Southeast Asia Politics*, Chapter 5, pp. 139–162. Boulder, CO: Lynne Rienner Publishers.

Dovert, S and B de Treglode (2004). *Vietnam Contemporain* (sous la direction de). Les Indes Savantes: IRASEC.

du Rocher, SB and B Fort (eds.) (2005). *Path to Regionalization: Comparing Experiences in Europe and East Asia*. Singapore: Maxhill Cavendish.

Duara, P (2010). Asia redux: Conceptualizing a region for our time. *The Journal of Asian Studies*, 69(4), 963–983.

Dubus, A (2011). *Policiers of the Thai State Toward the Malay Muslim South (1978–2010)*. Bangkok: IRASEC.

Dupont, A (1996). Is there an Asian Way. *Survival Global Politics and Strategy*, 38(2), 13–33.

Duval, Y (2008). Economic Cooperation and Regional Integration in the Greater Mekong Subregion (GMS). Trade and Investment Division, Staff Working Paper 02/08, UNESCAP. pp. 31–32.

Earle, JS and S Estrin (1996). Employee ownership in transition. In *Corporate Governance in Central Europe and Russia. Volume 2. Insiders and the State*, R Frydman, CW Gray and A Rapaczynski (eds.). Budapest/London/New York: Central European University Press.

Eaton, S and R Stubbs (2006). Is ASEAN powerful realist versus constructivist approaches to power in Southeast Asia. *The Pacific Review*, 19(2), 135–155.

Eliassen, KA and CB Arnesen (2007). Comparison of Europe and Southeast Asia. In *European Union and New Regionalism: Regional Actors and Global Governance in a Post-Hegemonic Era*, 2nd edn., M Telo (ed.), pp. 203–221. Aldershot: Ashgate.

Erikson, CL *et al.* (2003). From core to periphery? Recent development relations in the Philippines. *Industrial Relations*, 42(3), 368–395.

EU (2010). The European union strategy for the Baltic sea region: Background and analysis. *European Union Regional Policy*.

EU (2011). The EU strategy for the Danube region, A united response to common challenges. *EU Regional Policies Panorama Inforegio*, 37.

EU Commission (2012). Communication from the commission, Europe 2020, a strategy for smart, sustainable and inclusive growth. *COM 20*.

EU Report (2009a). Metropolitan regions in the EU, regional focus. *EU Regional Policy*, 01/2009, p. 8.

EU Report (2009b). Five years of enlargements, economic achievements and challenges. *European Economy*, 1/2009.

EU Regional Policy (2009). Metropolitan regions in the EU. *Regional Focus*, 01, 8.

European Commission (2003a). Wider Europe — neighbourhood: A new framework for relations with our eastern and southern neighbours report. *COM* 104.

European Commission (2003b). The European security strategy. Report.

European Commission (2004). Communication from the European Commission–European neighbourhood policy. *Strategy Paper*, *COM* 373.

Evans, P and J Rausch (1999). Bureaucracy and growth: A cross-national analysis of the effects of Weberian state structures on economic growth. *American Sociological Review*, 64, 748–765.

Evans, PB, D Rueschemeyer and T Skocpol (1985). *Bringing The State Back In*. Cambridge: Cambridge University Press.

Evans, P (1995). *Embedded Autonomy. States and Industrial Transformation*. Princeton, New Jerssy: Princeton University Press.

Evans, P (2005). Between regionalism and regionalization: Policy networks in the nascent east Asian institutional identity. In *Remaping East Asia, The Construction of the Region*, TJ Pempel (ed.), pp. 195–215. New York: Cornell University Press.

Evans, G (ed.) (1999). *Laos, Culture and Society*. Crows Nest, NSW: Silkworm Books.

Evans, G (2002). *A Short History of Laos: The Land in Between*. Crows Nest, NSW: Silkworm Books.

Faludi, A (2010). Territorial Cohesion Post-2013; To Whomsoever It May Concern. 24th AESOP Annual Conference, Finland 7–10 July 2010, p. 11.

Felker, GB (2003). Southeast Asian industrialization and the changing global production system. *Third World Quaterly*, 24(4), 255–282.

Ferge, Z (2001). European integration and the reform of social security in the accession countries. *Journal of European Social Quality*, 3(1,2), 9–25.

Ferge, Z and G Juhasz (2004). Accession and social policy: The case of Hungary. *Journal of European Social Policy*, 14(3), 233–251.

Ferry, M (2003). The EU and the recent regional reform in Poland. *Europe-Asia Studies*, 55(7), 1097–1116.

Ferry, M (2007). Policy developments in Poland, regional policy developments in member states and norway: Country reviews in 2006-07. *EPRC European Policies Research Centre*, Glasgow University of Strathclyde.

Fort, B and D Webber (eds.) (2008). *Regional Integration in East Asia and Europe, Convergence or Divergence?* London: Routledge.

Frost, EL (2008). *Asia's New Regionalism*. London Boulder.

Frydman, R, C Gray, M Hessel and A Rapaczynski (1999). When does Privatization work? The impact of private ownership on corporate performance in the transition economies. *Quaterly Journal of Economics*, 114, 1153–1191.

Frydman, R, K Murphy and A Rapaczynski (1998). *Capitalism with a Comrade's Face: Studies in the Postcommunist Transition*. Budapest: Central European University Press.

Furnivall, JS (1948). *Colonial Policy and Practice: A Comparative Study of Burma and Netherlands India*. Cambridge, UK: Cambridge University Press.

Gall, G (1998). The development of the Indonesian labour movement. *The International Journal of Human Resources Management*, 9(2), 359–376.

Gallagher, T (2009). *Romania and the European Union How the Weak Vanquished the Strong*, p. 207. England: Manchester University Press.

Gänzle, S (2009). EU governance and the European neighborhood policy: A framework for analysis. *Europe Asia Studies*, 61(10), 1715–1734.

Gardawski, J, J Bartkowski, J Mecina, and J Czarzasrty (2010). Working Poles and the Crisis of Fordism. Report, Scholar, Warsaw.

Gelauff, G, I Grilo and A Lejour (2008). *Subsidiarity and Economic Reform in Europe*. Berlin: Springer Verlag.

Ghesquière, H (2007). *Singapore's Success: Engineering Economic Growth*. Singapore: Thomson Learning.

Gillepsie, J (1999). Law and development in the market place. In *Law, Capitalism and Power in Asia*, K Jayasurija (ed.), pp. 118–150. London: Routledge.

Glaessner, G-J (1986). Le pouvoir bureaucratique. Solution des conflits en RDA. In *La Crise des Systèmes de type Soviétique*, Z Mlynar, W Brus and P Kende (eds.), Étude No. 13. Cologne.

Gottesman, E (2004). *Cambodia, after the Khmer Rouge: Inside the Politics of Nation Building*, p. 428. Thailand: Silkworm Books.

Grix, J and K Wanda (2002). The euroregion as a social capital maximizer: The German polish euroregion pro europa viadrina. *Regional and Federal Studies*, 12(4), 154–176.

Hadiz, VR (2002). The Indonesia labor movement. Resurgent or constrained. *Southeast Asian Affairs*, 130–142.

Haggard, S (1994). Business, politics and policy in northeast and southeast Asia. In *Business and Government in Industrializing Asia*, Chapter 10, A MacIntyre (ed.), pp. 268–301. Sydney: Allen and Unwin.

Hall, PA (1997). The role of interests, institutions and ideas in the comparative political economy of the industrialized nations. In *Comparative Politics. Rationality, Culture, and Structure*, M Lichbach and A Zuckerman (eds.), pp. 174–207. Cambridge: Cambridge University Press.

Hall, P and D Soskice (2001). *Varieties of Capitalism: The Institutional Foundations of Comparative Advantage*. Oxford: Oxford University Press.

Hamilton, HN (2004). The regionalization of Southeast Asian business: Transnational networks in national contexts. In *Remapping East Asia: The Construction of a Region*, TJ Pempel (ed.), pp. 170–191. Ithaca: Cornell University Press.

Handley, PH (2006). *The King Never Smiles. A Biography of Thailand's Bhumibol Adulyadej*. Yale Univesity Press.

Hann, C and E Dunn (eds.) (1994). *Civil Society: Challenging Western Models*. London: Routledge.

Hankis, E (1990). *East European Alternatives*. Oxford: Clarendon Press.

Harrison, RV and PA Jackson (eds.) (2010). *The Ambiguous Allure of the West: Traces of Colonial oin Thailand*. Thailand: Silkworm Book.

Hecklo, H (1994). Ideas, interest, and institutions. In *The Dynamics of American Politics. Approaches and Interpretations*, L Dodd and C Jillson (eds.). Boulder: Westview Press.

Hefner, RW (2010). Religious resurgence in contemporary Asia: Southeast Asian perspectives on capitalism, the state and the new piety. *Journal of Asian Studies*, 69, 1031–1047.

Hervieu, B, N Meyer, P Muller, F Purseigle and J Remy (2010). *les Mondes Agricoles en Politique*, (sous la direction de). Paries: Presses de Sciences Po.

Hibou, B (2004). *Privatizing the State*. London: Hurst.

Higgott, R (1997). De facto and de jure regionalism: The double discourse of regionalism in Asia Pacific. *Global society*, 11(2), 165–183.

Higgott, R (1998). The Asian economic crisis: A study in the politics of resentment. *New Political Economy*, 3(3), 333–356.

Higgott, R (2006). The theory and practice of a region. The changing global context. In *Regional Integration in East Asia and Europe, Convergence or Divergence?* B Fort and D Webber (eds.), pp. 17–38. London: Routledge.

Higgott, R (2007). Alternative models of regional cooperation? The limits of regional institutionalization in east Asia. In *European Union and New Regionalism. Regional Actors and Global Governance in a Post-Hegemonic Area*, Chapter 4, pp. 75–106.

Hooghe, L (ed.) (2006). *Cohesion Policy and European Integration: Building Multi level Governance*. Oxford: Oxford Univesity Press.

Hooghe, L and G Marks (eds.) (2001). *Multilevel Governance and European Integration*. Boulder: Roman and Littlefield.

Howard, MM (2003). *The Weakness of Civil Society in Post-Communist Europe*. Cambridge: Cambridge University Press.

Huchet, JF (2008). Du dirigisme au réalisme: La politique industrielle chinoise à l'heure de la globalization. In *Entreprises et Territoires. Une comparaison Europe*, Chapter 3, F Bafoil (ed.), pp. 83–148. Available at http://etats-entreprises-et-territoires. contenu-numerique.com/.

Hughes, C and K Un (eds.) (2011). *Cambodia's Economic Tranformation*. Singapore: Copenhague, NIAS Press.

Hunter, RJ and LV Ryan (2008). A field report on the background and processes of privatization in Poland. *Global Economy Journal*, 8(1), 1–18.

Intarakumnerd, P and Y Lecler (eds.) (2010). *Sustainability of Thailand's Competitiveness: The Policy Challenges*. Bangkok: IRASEC–ISEAS.

Ishida M (2005). Effectiveness and Challenges of the three Economic Corridors of the Greater Mekong Sub-region. Institute of Developing Economies, Discussion Paper No. 35. Available at http://www.ide-jetro.jp/English/Publish/Download/Dp/pdf/035.pdf.

Ivarson, S (2008). *Creating Laos: The Making of a Lao Space Between Indochina and Siam, 1860–1945*. Denmark: NIAS Press.

Jabko, N (2005). The political vision behind a regional currency. *Path to Regionalisation: Comparing Experiences in Europe and East Asia*, SB du Rocher, and B Fort (eds.), pp. 44–52. Singapore: Maxwell Cavendish.

Janos, A (2000). *East Central Europe in the Modern World: The Politics of the Borderland from the Pre-to the Post-Communist System*. San Francisco: Stanford University Press.

Jayasurija, K (1999). *Law, Capitalism and Power in Asia*. London: Routledge.

Jayasurija, K (2003). Embedded mercantilism and open regionalism: The crisis of regional political project. *Third World Quarterly*, 24(2), pp. 339–355.

Jayasuriya, K and A Rosser (2001). Economic crisis and the political economy of economic liberalisatin in SEA. In *The Political Economy of Southeast Asia: Conflicts Crises and Change*, 2nd edn., G Rodan, K Hewison and R Obison (eds.), pp. 233–258. Oxford: Oxford University Press.

Jerndal, R and J Rigg (2012). From bufferstate to crossroads state. Spaces of human activity and integration in the Lao PDR. In *Laos, Culture and Societies*, G Evans (ed.) pp. 35–60. Thailand: Silkworm Books.

Jones, L (2010). ASEANS's unchanged melody? The theory and practice of non interference in southeast Asia. *The Pacific Review*, 23(4), 479–502.

Jones, DM and MLR Smith (2007). Making process, no progress. ASEAN and the evolving east Asian regional order. *International Security*, 32(1), 148–184.

Jönsson, K (2010). Unity-in-diversity? Regional identity-building in southeast Asia. *Journal of Current Southeast Asian Affairs*, 2, 41–72.

Jowitt, K (1992). The Leninist legacy. In *New World Disroder*, K Jowitt (ed.). Berkeley: University of California Press.

Kaeser, MC and E-A Radice (1977). *The Economic History of Eastern Europe, 1919–1975*, 2 Bands. Oxford: Oxford Clarendon Press.

Kang, K and Y Wang (2002). An overview of currency union: Theory and practice. Discussion Paper 02/05, Korea Institute for International Economics Policies.

Karl, TL (1997). *The Paradox of Plenty: Oil booms and Petro-States*. California: University of California.

Katzenstein, PJ (1996). Regionalism in Comparative Perspective. Arena Working Paper. Available at www.arena.uio.no/.

Katzenstein, PJ (1999). Regionalism and Asia. *CSGR 3rd Annual Conference, After the Global Crises: What Next for Regionalism?* Scarman House, University of Warwick, 16–18 September.

Katzenstein, PJ (2005). *A World of Regions: Asia and Europe in the American Imperium.* Ithaca, NY: Cornell University Press.

Katzenstein, PJ and T Shirah (eds.) (1997). *Network Power: Japan and Asia.* Ithaca, NY: Cornell University Press.

Kaufmann, D and P Siegelbaum (1997). Privatization and corruption in transition economies. *Journal of International Affairs,* 50(2), 419–459.

Kawai, M (2003). Trade and investment integration and cooperation in east Asia: Empirical evidence and issue. In *Asian Economic Cooperation and Integration Progress, Prospects, Challenges,* pp. 161–193. Manila: ADB.

Keating, M (1998). *The New Regionalism in Western Europe: Territorial Restructuring and Political Change.* London: Elgar Edward.

Keating, M (2001). *Pluriannual Democracy: Stateless Nation in a Post-Sovereignty Era.* Oxford: Oxford University Press.

Kelly, J (2006). New wine in old wineskin: Promoting political reforms through the new European neighborhood policy. *Journal of Common Market Studies,* 44(1), 29–55.

Khong, YF and HES Nesadurai (2007). Hanging together, institutional design and cooperation. In *Crafting Cooperation: Regional International Institutions in Comparative Politics,* A Acharya (ed.), pp. 32–82. Cambridge: Cambridge University Press.

Kimchoeun, P, H Vuthy, E Netra, A Sovatha, K Sedara, J Knowles and D Craig (2007). Accountability and Neo Patrimonialism in Cambodia: A Critical Literature Reviews. Working Paper, 34, Cambodia Development Resource Institute, p. 80.

King, R (2008). *The Singapore Miracle — Myth and Reality: Brilliant Success of Flawed Experiment.* Chicago: Insight Press.

Kitschelt, H, Z Mansfeldova, R Markowski and G Toka (1999). *Post Communist Party Systems. Competition, Representation and Inter Party Cooperation,* p. 458. Cambridge: Cambridge University Press.

Kohl, H (2005). Arbeitsbeziehungen in den neuen EU Mitgliedsländern und ihre Implikation für das europäische Sozialmodell. In *Perspektiven der europäischen Integration nach der EU — Osterweiterung,* T Beichelt and J Wierlgohs (eds.), Workshop Documentation, FIUT Viadrina, 2005, pp. 51–71.

Kohler-Koch, B (1998). Organized interests in the EU and in the European parliament. In *Lobbysme, Pluralism and European Integration,* PH Claes, C Gobin, I Smets and P Winand (eds.), pp. 126–158. Brussels: European Interuniversity Press.

Koning, J (1997). Firms growth and ownership in transition countries. *Economic Letters,* 55, 413–418.

Konstadakopulos, D (2002). The challenge of technological development for ASEAN. Intraregional and international co-operation. *ASEAN Economic Bulletin*, 19(1), 100–110.

Kornai, J (1980). *Economics of Shortage*. Amsterdam: North-Holland.

Kratoska, PH, R Raben and HS Nordholt (2005). *Locating Southeast Asia: Geographies of Knowledge and Politics of Space*, Southeast Asia Series No. 11. Singapore: NUS.

Krongkaew, M (2004). The development of the Greater Mekong Subregion (GMS): Real promise or false hope. *Journal of Asian Economics*, 15, 977–998.

Kubik, J (2005). How to study civil society: The state of the art and what to do next? *East European Politics and Society*, 19(1), 105–120.

Kutter, A and V Trappmann (eds.) (2006). *Das Erbe des Beitritts, Eurtopäisierung in Mittel und Osteuropa*. Nomos: Verlag.

Landvai, N (2004). The weakest link? EU accession and enlargemetn dialoguing EU and post-Communist social policy. *Journal of European Social Policy*, 14(3), 319–333.

Lane, J-E (2000). *New Public Management*. London: Routledge.

Laothamatas, A (1995). From clientelism to partnership: Business–Government relations in Thailand. In *Business and government in industrializing Asia*, A MacIntyre (ed.), pp. 195–215. Sydney: Allen and Unwin.

Lavenex, S and F Schimmelfennig (2009). EU rules beyond EU borders: Theorizing external governance in European politics. *Journal of European Public Policy*, 16(6), 791–812.

Lavigne, M (1999). *The Economics of Transition. From Socialist Economy to Market Economy*. London: MacMillan.

Lawson, S (1998). Confucius in Singapore: Culture, politics and the PAP state. In *Weak and Strong States in Asia — Pacific Societies*, Chapter 7, P Dauvergne (ed.), pp. 114–134. Sydney: Allen & Unwin.

Lebel, L, J Dore, R Daniel and YS Koma (eds.) (2007). *Democratizing Water Governance in the Mekong*. Thailand: User Mekong Press.

Lepesant, G (2012). The structural funds in Central Europe. Support for infrastructure and for Innovation. In F Bafoil, S Chirativat and JP Verbiest (forthcoming).

Lieberman, V (1993). Local integration and Eurasian analogies: Structuring southeast Asian history, c. 1350–1830. *Modern Asian Studies*, 27, 475–572.

Linz, JJ and A Stepan (1996). *Problems of Democratic Transition: Southern Europe, South America and Post Communist Europe*. Baltimore, MD: John Hopkins University.

Lippert, B (2006). Erfolge und grenzen der technokratischen EU–erweiterungspolitik. In *Das Erbe des Beitritts. Europäisierung im Mittel- und Osteuropa*, A Kuttera and V Trappmann (eds.), pp. 57–74. Baden-Baden: Nomos Verlagesgesellscha.

Lippert, B and G Umbach (2005). *The Pressure of Europeanisation: From Post-Communist State Administrations to Normal Players in the EU System*. Baden-Baden: Nomos Verlagsgesellschaft.

Lolle, W (2006). Evaluating the EU Cohesion policy, paper to the Regional studies Association conference, Leuven, 8–9 June.

MacIntyre, A (1995). Power, prosperity and patrimonialism: Business and government in Indonesia. In *Business and Government in Industrializing Asia*, A MacIntyre (ed.), pp. 244–267. Sydney: Allen and Unwinin.

Major, I (1999). *Privatization and Economic Peformance in Central and Eastern Europe: Lessons to be Learnt from Western Europe*. Cheltenham: Edward Elgar.

Mansfeldová, Z, S Nalecz, E Priller and A Zimmer (2004). Civil society in transition: Civic engagement and nonprofit organizations in central and eastern Europe. In *Future of Civil Society, Making Central European Nonprofit-Organizations Work*, A Zimmer and E Priller (eds.), pp. 99–119. Wiesbaden: VS Verlag für Sozialwissenschaften.

March, J and J Olsen (1989). *Rediscovering Institutions. The Organizational Basis of Politics*. New York: The Free Press.

Marcou, G (2004). Nouveaux cadres territoriaux et institutionnels de la gestion administrative en Europe centrale et orientale. In *L'Élargissement de l'Union Européenne: Réformes Territoriales en Europe Centrale et Orientale*, V Rey, LC de Lille and E Boulineau (eds.), pp. 153–168. Paris: L'Harmattan.

Margolin, J-L (2010). The people's action party. Blueprint for Singapore, 1959–1965. In *Singapore From Temasek to this 21st Century*, K Hack, J-L Margolin and K Delaye, pp. 292–322. Singapore: NUS Press Singapore.

Martin, M (2003a). Civil society and political parties in the Czech Republic. In *Communists and Post-Communist Transformation. Czechoslovakia, Czech Republic and Slovakia*, S Smith (ed.). London: Routledge.

Martin, M (2003b). *The Rise and Fall of Czech Capitalism: Economic Development in the Czech Republic Since 1989*. Cheltenham: Edward Elgar.

Massicar, E (2010). Regionalization process in Turkey? In *Regional Development and the European Union. A comparative Analysis of Karabück, Valenciennes and Katowice*, F Bafoil and A Kaya (eds.), pp. 19–35. Istanbul: Istanbul Bilgi University Press.

McKey, SC (2006). The squeaky wheel's dilemma new forms of labor Organizing in the Philippines. *Labor Studies Journal*, 30(4), 41–63.

Migdal, JS (1994). Strong states, weak states: Power and accommodation, understanding political development (MyronWeimar, Samuel P. Huntington), pp. 391–434.

Migdal, JS (2001). *State in Society. Studying how States and Societies Transform and Constitute one Another*. Cambridge: Cambridge University Press.

Mihaly (1985). Industry and foreign capital. In *Economic History of Eastern Europe, 1919–1975*, MC Kasers and EA Radice (eds.), p. 114. Oxford: Clarendon Press.

Monfort, P (2009). Territories with Specific Geographical features, Working Papers, EU, Regional Policy, No. 02/2009, 22p.

Murray, P and N Rees (2010). Introduction. European and Asia regionalism: Form and function. *International Politics*, 47, 269–275.

Myers, A and D Wharton (2007). *The Cross Border Economies of Cambodia, Laos, Thailand and Vietnam*. *Development Analysis Cambodian Development Resource Institute*, 247 pages, Framework with Funding from the Rockfeller Foundation.

Nacu, A (2008). *L'Européanisation d'Ouest en Est*, English translation by F Bafoil and T Beichelt (eds.). Cambridge, Massachussets: l'Harmattan.

Naughton, B (2009). *The Chinese Economy: Transition and Growth*. Chapter 5, pp. 165–192. Paris: The MIT Press.

Nesadurai, HES (2003a). *Globalisation, Domestic Politics and Regionalism: The ASEAN Free Trade Area*. London: Routledge.

Nesadurai, HES (2003b). Attempting developmental regionalism through AFTA: The domestic sources of regional governance. *Third World Quaterly*, 24(2), 225–253.

Neumann, L (2000). Decentralised collective bargaining in hungary. *International Journal of Comparative Labor Lawand Industrial Relations*, 16, 113–128.

Niyomsilpa, S (2008). Industry globalized: The automotive sector. In *Thai Capital After the 1997 Crisis*, P Phongpachit and C Baker (eds.), pp. 61–83. Thailand: Silkworm Books.

Nölke, A and A Vliegenthart (2009). Enlarging the varieties of capitalism: The emergence of dependent market economies in east central Europe. *World Politics*, 61(4), 670–702.

North, DC (1990). *Institutions, Institutional Change and Economic Performance*. Cambridge: Cambridge University Press.

North, DC, JJ Wallis and BR Weingast (2009). *Violence of Social Orders; A Conceptual Framework for Reinterpreting Human History*. New York: Cambridge Univresity Press.

Nove, A (1961). *The Soviet Economy: An Introduction*. London: George Allen and Unwin.

Ockey, J (2004). *Making Democracy Leadership, Class, Gender and Political Participation in Thailand*. Thailand: Silkworm Books.

OECD (2005). *Business Clusters Promoting Enterprises in Central and Eastern Europe*. Paris: LEED.

OECD (2006). *Territorial Reviews of Competitive Cities in the Global Economy*. Paris: OECD.

OECD (2007). *Competitive Regional Clusters: National Policy Approaches*. Paris: OECD.

OECD (2008). *Territorial Reviews*. Paris: Poland.

OECD (2009). *Territorial Reviews, Trans-border Urban Co-operation in the Pan Yellow Sea Region*. Paris: OECD.

Orenstein, MA (2000). *Out of the Red: Building Capitalism and Democracy in Post-Communist Europe*. Ann Arbor: University of Michigan Press.

Osborne, M (2005). *History of Southeast Asia*, 8th edn. London: Allen & Unwin.

Osborne, M (2010). *Southeast Asia: An Introductory History*, 10th edn. London: Allen & Unwin.

Ost, D (2000). Illusionary corporatism in eastern Euopre: Neo liberal tripartism and post–communist class identities. *Politics and Society*, 28(4), 508–530.

Ost, D and S Crowley (eds.) (2001). *Workers after Workers' States. Labor Politics in Postcommunist Europe.* Boston and Oxford: Rowman & Littlefield.

Owen, NG (1992). Economic and social change. In *The Cambridge History of South East Asia*, Chapter 3, N Tarling (ed.), pp. 145–146. Cambridge: Cambridge University Press.

Owen, NG (ed.) (2005). *The Emergence of Modern Southeast Asia, A New History.* Singapore: University Press.

Owen, NG (2006). *History of Modern South East Asia.* Singapore: NUS.

Palat, RA (2004). Strong states, weak societies: State and class in the Asian rimlands. In *Capitalist Restructuring and the Pacific Rim*, Chapter 2, pp. 57–58. London: Routledge Curzon.

Palier, B and Y Surel (2005). Les Trois I et l'analyse de l'etat en action. *Revue Française de Science Politique*, 55, 7–32.

Papin, P (2004). *Vietnam, Parcours d'une Nation*, Editions Belin. Paris: La Documentation Française

Parsonage, J (2003). Southeast Asia's growth triangle: A sub-regional response to global transformation. *Events and Debates*, 307–317.

Pasquier, R and C Perron (2008). Régionalisations et régionalismes dans une Europe élargie: Les enjeux d'une comparaison Est-Ouest. *Revue d'Etudes Comparative Est–Ouest*, 39(3), 5–18.

Pavlinek, P (2002). The role of foreign direct investment in the privatisation and restructuring of the Czech Motor Industry. *Post-Communist Economies*, 14(3), 359–379.

Pempel, J-T (ed.) (2005). *Remaping East Asia, the Construction of a Region.* Ithaca, NY: Cornell University Press.

Perron, C (2003). *Les Pionniers de la Démocratie.* Paris: Gallimard/Le Monde.

Perroux, F (1980). *Philosophie du Développement.* Paris: Gallimard/Le Monde.

Petman, R (2010). Asian perspectives on the European experience of regionalism. *International Politics*, 47, 293–307.

Phelps, NA (2004). Triangular diplomacy writ small: The political economy of the Indonesia–Malaya–Singapore growth triangle. *The Pacific Review*, 17(3), 341–368.

Pholsena, V (2006a). Ethnic Classification and Mapping Nationhood. In *Post-war Laos: The Politics of Culture, History and Identity*, Chapter 6, pp. 151–179. Ithaca, NY: Cornell University Press.

Pholsena, V (2006b). From Indochinese dreams to post-Indochinese realities. In *The Mekong Arranged and Rearranged*, Chapter 2, M Serena, I Diokno and NV Chinh (eds.), pp. 43–64. Chiang Mai, Thailand: Mekon Press.

Pholsena, V and R Banomyong (2004). *Le Laos au XXI. Les Défis de L'intégration Régionale.* Bangkok: IRASEC, (in English, 2009).

Phongpaichit, P and S Piriyarangsan (1994). *Corruption and Democracy in Thailand,* p. 52. Radcliff (KY): Silkworms Books.

Phongpaichit, P and C Baker (2005). *Taksin,* 2nd edn. Radcliff (KY): Silkworm Books.

Phongpaichit, P and C Baker (eds.) (2008). *Thai Capital, After the 1997 Crisis.* Radcliff (KY): Silkworm Book.

Pierson, P (1996). The path to European integration: A historical institutionalist analysis. *Comparative Political Studies,* 29(2), 123–163.

Pierson, P (2000). Path dependence, increasing returns, and the study of politics. *American Political Science Review,* 94(2), 251–267.

Pirker, T, MR Lepsius, R Weinert and HH Hertle (1995). *Der Plan als Befehl und Fiktion. Wirtschaftsführung in der DDR.* Opladen: Westdeutscher Verlag.

Portet, S (2005). Poland circumventing the law or fully deregulating? In *Working Employment Conditions in New Members States,* D Vaughan-Whitehead (ed.). Geneva: ILO.

Prodi, R (2002). A wide Europe–A Proximity Policy as the Key to Stability Peace, Security and a Dialogue and the Role of the EU Sixth ECSA–World Conference, Jean Monnet Project, Brussels, 6th December Speech 02/619.

Putnam, RD (1988). Diplomacy and domestic politics: The logic of two-level games. *International Organization,* 42, 427–460.

Pye, L (1985). *Asian Power and Politics: The Cultural Dimension of Authority.* Cambridge, Massachussets: The Belknap Press of Harvard University.

Quevit, M (2005). La grande région et la problématique des rapports etat–nation–région, dans l'union Européenne. *Revue Internationale de Politique Comparée,* 12(2), 207–221.

Radelet, S and J Sachs (1997). Asia's reemergence. *Foreign Affairs,* 76(6), 44–59.

Ragaru, N (2005). Apprivoiser les Transformations Post–Communistes en Bulgarie: la Fabrique du Politique (1989–2004), doctoral Thesis, 2 Vols.

Ragaru, N (2008). La rivière et les petits cailloux. Elargissement européen et européanisation en Europe centrale et orientale. In *L'Europeanisation d'Ouest en Est,* F Bafoil and T Beichelt (eds.), pp. 241–283. Paris: L'Harmattan.

Rey, V (1996). (études coordonnées par) *Les Nouvelles Campagnes de l'Europe central et Orientale.* Editions du CNRS.

Rieger, HC (1991). The treaty of Rome and its relevance for ASEAN. *ASEAN Economic Bulletin,* 8(2), 160–172.

Rigg, J (2003). *Southeast Asia: The Human Landscape of Modernization and Development,* 2nd edn. London: RoutLedge.

Ritchie, BK (2009a). Economic upgrading in a state-coordinated, liberal market economy. *Asia Pacific Journal of Management,* 26(3), 435–457.

Ritchie, BK (2009b). Characteristics of varieties of capitalism in developed and developing countries in Ritchie. *Asia Pacific Journal of Management,* 26.

Rodan, G (2001). Singapore: globalization and the politics of economics restructuring. In *The Political Economy of Southeast Asia: Conflicts Crises and Change*, 2nd edn., G Rodan, K Hewison and R Obison, pp. 138–177. Oxford: Oxford University Press.

Rolant-Holst, D, J-P Verbiest and Z Fan (2008). Growth and trade horizons for Asia: Long-term forecasts for regional integration. Working Paper UNU-WIDER Research Papers, World Insitute for Development Economic Research (UNU-WIDER).

Rudolf, LI and SH Rudolf (1979). Authority and power in bureaucracy and patrimonial administration: A revisionist analysis of Weber on bureaucracy. *World Politics*, 31(2), 195–227.

Rupnik, J (1979). Dissent in Poland, 1968–1978: The end of revisionism and the rebirth of civil society. In *Opposition in Eastern Europe*, RL Tokes (ed.), pp. 60–111. London: Macmillan.

Rupnik, J (2008). De l'antipolitique à la crise de la démocratie: Que reste-t-il de l'héritage de la dissidence? In *La Citoyenneté Démocratique dans l'Europe des Vingt-sept*, C Lequesne and M MacDonagh-Pajerova (eds.), pp. 101–125. Paris: L'Harmattan.

Rys, V (2001). Transition countries of central Europe entering the European union: Some social protection issues. *International Social Security Review*, 54(2/3), 177–189.

Sabel, CF and J Zeitlin (2008). Learning from differences: The new architecture of experimentalist governance in the EU. *European Law Journal*, 271–327.

Sapir, A (2003). An agenda for a growing Europe. Making the EU economic system deliver. Available at www.euractiv.com/ndbtext/innovation/sapirreport.pdf.

SarDesai, R (1994). *South East Asia, Past and Present*, 3rd edn. Boulder, Colorado: Westview Press.

Schimmelfennig, F (2005). Strategic calculations and international socialization: Memberships, incentives, party constellations, and sustained compliance in central and eastern Europe. *International Organization*, 59, 827–860.

Schimmelfennig, F, S Engert and H Knobel (2006). *International Socialisation in Europe. European Organisations, Political Conditionality and Democratic Change*. Canada:Palgrave.

Schimmelfennig, F and Sedelmeier, U (2005). Conceptualizing the Europeanization of Eastern and Central Europe. In *The Europeanization of Central and Eastern Europe*. Ithaca: Cornell University Press.

Scott, WJ (2002). Cross, border governance in the Baltic sea region. *Regional and Federal Studies*, 12(4), 135–153.

Sedelmeier, U (2005). Eastern enlargement: Towards a European EU? In *Policy-Making in the European Union*, 5th edn., H Wallace and W Wallace (eds.), pp. 402–428. Oxford: Oxford University Press.

Sedelmeier, U (2010). The EU and democratization in central and Southeastern Europe since 1989. In *Central and Southeast European Politics since 1989*, SP Ramet (ed.). Cambridge: Cambridge University Press.

Segert, L and P Machos (1995). *Parteien in Osteuropa*. Opladen: Springer VS.

Seibel, W (1994). Das Zentralistische Erbe, die institutionnelle Entwicklung der Treuhandanstalt und die Nachhaltigkeit ihrer Auswirkungen auf die bundesstaatlichen Verfassungstrukturen. *Aus Politik und Zeitgeschichte*, B 43–44/94, pp. 3–13.

Seliec, MB and A Trouvé (2010). La politique agricole commune est-elle territoriale? In *Les Mondes Agricoles en Politique*, B Hervieu, N Meyer, P Muller, F Purseigle and J Remy (eds.), pp. 397–413. Paris: Presses fondation sciences politiques.

Shields, S (2004). Global restructuring and the polish State: Transition transformation or transnationalisation? *Review of International Political Economy*, 132–154.

Sing, M (2004). Weak labor movement and opposition parties: Hong Kong and Singapore. *Journal of Contemporary Asia*, 34(4), 449–464.

Sissenich, B (2010). Weak states, weak societies: Europe's east–west gap. *Acta Politica*, 45, 11–40.

Skilling, HG (1976). *Czechoslovakia's Interrupted Revolution*. Princeton, NJ: Princeton University Press.

Slocomb, M (2010). *An Economic History of Cambodia in the Twentieth Century*. Singapore: NUS Press.

Smith, SLD (1997). The Indonesian–Malaysia–Singapore growth triangle: A political and economic equation. *Australian Journal of International Affairs*, 51(3), 369–382.

Solingen, E (2005). East Asian regional institutions. In *Remaping East Asia, The Construction of the Region*, Chapter 2, TJ Pempel (ed.), pp. 31–53. Ithaca: Cornell University Press.

Staniszkis, J (1991). *The Dynamics of Breakthrough in Eastern Europe: The Polish Experience*. Berkeley: University of California Press.

Stark, D (1996). Recombinant property in Eastern European capitalism. *American Journal of Sociology*, 4, 993–1027.

Stark, D and L Bruszt (1998). *Postsocialist Pathways: Transforming Politics and Property in East Central Europe*. Cambridge: Cambridge University Press.

Stubbs, R (2002). ASEAN plus three: Emerging East Asian regionalism? *Asian Survey*, 42(3), 440–455.

Sullivan, M (2011). China's aid to Cambodia. In *Cambodia's Economic Transformation*, C Hughes and K Un (eds.). Singapore: Copenhague, NIAS Press.

Szelenyi, I and S Szelenyi (1995). Circulation or reproduction of elites during the post-communist transformation of Eastern Europe. *Theory and Society*, 24, 613–628.

Tarling, N (1998). *Nations and States in Southeast Asia.* Cambridge: Cambridge University.

Tarling, N (1999). *The Cambridge History of South East Asia, Vol. 2, Part 1, From 1800 to the 1939s.* Cambridge: Cambridge University Press.

Tarling, N (2000). *Cambridge History of Southeast Asia Vol. 2, Part 2, From World War II to the Present.* Cambridge: Cambridge University Press.

Tarling, N (2001). *Imperialism in Southeast Asia.* London: Routledge.

Tarling, N (ed.) (2004). *Cambridge History of Southeast Asia, Vol. 4, Part 2, From World War II to the Present.* Cambridge: Cambridge University Press.

Tarling, N (2006). *Regionalism in Southeast Asia: To Foster the Political Will.* London: Routledge.

Telo, M (ed.) (2007). *European Union and New Regionalism: Regional Actors and Global Governance in a Post-hegemonic Area,* 2nd edn. Farnham (Surrey): Ashgate.

Terada, T (2003). Constructing an East Asian concept and growing regional identity: From EAEC to ASEAN+3. *The Pacific Review,* 16(2), 251–277.

Thambipillai, P (1991). The ASEAN growth triangle: The convergence of national and sub national interests. *Contemporary Southeast Asia,* 13(3), 299–314.

Thambipillai, P (1998). The ASEAN growth areas: Sustaining the dynamism. *The Pacific Review,* 11(2), 249–266.

Thant *et al.* (1998). *Growth Triangles in Asia: A New Approach to Regional Economic Cooperation.* Oxford: ADB/Oxford University Press.

Tipton, FB (2009). Southeast Asian capitalism: History, institutions, states and firms. *Asia Pacific Journal of Management,* 26, 401–434.

Tulmets, E (2007). Alterwien in neuen programmen. Von der osterweiterung zur ENP. *Osteuropa,* 57, 2–3.

Turnbull, CM (1992). Regionalism and nationalism, In *The Cambridge History of Southeast Asia,* N Tarling (ed.). Chapter 5, Vol. 4. Cambridge: Cambridge University Press.

Turnbull, CM (2009). *Singapore Present and Past.* Singapore: NUS.

Turner, M (2002). Choosing items from the menu: New public management in Southeast Asia. *International Journal of Public Administration,* 25(12), 1493–1512.

UNDP (2008). Human Development Report.

Vachudova, MA (2005). *Europe Undivided: Democracy, Leverage and Integration After Communism.* Oxford: Oxford University Press.

Vaughan-Whitehead, D (2003). *EU Enlargment Versus Social Europe? The Uncertain Future of the European Social Model.* Cheltenham: Edward Elgar.

Von Hirschhausen, B (1997). *Les Nouvelles Campagnes Roumaines: Paradoxes d'un Retour Paysan.* Paris: Belin.

Verbiest, JP (2012a). Myanmar, in ASEAN 2030 Report, 2011 (Forthcoming, ADB).

Verbiest, JP (2012b). Regional integration in both regions. In *Asian and European Regional Integration Process in the New Context of Development Challenges*, Southeast Asia and Eastern Europe from a Comparative Perspective, F Bafoil, S Chirativat and JP Verbiest (Forthcoming 1996).

Wah, LE (1996). Public service innovation in Singapore. In *Public Sector Innovations: The ASEAN Way*, SH Salleh (ed.). Kuala Lumpur: Asia Pacific Development Centre.

Wädekin, KE (1977). The place of agriculture in the European communist economies: A statistical essay. *Soviet Studies*, 29(2), 238–254.

Weatherbee, DE (1995). The foreign policy dimensions of sub-regional economic zones. *Contemporary Southeast Asia*, 16(4), 421–432.

Weatherbee, DE (2009). *International Relations in Southeast Asia. The Struggle for Autonomy*. Lanham–Boulder: Roman & Littlefield Editions.

Weber, M (1958). The social psychology of the world religions. In *From Max Weber: Essays in Sociology*, HH Gerth and CW Mills (eds.), pp. 267–301. New York: Routledge.

Weber, M (1978). *Economy and Society*. Berkeley: University of California Press.

Weber, M (1991) Politics as a vocation. In *From Max Weber: Essays in Sociology*, HH Gerth and CW Mills (eds.), pp. 77–128. New York: Routledge.

Webber, D (2001). Two funerals and a wedding? The ups and downs of regionalism in East Asia and Asia-Pacific after the Asian crisis. *The Pacific Review*, 14(3), 339–372.

Webber, D (2007). Trade and security? Political integration in an insecure tegion. In *The Evolution of Regionalism in Asia*, H Dieter (ed.), pp. 147–159. New York: Routledge.

Wenden, C (2010). *Atlas des Migrations*. Paris: Presses de Sciences Po.

Whitehead, V (2005). *Working Employment Conditions in New Member States*. Geneva: ILO.

Wild, G (2002). Economic de la transition: Le dossier. In *L'Europe Past-Communiste*. Paris: PUF.

Winichakul, T (1997). *Siam Mapped: A History of the Geo — Body of a Nation*. Honolulu: University of Hawai.

Winiecki, J (2004). Determinants of catching up or falling behind: Interaction of formal and informal institutions. *Post-Communist Economies*, 16(2), 137–152.

Wnuk-Linpinski, E (1982). Dimorphism of values and social schizophrenia, a tentative description. In *Sysiphus, Sociological Studies, Crisis and Conflicts, the Case of Poland* 1980–1981, Vol. III, pp. 81–90. Warsaw: PWN.

Wollmann, H (1997). Institution building, and decentralization in formerly socialist countries: The cases of Poland, Hungary, and East Germany. *Environment and Planning, Government and Policy*, 15, 463–480.

Womack, JP, DT Jones and D Roose (1990). *The Machine that Changed the World*. New York: Rawson Associates.

Wong, M–H, R Shankar, R Toh (K Kessel, Special Advisor) (2011). ASEAN Competitiveness Report, 2010, NUS Singapore.

Wyatt, DK (2002). *Thailand, A Short History*, 2nd edn. Thailand: Silkworm Books.

Yap, JT (2007). Integrating the lower income countries in Europe and East Asia: Some comparative issues. In *Path of Regionalization — Comparing Experiences in East Asia and Europe*, Asia-Europe Research Series, SB du Rocher and B Fort (eds.). Singapore: Marshall Lavendish.

Yap, S, R Lim and LW Kam (2009). *White Men in White, The Untold Story of Singapore's Ruling Political Party*. Berhad, Malaysia: Straits Times Press.

Yeo, LZ (2009). The everlasting love for comparison. Reflections on the EU's and ASEAN's integration. In *The United States and Europe in a Changing World*, RE Kanet (ed.), pp. 185–205. Dordrecht: Republic of Letters, Publishing.

Yeo, LZ (2010). Institutional regionalism versus networked regionalism: Europe and Asia compared. *International Politics*, 47, 33.

Yeung, W-C (2009). Regional development and the competitive dynamics of global production networks: An East Asia perspective. *Regional Studies*, 43(3), 325–351.

Yong, MC (1992). The political structures of the independent states. In *The Cambridge History of Southeast Asia*, N Tarling (ed.), Vol. II, Part Two, pp. 59–138. Cambridge: Cambridge University Press.

Yoshihara, K (1988). *The Rise of Ersatz Capitalism in South East Asia*. Oxford: Oxford University Press.

Zecchini, S (ed.) (1997). *Lessons from the Economic Transition, Central and Eastern Europe in the 90s*. Dordrecht/Boston: Kluwer Academic Publishers.

Zimmer, A and E Priller (eds.) (2004). *Future of Civil Society, Making Central European Nonprofit-Organizations Work*. Wiesbaden: VS Verlag für Sozialwissenschaften.

INDEX